Confucius and Confucianism

D1714733

Confucius
& Confucianism

The Essentials

Lee Dian Rainey

WILEY-BLACKWELL

A John Wiley & Sons, Ltd., Publication

This edition first published 2010

Blackwell Publishing was acquired by John Wiley & Sons in February 2007. Blackwell's publishing program has been merged with Wiley's global Scientific, Technical, and Medical business to form Wiley-Blackwell.

Registered Office
John Wiley & Sons Ltd, The Atrium, Southern Gate, Chichester, West Sussex, PO19 8SQ, United Kingdom

Editorial Offices
350 Main Street, Malden, MA 02148-5020, USA
9600 Garsington Road, Oxford, OX4 2DQ, UK
The Atrium, Southern Gate, Chichester, West Sussex, PO19 8SQ, UK

For details of our global editorial offices, for customer services, and for information about how to apply for permission to reuse the copyright material in this book please see our website at www.wiley.com/wiley-blackwell.

Library of Congress Cataloging-in-Publication Data

Rainey, Lee Dian.
Confucius and Confucianism : the essentials / Lee Dian Rainey.
    p. cm.
  Includes bibliographical references (p.   ) and index.
  ISBN 978-1-4051-8841-8 (hardcover : alk. paper) – ISBN 978-1-4051-8840-1 (pbk. : alk. paper)
  1. Confucius. 2. Confucianism. 3. Philosophy, Confucian. I. Title.
  B128.C8R35 2010
  181′.112–dc22

                                                                2009044654

A catalogue record for this book is available from the British Library.

Set in 10 on 12pt Sabon by Toppan Best-set Premedia Limited
Printed in Singapore by Ho Printing Singapore Pte Ltd

01   2010

For my mother and father,
Phyllis MacGregor and William Rainey

飲 水 思 源

When you drink the water, remember its source.
                                          Chinese proverb

Contents

List of Illustrations

Preface: Why Confucius?

Confucius was born over 2,500 years ago. Why would we want to know what he said? How could someone from that long ago be of any importance to us now?

Confucius faced many of the same problems we do: governments telling lies; an enthusiasm for military adventures; great social, economic, and technological changes; a society that seemed to be losing any respect for education and for moral behavior; growing sleaziness and ignorance. Confucius offers solutions to these problems. You will find that what he has to say applies to our dilemmas and to us today.

Confucius said that we can become responsible, adult people who behave properly. If we can do that, we can change the world we live in. Unlike many people today, when Confucius talks about morals and virtues, he does not do it to accuse others or to force his thinking on anyone. Confucius tells us that we should become educated, not to get a job, but to become better people. He, and his followers, talk about cultivating the self, just as one grows a garden. Do that properly and you change your family, neighborhood, and country.

Readers who are just beginning in this area should be aware that every section of this text is debated and that the issues are far more complex than a text of this sort can convey. They should bear in mind that this is an introductory text. References to arguments about issues and terms are in the endnotes, along with suggestions for further reading, and I would encourage readers to follow up with them.

This book is based on the work of hundreds of scholars. The study of Chinese philosophy in the West has, in the last 20 years, become increasingly sophisticated and exciting. Scholars in the area must also bear in mind that this book is an introduction and that many complex ideas have often had to be conflated or relegated to endnotes.

I can still remember my excitement when I first stumbled, quite by accident, on classical Chinese thought. I hope to be able to convey some of that in this small volume and to give the reader a glimpse into a world that has so much to say to us.

I would like to thank the anonymous readers of both the proposal and the draft, who have been generous in their suggestions and corrections; I am deeply grateful for their careful reading. Heartfelt thanks are also due to the editors and the staff at Wiley-Blackwell. The enthusiasm, insight, and support from such outstanding professionals have made writing this book a pleasure. I would like to thank the marvelous librarians of the Queen Elizabeth II library at Memorial University. Generations of students at Memorial University have helped me deepen my understanding, and their, somewhat unexpected, enthusiasm for Chinese philosophy has been a great joy. The never-ending kindness and hospitality of Su Xinghua and her family in Taiwan for over twenty years is a debt they have never allowed me to repay. I would also like to thank Professor Simon Wong and Dr. Terry Woo for their *rennai*, patience, in our ongoing, and sometimes contentious, discussions of Confucianism. I owe many, many debts to Professor Tracy Su, who has been a shining example to me of the Confucian virtue of *ren*, humanity. Dr. Jean Snook freely brought her sharp editing skills to this manuscript. It was her advice, encouragement, and support that made writing this possible, all the while exemplifying the Confucian virtues of *cheng*, sincerity, and *yong*, courage. Finally, I would like to thank Dr. Richard Teleky for his editing of the manuscript, but mostly for a friendship that spans half of our lives and for his *yi*, rightness, and *zhi*, wisdom, that guide it.

Book Notes

The Pinyin system of transliterating Chinese is used throughout, rather than the older Wade–Giles system. The Wade–Giles transliteration can be found, after the Pinyin, in the endnotes and the glossary of names and terms. The exception to this is with authors' names and book titles, where Wade–Giles has been used. The Pinyin is then in brackets in the endnotes.

As the Pinyin system is problematic for many English speakers, an approximate pronunciation of names or terms can be found in the Glossary.

The translations here, with a few exceptions, are mine: I will cite the text, and where possible a chapter title or the standard numbering system, and I will refer the reader to an alternate translation. Some texts, such as *The Book of History*, have not been fully translated for many years and so the alternate translation is an old one.

This text is meant as a basic introduction. Suggestions for texts, standard translations, and other views can be found in "Suggestions for Further Reading."

Chronology

16th to 11th century BCE: Shang dynasty

11th century to 256 BCE: Zhou dynasty
  11th century to 771 BCE: Western Zhou dynasty
  771–256 BCE: Eastern Zhou dynasty
    722–481 BCE: Spring and Autumn era
    403–256 BCE: Warring States era

221–207 BCE: Qin dynasty

206 BCE–220 CE: Han dynasty
  206 BCE–25 CE: Western or Former Han
  25–220 CE: Eastern or Later Han

220–80: Three Kingdoms period

220–589: Period of Disunity

581–618: Sui dynasty

618–906: Tang dynasty

907–960: Five Dynasties

960–1125: Northern Song dynasty

1127–1279: Southern Song dynasty

1279–1368: Yuan (Mongol) dynasty

1368–1644: Ming dynasty

1644–1912: Qing (Manchu) dynasty

established 1911: Republic of China

1949: People's Republic of China

1

Confucius' World and His Life

Confucius say, "Man who shoots off mouth, must expect to lose face."[1] Who is this Confucius with his fractured English and trite sayings?

In the West we tend to have a cartoon-like view of Confucius: as a man who churned out dull maxims – the "dictum coining sage," says the Lonely Planet travel guide[2] – or as a conservative old fogy whose sayings show up in fortune cookies.

In the Chinese city of Qufu, Confucius' birthplace, on any given day you will see hundreds and hundreds of people, most in family groups or tour groups. The majority of the three million visitors a year are from elsewhere in China, or from Korea or Japan. They wend their way through the historic sites in the area – the temple of Confucius, the Apricot Pavilion where Confucius taught his students, Confucius' grave, and Confucius' family home. Some burn incense and bow before the central statue of Confucius. Everyone takes pictures and listens to the tour guides' spiel. While not especially reverent, everyone seems attentive and interested. This is a UNESCO World Heritage Site. Throughout the city, hawkers will sell you Confucius medallions, key chains, books, pictures, statues, and even tea "from the Sage Confucius' land." There is no trace of a boring, trite Confucius here.

It is not just the Western image of Confucius that is a problem. In modern China, if you talk about "Confucius" most people will not know who you are talking about. That is because Confucius' name is not actually Confucius. The name "Confucius" was coined by Catholic missionaries to China in the sixteenth century. It is the Latin form of the Chinese "Kong Fuzi," or Master Kong (the "Fu" is an honorary addition). In Chinese he is "Kongzi."[3] "Kong" is Confucius' family name and the "zi" means "Master" or "Teacher"; in Chinese, titles come after the family name, not in front of it as in English. I will use the Western convention, "Confucius," because it is most familiar to English speakers, but we should probably begin by knowing his real name.[4]

Westerners also tend to see China and things Chinese as very much the opposite of the West: for example, Western philosophy is rational while Chinese thought is mystical. As children many of us in North America believed that if we dug a hole through the earth we would come out on the "other" side, in China. A "Chinese fire drill" is a messy and disorganized event; "Chinese whisper" is a children's game where a sentence is whispered from one to another, finally ending as nonsense. Is stereotyping one of the reasons why Confucius, central to Chinese culture, is solely a figure of fun, while our important religious and philosophical figures are not?

Confucius' World: Looking Back to a Long, Unified Civilization

By the time Confucius was born in 551 BCE, there had been a civilization and a political structure in China for about 1,500 years, and possibly longer than that. He and his contemporaries looked back to the reigns of the sage-kings who were said to have lived two to four thousand years earlier. These sage-kings were described as bringing the arts of civilization and government to China, inventing everything from farming to flood control. Modern scholars argue whether these sage-kings were early rulers around whom fabulous supernatural stories were built or ancient gods who were reinvented as historical rulers of a very ancient past.[5] For Confucius and those of his time, the sage-kings represented the best of rulers and the heritage of Chinese civilization.

Dynastic rule came with the Xia dynasty (*c*.2183–1500 BCE) and the Shang dynasty (*c*.1500–1100 BCE). Their China was not the China we now know. The area they ruled was centered around the Yellow River basin; gradually political authority would stretch north, west, and south to take in the China of Confucius' time (see map), though even that China was not as large as contemporary China.

The Zhou Dynasty

King Wu, one of the founders of the Zhou dynasty, fell ill. His brother, the Duke of Zhou, was so distressed that he prayed to their ancestors, asking that he might be taken instead of his brother. While King Wu recovered on that occasion, when the King did die, his son, King Cheng, was very young and the Duke of Zhou ruled on his behalf as regent. The Duke rejected suggestions from other nobles that he should kill the child and take the throne himself. The Duke's rule was considered to be the model of good government. When King Cheng was old enough, the Duke handed over the government to him and, so it is said, retired to write the hexagrams of the *Book of Changes* and ritual texts. (See chapter 8.)[6]

The Zhou dynasty defeated the Shang rulers in about 1027 BCE, bringing under their rule what was then western and central China. The Zhou government, like the Shang before it, was a feudal state where the king claimed ownership of all the land and then parceled territories out to lords who pledged allegiance to him. Government offices were hereditary among noble families and it was birth, not merit, that determined one's place in society.

When we use the word "feudal" we should not think of a king and his few advisors sitting about in a castle. The Zhou government structure was complex. There was a prime minister, a minister of the household, a minister of justice, and a director of public works whose job it was to build and repair dykes, bridges, irrigation channels, and water reservoirs. There was a minister of war and ministers who were in charge of fortifications. The ministry of religion carried out divination, interpreted dreams and celestial phenomena, and saw to sacrificial offerings. Other departments dealt with everything from entertaining foreign guests, directing the music conservatory, overseeing and storing the harvest, hunting, and crafts. Other officials advised the ruler on the law, rewards for service to the crown, and proper conduct.

By the time of Confucius, not only was there a complex government, but China had a sophisticated society and culture. By the time of the Zhou dynasty, there was a writing system that was already centuries old, books, histories, music, and poetry. Skill in metal work was so refined that great sets of bells could be cast, each one playing more than one note when struck. The Chinese used the decimal system and a metallic form of money; they traded with people outside the China of the time. There were large market towns, roads, bridges, and irrigation systems using canals, bridges, and dams. By the time of Confucius, China is estimated to have had a population of about 50 million people.

The rulers and nobles were a warrior aristocracy whose prestige and power was based on warfare, hunting, and sacrificial rituals to their ancestors. These things set nobles apart from commoners. Noble families were defined by kinship ties and each great family had its own estate, temples, and military forces. Nobles lived on their own estates and on the wealth they produced there. Commoners and farmers were like serfs, working on the estates and called on for military service by their local lord.

When an elite is defined by prowess in war, manhood is defined by military courage and honor is central. Nobles saw themselves as obliged to take vengeance on anyone who took liberties with their honor; any small slight had to be avenged to preserve one's honor. Courage, loyalty, honor, family name, and sacrifices to the ancestors who founded the lineage were central to the nobility's understanding of who they were.

Ancestors and Spirits

The ancestors of those nobles were powerful. They were thought to control success in war, hunting, and agriculture. They were capable of punishing the living for any neglect in the regular offerings that were made to them; the ancestors might also appear to punish their enemies, and to cause trouble for the living.

The ancestral halls of the nobles contained tablets representing the ancestors. Ceremonies were performed in which food and drink were offered to ancestral spirits; descendents took on the role of the ancestors in these rituals. There was no clear line between the living and the dead as the living nourished the ancestors and the ancestors cared for the family.

It is not clear where these ancestors were. They are often referred to as "ascending" but we are not told where. The dead (that is, all the dead, not just the ancestors of noble families) were also said to go to the Yellow Springs, a gloomy underworld where what was left of their life force gradually disappeared.

Ancestors who had become too remote to be known, the dead who had no one to sacrifice to them, and the dead of other families were thought to be supernatural too. Often dangerous, these ghosts could bring disease, death, or calamity and had to be guarded against. Another range of supernatural beings, the spirits, included ancestors and what we would call gods. These were the gods of natural phenomena, of particular areas, and gods with specific responsibilities such as fire, childbirth, or rain. Later texts would refer to all of these kinds of beings as "ghost-spirits"[7] when talking about some sort of survival after death or supernatural beings. The beings of the other world continued to be involved in this one, in both positive and negative ways.

Religious ceremonies for ancestors were performed by their noble descendents. There were also religious professionals, like shamans, who treated the sick with ritual and with herbal medicine; they exorcized evil spirits and opened up communication with the dead through divination. These shamans had a number of ways to foretell the future. They held official positions at court and were mostly women.

Heaven and the "Choice of Heaven"

Central to Zhou dynasty religious thinking was the concept of Heaven. This is not a heaven as we might think of it, that is, a place where one goes after death. Heaven may be a god, but not the creator God of the biblical traditions. This is a central deity or concept that was understood as the primary supernatural power. There are some ancient texts that talk about Heaven as a god, and a god with a personality, who is pleased or angered by the actions of human beings and who then blesses or punishes based on Heaven's standards. On the other hand, Heaven is sometimes described as being something closer to nature, an impersonal and automatic force not at all like human beings.

Whether Heaven was understood as a god or as nature, we frequently find Heaven closely allied to the interests of the common people: "Heaven hears and sees as our people hear and see; Heaven approves of actions and displays its warnings, as our people approve of actions and hold things in awe: this is the connection between the upper and lower worlds."[8] While there is a separation between the supernatural world and ours, these two worlds were thought to hear, see, and approve of things, in the same ways.

The Zhou dynasty made use of the idea of Heaven in what began as a neat bit of propaganda called the "choice of Heaven" (sometimes translated as the "mandate of Heaven"). The theory behind the choice of Heaven is simple: Heaven dislikes bad rulers and sends sign of displeasure – drought, earthquakes, or floods. If the bad ruler ignores these signs and does not reform, Heaven chooses an upstanding and moral man to replace the bad and corrupt ruler. With Heaven's support, the upstanding man will overthrow the corrupt ruler and become the new ruler. So, if you are the ruler, you have the choice of Heaven; if you are overthrown, you have lost Heaven's favor and the new ruler now has it.

The reason the leaders of the Zhou dynasty used the choice of Heaven theory was that they had overthrown the Shang dynasty. They claimed that it was the choice of Heaven that gave them the authority to do so; that they became the rulers shows that they did indeed possess the choice of Heaven. What began as an effort of self-justification by the early Zhou dynasty rulers continued on throughout Chinese imperial history where emperors were thought to have the choice of Heaven by virtue of being emperor. Confucius and other thinkers will also use the concept of the choice of Heaven to widen the concept and to demand accountability from rulers.

The Decline of the Zhou Dynasty and the Rise of the Warring States

For almost three hundred years, the Zhou dynasty used the choice of Heaven to justify their rule and ruled successfully over China. In 771, the Zhou capital in the west was captured by non-Chinese enemies and the Zhou king was killed. Some of the royal family escaped and established their new capital further to the east in the present-day city of Luoyang. This loss of the western territories, and, even more, the loss of prestige, signaled the beginning of the decline of the Zhou rulers' political power. If the Zhou rulers could not even protect their own capital city, then they were incompetent or weak – or both. Local lords took more and more control of their own estates and saw no reason for obedience to a weak Zhou ruler.[9]

As the Zhou ruler's power declined, local lords set up their own governments, often mirroring those in the Zhou court; they took on royal roles and titles and their estates became independent states. The power of a local lord came from his ability to call up men and assemble a strong army. The bigger his territory, the more men a lord would have to call on. This gave lords a considerable incentive to try to annex their neighbors' land and increase their territory.

Local lords faced threats everywhere they looked. Family members could be plotting to assassinate them. Other noble families in their state could be planning to overthrow them. Neighboring states might be working out plans to invade them.

One of the major problems facing these local lords was that they had no political legitimacy. There was no reason for any particular lord to be the ruler of that state. He did not have the choice of Heaven; if he did, he would rule the entire kingdom. He might claim a right to rule on the basis of his relation to the Zhou ruler, or as the head of his noble family. But there were other members of his own family – brothers, sons, uncles, nephews – who could make the same claim. Added to that, there were other noble families in his own state who saw no reason why the present ruler's family should be the ruling family. If his rule was based solely on the nobility of his family, any other noble family might be just as noble. This meant that any ruler faced rebellion both from within his family and from other noble families. As we move into the Warring States era (403–221 BCE) most of the original lords were overthrown by other noble families. Families that had overthrown their rulers faced similar challenges from other noble families and, increasingly, from newly rich families who had little claim to nobility but whose power lay in their wealth.

Members of ruling families plotted against each other. For example, in 696 BCE, in the state of Wei, the Duke of Wei had an affair with one of his dead father's concubines and he favored the son born from that union. When this son grew up and married, the Duke liked his son's bride very much indeed and had an affair with her from which two sons were born. The bride, confident of the support of her father-in-law, the Duke, plotted with her sons to kill her husband, the Duke's son. This would allow at least one of her sons (the Duke's illegitimate sons) to become ruler. The plot was only successful when the Duke came in on it. And so it was that the son was killed by his father, his wife, and his half-brothers.[10]

A prince might be supported by another of the state's noble families in his bid to overthrow his father. When the son was successful in killing his father and becoming ruler, he was indebted to the noble family that had supported him. If conspirators were unsuccessful, they were beheaded, drawn and quartered, their families were all killed, and their wealth went to the ruler. So it was to the ruler's financial advantage to charge his subjects with treason.

Life at the courts of these rulers could well be full of assassinations, poisonings, and plots. Sons rebelled against fathers, younger brothers against older brothers, families against families. Inter-family plotting was not the only danger for a ruler, or his successor.[11] Externally, states threatened and attacked one other or made temporary alliances that shifted easily.

As part of their duties as ruler of a state, rulers would travel, with great pomp, to the courts of other rulers where they would be greeted with feasts, musical performances, and gifts. Treaties would be signed and terrible oaths of lifelong friendship and political alliance sworn. This would be followed, almost inevitably, by treachery and attack.

Warfare was unending. By the 720s BCE, with the Zhou dynasty in decline, there were about 120 feudal states. Two hundred and fifty years later, by the time of the death of Confucius in 479 BCE, only 40 states survived. These 40 states continued to fight each other until, 250 years later, there were only seven states left.

The rulers of these states answered to no one. If you are looking for examples of despicable behavior, reading through the histories of the time, you will be spoiled for choice. Rulers were able to follow their own inclinations, and these inclinations were often greedy and immature. When Duke Zhuang, the ruler of the state of Zhu, was not able to punish an officer when he wanted to, he flew into a violent rage and flung himself onto his bed with such force that he fell off into the embers of the fire and burned to death. Before dying he gave orders that five men be put to death to accompany him in the tomb along with five chariots. The history says, "Duke Zhuang was an excitable and ferocious man."[12]

Living in a state of war and threat did not mean that nobles and rulers in these small states lived frugally. They had enormous gardens, and great orchestras and dancers providing music and entertainment at parties and feasts. They dressed in the latest fashions and enjoyed pastimes like hunting. One ruler, Duke Ling of the state of Qin (608 BCE), amused himself by shooting a crossbow at ordinary people from his city walls. When his chef did not prepare a dish properly, the duke had him killed and his body stuffed in a basket and paraded through the palace as a warning to others.[13] In 494 BCE King Fuchai of the state of Wu was described by his contemporaries as so self-indulgent that whenever he traveled, even if he was just staying for one night, he would insist on towers and pavilions being built for him. Ladies and maids must be ready to serve him. Even when he went out just for the day, all his games and pastimes had to accompany him. He was an avid collector of art and precious rarities and enjoyed spectacles and grand musical performances.[14] The nobility and rulers of the time were frequently corrupt, immoral, interested in extravagance and luxury, and often not very bright.

Shifting alliances and intrigues, both inside and outside the state, meant that concepts like honesty and loyalty were considered hopelessly old-fashioned. Anyone trying to behave well was obviously not smart enough to figure out the *realpolitik* of the day. There were good and responsible rulers and loyal and honest government officials, but often they did not fare well. One official, Shi Qi, was captured by enemy forces. He refused to disclose the whereabouts of his lord's body, because he had taken an oath to keep the burial site secret. They threatened to kill him. Shi Qi responded by saying, "When it comes to this kind of thing, if I had won, I would have become a high official; as I've lost, I'm going to be boiled alive. That's how it goes; I can hardly object." His torturers then boiled him alive.[15]

In another story of courage, a noble, Cui Zhu, had killed his ruler and so took the title of prime minister, setting his son up as the new ruler. The state's Grand Recorder, the historian who kept the records of the court, wrote in the record, "Cui Zhu assassinated his ruler." Cui Zhu had him killed. The Grand Recorder's younger brother then took over the post and recorded the same thing. He too was killed, as was yet another brother who succeeded to the position. When the fourth brother took over the job and made the same entry, Cui Zhu finally gave up. While all this was going on, a minor historian who was living in the south of the city heard that the Great Recorder had been killed. He gathered up his writing kit and headed to the court, only to turn back when he heard that the facts had indeed been recorded.[16] There were examples of loyalty and dutifulness, but they were few and far between.

The collapse of the feudal system headed by a dynastic ruler and the social breakdown that followed meant that there were also major social, cultural, and economic changes. Many of the older noble families fell on hard times financially or in the struggle for dominance in their state. A new merchant class rose along with a money economy, replacing the feudal bonds that had traditionally kept relationships together.

As the old nobility declined, their inherited government positions were increasingly filled by salaried appointed officials. These new bureaucrats were scholars, an intelligentsia who moved from one state to another as they liked, or as they were offered jobs. Although they were members of the nobility, they were not necessarily tied by family or clan bonds to the ruler or the state they served.

As well, there were innovations in warfare: iron weapons were now used, the crossbow had been invented, traditional chariot attacks by noble charioteers were replaced by massive infantry and cavalry formations and generals were chosen for their skill in tactics, not for their noble birth. There were innovations in farming too. Agriculture increased because of better irrigation and the use of iron tools. With the breakdown of feudalism, farming was more and more in the hands of nuclear families. Cities expanded as political and trade centers.[17]

The breakdown of the Zhou dynasty's rule led to major changes in Chinese politics, society, and culture. A once unified China was divided into many warring, small states. War, and the pestilence that often followed it, brought death and suffering to ordinary people. Even without war, life could be hard with high taxes and the ever-present threat of conscription into the army. Amongst the nobility, notions of loyalty and honor changed to calculating self-interest and a passion for money. A great deal of this may sound familiar to us in our world. For Confucius, and many of the thinkers who came after him, all of these things were signs of the decline of society and the loss of civilization itself. The past centuries of Chinese civilization were about to be lost.

> One of Confucius' students spent the night at Stone Gate. In the morning the gatekeeper asked him where he had come from. The student answered, "From Confucius' home." The gatekeeper replied, "Confucius – isn't he the one who knows what he wants to do is impossible, but keeps trying anyway?"[18]

The Life of Confucius

Confucius was born in 551 BCE into the troubled times of war, intrigue, and great economic and social changes; his life and teachings need to be understood in light of them. When it comes to the facts of Confucius' life and teachings, we have a number of written sources. As we shall see, ancient texts, and the versions of these texts, like all ancient texts, present problems. The next section is an introduction to some of these texts and some of the problems around them. There are additional problems given that Confucius was so famous that it was only natural that all sorts of myths would be built up around him. There is an extensive hagiography, pious stories that have accumulated over 2,000 years. In the final section we will see that scholars have been able to put together a biography of Confucius that, while still sketchy, is considerably more probable than the legends. While we have a good idea of what Confucius taught, just who Confucius was in terms of the events of his life, or his personality, are much more difficult matters. We do not even know what he looked like – though traditionally he was said to have been tall and well built. Our sources do not always tell us things we might like to know.

Sources

When we try to piece together the life of Confucius we come across the same problem that we have with the life of any figure from long ago. While we have texts that give us a great deal of information, how trustworthy and accurate are they? Who wrote them? Why? Is the picture they give us accurate?

After the death of Confucius in 479 BCE, his students, and their students after them, generated texts that claimed to set out, or elaborate on, his thought. We will look at these texts in more detail in chapter 8. We have, for example, texts like the *Analects* (*Lun Yu*), a collection of the sayings of Confucius. The *Analects* is said to have been put together by his students. For the last one thousand years, the *Analects* has been seen as the primary source of direct quotations from Confucius, though, as we will see, the text presents its own problems. It does not contain a complete biography of Confucius. There are other texts that purport to give us information about Confucius' life, though they are considered less reliable: for example, the *Kongzi Jia Yu*, a record of sayings of Confucius and his students; the *Three Character Classic*, a primer for boys; and the *Classic for Girls*. While they too give us information about Confucius' life and teachings, they are much later texts from the Han dynasty (206 BCE–220 CE). Generated by Confucius' followers, all of these texts claim that they are quoting Confucius, describing episodes in his life, and accurately reporting his teachings. So there are a great number of sources.[19]

Versions of the Texts

To confuse the sources further, there are not only texts, but there were versions of these texts. Texts evolved, first transmitted by students, then copied by others. If we take the *Analects* as an example, we can see how this works. The *Analects*, or sayings of Confucius, were traditionally understood to be the notes taken by Confucius' students at the time or recollections that his students gathered together later. The text presents quotations from Confucius, or a conversation between Confucius and others, but often without a context, so that we do not know what question was asked, or why Confucius was prompted to say certain things. The text we now have is divided into 20 chapters or parts; these are subdivided by numbering the sayings within each chapter. While scholars continue to debate which of these sayings are authentic, it is agreed that the text was written, or compiled, by a number of people over the course of about two hundred years. By the Han dynasty, two to three hundred years after Confucius' death, there seem to have been three versions of the *Analects* in circulation, and the text we have now is likely a synthesis of all three.[20]

There are some sayings in the *Analects* that are quite clear and there are others that are far more cryptic. An example of the former is a story about one of Confucius' students, Zai Wo, who was found having a nap during the day. Confucius commented that, as one cannot carve rotten wood, there was no point in scolding Zai Wo.[21] Evidently Zai Wo's lack of energy made him "rotten wood," so there was no point in Confucius correcting him. An example of a somewhat more cryptic saying is this one: "One day the stables burned down. When Confucius returned from court, he asked, 'Was anyone hurt?' He did not ask about the horses."[22] It is only when we know more about Confucius' teachings that we can understand his remark. It does not mean that Confucius did not care for animals. His first concern was with the stable hands and whether any had been killed or injured. He was concerned with people first; the horses, expensive and prized possessions of the ruler, came second. So reading the *Analects* requires information from the text itself, from commentaries written about it, and information about Confucius' teachings from other Confucian texts.

Modern scholars sift through classical Chinese texts like the *Analects* using modern tools such as linguistic and textual analysis to try to date them, trace their transmission, and penetrate the layers of interpretation. The result is a consensus about many of the important parts of Confucius' life and thought, while interpretations of them, and arguments about these interpretations, continue.

Confucius is like other important figures from the past, Jesus and the Buddha, for example, in that complex traditions grew up around them. While scholars agree on many of the basics of their lives and teachings, there can still be wide variations in interpretation. Within these limitations, we can reconstruct the broad outline of Confucius' life and teachings.

Hagiography, the Pious Stories of Confucius' Life

The first attempt at a full biography of Confucius can be found in the *Historical Records (Shi Ji)* written in the Han dynasty, 250 years after Confucius' death. Unfortunately, this biography contains many of the legends and fancies that had already gathered around the life of Confucius.[23]

These legends maintain that Confucius' ancestors were descended from royalty and moved to the state of Lu, modern Shandong province, from the state of Song. Confucius' father is traditionally identified as Kong Shu Lianghe. The histories record that he used his terrific strength and courage to save his fellow soldiers.[24] While he may have been a great soldier, he was less successful at being a civil servant. When he was 60, he married

Figure 1.1 Traditional rendering of Confucius

Confucius' mother, Yan Zhizai, who was only 20. Either with her husband, or alone, Confucius' mother went to Mount Niqiu to pray for a son[25] and there received the spirit of Heaven.

Other stories tell us that shortly before Confucius' birth, a unicorn appeared to Confucius' mother carrying a plaque that said that, with the decline of the Zhou dynasty, the child would be the "uncrowned king." After it left, Yan Zhizai gave birth to her son. Two dragons descended from heaven, circling the house, and five gods descended to the courtyard. His mother heard celestial music announcing the birth of a sage. At birth, the crown of Confucius' head looked like the shape of Niqiu mountain and so he was named "Kong Qiu."[26]

When Confucius was three, his father died. As a very young child, Confucius could play music and practiced rituals (see chapter 2 for a discussion of these rituals). As a boy he attended a school set up by a prime minister. When he was 17, his mother died. Even as a teenager, he was recognized by some officials in the state of Lu as a descendent of sages and as having a natural ability to understand and perform even the most ancient of rituals.

When he was 20, Confucius began his career as minor official. When his first son was born, the Duke of Lu sent the gift of a carp in honor of the birth, and so the son was named Kong Li (Li, "carp").

Tradition also has it that, at an early age, Confucius was appointed by the rulers of Lu to the post of police commissioner, then to a higher level as Minister of Public Works, moving on to become Minister of Justice, and finally to the position of prime minister of Lu.[27]

In the histories Confucius is shown as using his knowledge of diplomatic protocol to help the Duke of Lu set up an advantageous treaty with the state of Qi. The envoys from Qi, aware of Confucius' intelligence and skill, tried to intimidate him by sending armed men to the negotiations. Confucius, however, handled the situation so that Lu got what it wanted in the treaty. A paragon of virtue, Confucius did not fold when faced by force; without swagger, Confucius was courageous enough to correct his lord and wise enough to know the precedents.

Confucius continued to study with the most renowned Music Masters and Masters of Ritual. There are tales that say that, when a new ruler took over in the state of Lu, the state of Qi sent three beautiful women to the new ruler; the women were successful in making the new ruler distrust Confucius. Offended, Confucius withdrew from government, and began his fourteen years of travel throughout China (497–484 BCE), giving wise advice to other rulers and teaching the students who gathered about him. Traditionally it was thought that he had 72 students who were close to him and more than three thousand students altogether. These travels were sometimes dangerous with so many groups of armed men everywhere. In the state of Wei, Confucius and his students were attacked and beaten; on his way to the state of Chu, he and his followers were surrounded and besieged by a group of undisciplined soldiers. Sometimes political intrigue threatened Confucius: in the state of Song there was an attempt to assassinate him. During his travels he dealt with hunger and hardships. Still, he taught his students and attempted to advise rulers.

If Confucius was such an accomplished sage, why did rulers not take his advice? Later texts tell us that despite consistently wise advice to the rulers of the states of Wei and Lu, Confucius was ignored. The texts give three reasons for this. First, in order to follow Confucius' advice, rulers would have had to accept Confucius' criticism of their behavior and reform themselves; they would then have been required to govern with care and restraint. No ruler of that time was interested in doing any of these things. Second, other government officials were envious of Confucius and feared him; they did their best to thwart his plans. They slandered Confucius to their rulers, undercut his authority, and encouraged their rulers to behave badly in the hope that Confucius would become disgusted and leave. The corruption of the time meant that Confucius was not able to find a job in the

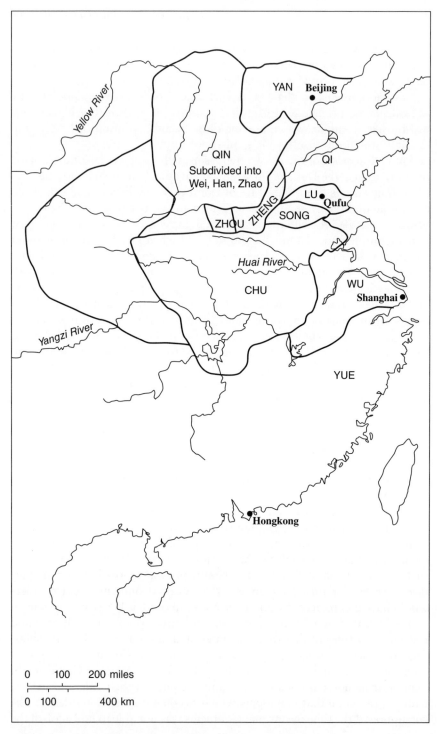

Figure 1.2 Map of Warring States, China (with modern cities)

many states he traveled to. Third, people of the time were incapable of really understanding what Confucius was teaching. Had the rulers and officials of the state of Lu, the inheritors of the Zhou tradition, really understood and followed what Confucius advised, they would have attained the choice of Heaven and become founders of a new dynasty that unified China. The stories that accumulated around Confucius contain these justifications for his lack of political success.

The stories continue by saying that, when Confucius returned to the state of Lu, he was not offered an office, so he spent his time teaching and writing or editing the ancient texts, *The Book of History*, *The Book of Poetry*, the *Spring and Autumn Annals*, and the *Book of Changes* (see chapter 8). When he had completed the texts, he lived on a vegetarian diet and prayed to the spirit of the Pole Star; a red rainbow flashed down from the heavens and changed into an inscribed tablet of yellow jade. Other traditions hold that Confucius himself was the Pole Star, representing the god of literature, who had come down to earth.

As death neared, Confucius was such an accomplished sage that he could often tell the future: predicting the outcome of natural events and the futures of some of his students. We are told that, near the end of his life, some hunters in the state of Lu captured a beast and killed it. Confucius was the only person who could correctly identify the beast as a unicorn. He wept and asked aloud why the unicorn had appeared at this time. The unicorn, a sign of a new dynasty, had been killed. This was taken to mean that Confucius understood that the state of Lu would never rise to greatness. In another version of this story, hunters killed a beast they did not recognize. When Confucius saw it, he knew it was a unicorn. He wept to see it dead because a unicorn appears when morality and justice will prevail. The hunters had killed the unicorn, an omen of good government. This was also a portent of Confucius' impending death.

After Confucius' death, some of his students kept a vigil at his grave. They brought trees from their native places to plant. This custom has continued and to this day one finds trees from all over in the Kong family graveyard.

Traditions around these stories and scenes are still recounted and can now be found in books and at tourist sites. For example, in the city of Qufu, which claims to be the birthplace of Confucius, one can be shown the seat where Confucius wrote the *Spring and Autumn Annals*, the pavilion where Confucius taught his students, the well that belonged to Confucius' family, and other sites to match these stories.

We can see a number of themes in these stories. First, as with many important figures from the past, Confucius had a special birth, complete with supernatural figures and events. His birth and death are rounded by appearances of unicorns; Confucius' failure to reform the times is represented by a dead unicorn just before Confucius' own death. Throughout his life, there are signs of Confucius' special status. As he matures, his sagely abilities border on the supernatural. Second, Confucius' abilities, even at a young age, are noted by the wise men of his time. Third, it is clear to some that Confucius is the greatest sage and he gathers around him thousands of students eager to learn from him. Fourth, despite recognition by some of the people of his time, Confucius is not recognized for what he is by any of the rulers. He fails, not through any fault of his own, but because the authorities at the time could not understand his vision. Confucius is the frustrated visionary who is always right, but never listened to. Had he been listened to, history would have been different. Confucius was the "uncrowned king" of the era. He was the Sage who attained the choice of Heaven, but he was, tragically, never given the chance to rule.

It is possible that some of these stories are true. But it is more likely that they were created to honor the Sage. They are charming, just as charming as the story of the three wise men at Jesus' birth, but pious stories of Confucius' life are not things we need to rely on.

Scholarly Versions of Confucius' Life

It is generally agreed that Confucius was born in the village of Zou or Zouyi in the state of Lu, near the modern city of Qufu in Shandong province, in 551 BCE. This would make him an approximate contemporary of the Greek thinker Pythagoras (585–497 BCE). He was named Kong Qiu. As was often the case, Confucius had a second given name, a "style," Zhong Ni. His father, Kong Shu Lianghe, was a well-known military figure in the army of Lu with a reputation for courage and loyalty. Of his mother, little is known as Confucius did not refer to her directly. All we know for certain is that her family name was Yan. His parents may not have been married or it may be that Confucius' mother was a concubine. Confucius' father seems to have separated from his mother, and she died early.

By the time Confucius was born, the state of Lu was besieged by its neighbors and internally divided among three powerful noble families; the hereditary duke was a mere figurehead. One of the three great families, the Ji family, took over the post of chief minister of Lu and from this position of power carried on as if they were royals, even offering sacrifices at Mount Tai – a royal prerogative.

Little is reliably known about Confucius' childhood, though Confucius himself remarked: "I was of lowly status when I was young. That is why I am skilled in many things."[28] There is a long tradition that Confucius' immediate family, while of noble lineage, were poor, and lived in genteel poverty.

It is likely that Confucius was a minor noble of a class called "knights" – the lowest rank of the noble class.[29] As a member of the nobility, a knight might be able to get one of a number of jobs at court: historian or record keeper, secretary, the tutor of princes or the sons of nobility, the overseer of rituals and music, or the master of ceremonies. By the sixth century BCE knights were part of the groups of professionals who performed funeral, marriage, and sacrificial rituals; they might also find employment as tutors or advisors. The usual translation of "knights" then becomes "scholars" or "bureaucrats."

These scholar/bureaucrats served as officials in various capacities at the royal Zhou court and in the courts of the independent states. They formed an emerging professional group. To a large extent they blamed extravagant rulers who listened more to friends, family, and shamans than to officials, like them, who knew their job.

One of the reasons we know Confucius was a member of the nobility was that he had an education, possibly in a local school, possibly in the company of other noble boys at a noble house. We know that, because Confucius was skilled in what were called the "six accomplishments." These were: rites, music, archery, charioteering, the study of history and literature, and the study of mathematics.[30] They were noble accomplishments, things a gentleman was expected to be conversant with. We can think of an English gentleman of the nineteenth century, for example, who would have known some Greek and Latin, been able to quote the Bible and Shakespeare, and known how to ride well. Like them, Confucius had the skills and training a man of his class would be expected to have.

In his early adulthood, Confucius visited the neighboring state of Qi (to the northeast of Lu) and spoke to its ruler, Duke Jing. Presumably he was looking for employment in that state. He returned home to Lu just as a noble began a rebellion against the Ji family. Confucius apparently considered joining this rebellion in the hope, he said, of gaining a position of influence in the new government and returning the state of Lu to the glories of the old Zhou dynasty.

The rebellion was unsuccessful and Confucius accepted some minor posts in the government of Lu, but then resigned them. Later commentators say that Confucius was disgusted by the improper behavior he saw in the government.

His resignation left Confucius unemployed and so, in his fifties, he traveled to a number of states over the next dozen years, going first to Wei and then to Song, hoping for employment. As a scholar visiting the court of one of these small states, Confucius would have been welcomed as a guest and given a place to stay and possibly something to cover living expenses for a while. At some point in his stay, the ruler or his ministers would have asked him about his opinion of current affairs or government. Depending on his advice, the ruler and senior ministers would decide about hiring him. Confucius seems to have been spectacularly unsuccessful in these interviews. Like many of his class, Confucius hoped that his ideas would be accepted by one of the rulers and that he would be given an influential post in government. This did not happen.

In 484 BCE, unable to find a job or to influence rulers, Confucius returned to Lu where he was given what was probably a merely ceremonial position. On the one occasion that Confucius gave advice to the rulers of Lu, his advice was rejected.

Confucius is often credited with establishing the first school – accepting fees from his students in return for his teaching. Confucius taught his students the classical learning that included the things that Confucius himself had learned as a boy and young man: poetry, history, literature, ritual, and music. While he taught traditional subjects, he always interpreted these classical studies in his own way. The education Confucius offered was not merely rote learning nor was it aimed only at making his students employable. Confucius interpreted history, poetry, ritual, and music, teaching them as a foundation for moral behavior and good government, as we will see in chapters 2 and 3.

While Confucius might have been one of the first to make teaching his sole occupation, there is no evidence that he established a formal school. Rather, students, mostly people from the same class of knights or nobility that Confucius belonged to, paid him for training. Confucius himself says that he accepted even the poorest of these men as long as their character and hard work made them good students. It is not clear just where he taught his students. It may be that lessons took place in rooms or courtyards in his home, but there was no school building. Rather than the 3,000 students attributed to him, scholars have identified 110, and, though there may have been more, it is unlikely that there were the thousands the legends speak of.

Confucius' students describe him as talking mainly about *The Book of Poetry*, history, and ritual. In his discussion of poetry, Confucius said, "*The Book of Poetry* has three hundred poems that can be summed up in one sentence: 'Have no evil thoughts.' "[31] Confucius' son reported that his father had asked him if he had studied *The Book of Poetry*. Confucius said, "If you do not, you will be unable to speak."[32]

The kind of speech that Confucius was referring to was quite practical: Confucius argued that poetry had many applications; he said to his students,

> My children, why do you not study *The Book of Poetry*? For it inspires thought, increases one's scope, cultivates one's ability to be sociable, and shows one how to express feelings of resentment. At home one learns the

personal duty of serving one's father, and in public the duty of serving one's lord. In addition, one learns the names of birds, beasts, and plants.[33]

The reason for Confucius' emphasis on poetry was that quotations from poems were used in diplomatic etiquette, in documents, and in speeches. A cultivated gentleman quoted poems and understood quotations, just as, in earlier times in the West, people quoted the Bible or Shakespeare. The inability to follow poetic references meant that one was low-class and ignorant.

Confucius taught history, but not just as the study of historical facts and dates. History was to be understood as a study in morality: students learned the events of earlier times so as to model themselves on the great founders of the Zhou dynasty, for example.

When Confucius taught his students ritual, he was teaching them the requirements of court ritual: proper greetings for guests, state marriages and funerals, rituals of ancestral veneration. Again, all of this was to prepare his students for jobs in government.

Not only did Confucius teach his students about music, he himself was an avid musician. Throughout the *Analects*, Confucius is described as singing, playing, and talking about music. When Confucius was with a person who was singing and who sang well, he would ask him to repeat the song, while he joined in.[34] One of Confucius' students was playing a zither when he replied to Confucius' question about what he had his heart set on. He put down the instrument to answer, "In the third lunar month of the late spring, dressed in our spring clothes, I would like to go with five or six grown men and six or seven boys to bathe in the river Yi. There, in the breeze, we would dance and come home singing." Confucius sighed and said, "I agree. ..."[35] Confucius not only sang, but played as well. He is described as playing the sounding chimes and the zither. Some music moved him deeply: the *Analects* says that when Confucius was in the state of Qi he heard classical music called the *Shao*, and for three months after he was so distracted thinking about it that he did not notice the taste of his food.[36]

There are some hints of Confucius' personality from the texts especially the *Analects*. His students were not always the sharpest pencils in the box and he was sometimes impatient with them. He said that if he had pointed out one corner of the mat to a student, he expected the student to find the other three; one student was so lacking in understanding that Confucius called him "a boor."[37] Confucius said that he was not about to teach anyone who "has not been driven crazy trying to understand a problem or has not gotten into a frenzy trying to put his ideas in words."[38] On the other hand, Confucius' heart was broken when his favorite student died young. And Confucius, described so often as an old fogy, said, "We should look upon the younger generation with awe, because how do we know that those who come after us will not surpass us now?"[39]

Confucius' students describe him as never having the faults of dogmatism, inflexibility, or egoism.[40] This seems to have been true. Confucius never claimed to be a sage or even more intelligent than others; he claimed only to love learning and to be quick in seeking out knowledge. This was matched by the eagerness he said he felt to teach what he had learned.

He gave a description of his own inner journey by saying, "At the age of fifteen, I set my mind on study. At the age of thirty, I established myself; at forty, I had no doubts. At fifty I knew the choice of Heaven; at sixty, my ears were tuned to it; and, at seventy, I could follow the desires of my heart without going beyond the bounds of proper behavior."[41] He had finally learned enough that he could match his desires completely to what is proper. In case this sounds a bit pompous, Confucius never stopped criticizing his own behavior and he did not think he was perfect. He once said that "When I fail at cultivating virtue, when I do not put into practice what I have learned, when I know what is right and still cannot follow it, when I am not able to change what is not good within me – these are the things that worry me."[42] Like all of us, Confucius may have known what was right, but that did not mean he was always able to do it.

Nor was Confucius someone who felt superior about his intelligence or learning. He once said, "Do I possess wisdom? Indeed I do not. There was a fellow who asked me a question and I was completely blank. So, we discussed the issue from beginning to end until we finally sorted it out." Acknowledging that he did not know, Confucius then went on to figure out the answer to the problem.

Confucius was not caught up in worrying about wealth and status – unlike some of his students. As we have seen, he was quite happy to go swimming with his friends and come home singing. He said, "Eating plain food, drinking water, and having one's elbow as a pillow – there is joy in this! Wealth and high position – when gotten improperly – as far as I am concerned are nothing more than passing clouds."[43] When asked about his ambitions, Confucius answered, "I would like to bring comfort to older people, to inspire trust in my friends, and to be cherished by the young."[44] Confucius described himself as a man who would forget to eat when trying to solve a problem, was so joyful that he could forget his worries, and did not notice old age creeping up on him.[45]

Confucius was married and had a son and a daughter, but he seems to have spent little time with his family; from what we see of him in texts like the *Analects*, his attention and affections are aimed at his students and male friends.

Figure 1.3 Confucius' tomb

Confucius died in 479 BCE at the age of 72. There is a story that when Confucius fell gravely ill, his students attended him as if he were a great lord and they were his ministers – serving him with elaborate protocol. They did this because they believed Confucius to be a great sage and his lack of high rank was embarrassing to them. At one point, when Confucius regained consciousness, he saw what they were doing and said, "You've been carrying out this make-believe for a while, haven't you? I have no government ministers, but you are acting as if I do. Who do you think I am going to fool? Can I fool Heaven? Anyway, why wouldn't I rather die in the arms of my students than in the arms of government ministers? I may not have a grand funeral, but it's not as if I'm going to die by myself on the side of the road."[46] His students had no choice but to carry out his funeral according to his low rank. Confucius' affectionate reproach in this story gives it the ring of truth.

One wonders what he thought about his life as it came to a close. On the one hand, he had never been able to put his ideas into practice because he had never been able to get a senior government position. Many of his former students who did achieve high government positions seem to have forgotten most of what he had taught them about proper behavior and good government. He might have thought that his life was in vain and his teachings would be lost. On the other hand, he was a passionate man who believed that the standards he followed were timeless, so he may yet have had hope for the future. The one thing that is certain is that he had no idea that he would be seen as the most influential thinker in Chinese history and that his name would be known in countries he had never imagined.

2

Confucius' Teachings I: The Foundation of a Good Person

While we may not know much about the details of Confucius' life, we are on firmer ground when it comes to his thought. Here people argue not so much over what Confucius taught but what that means.

As a teacher, Confucius taught traditional subjects like poetry and history. However, he taught these things by shaping them to fit his own ideas. His teachings were based on the terms and ideas of his time, but as we shall see, Confucius often radically reshaped these terms and ideas to fit what he wanted to say.

How do you fix a world that is falling apart? Confucius offered a thorough-going plan that addressed what we, as individuals, have to do and then how we must change society. In the first section we will look at how we can become adult, proper, people and then in the next section go on to see how we can then change society and government.

We will begin with the building blocks of an inner disposition – filial piety, dutifulness, honesty, sincerity, rightness, wisdom, and courage – and see how all of this comes together in the attitude of humanity.

Filial Piety

When grandfather discovered that his ten-year-old grandson was lazy in his studies, he had the boy flogged. The boy's parents were worried that these floggings would one day kill the child. The boy's father tried to intervene with his father and beg for leniency. The grandfather insisted that the grandson must study, and so flogged him harder.

One day, the grandfather discovered his grandson playing in the snow when he should have been studying. Grandfather had the boy stripped naked and left him kneeling in the snow while he considered the punishment. The boy's father did not dare say anything, but just stripped himself naked and kneeled down in the snow beside his son.

> The grandfather said to his son, "Your son is about to be punished for his faults, but what are you doing kneeling in the snow beside him?" The boy's father replied, "You are freezing my son, so I am freezing yours!"

Filial piety is a phrase that has probably not been used in everyday speech for over a hundred years, so we first need a definition. Filial piety means respect and reverence for one's parents – this is then extended to one's teachers and elders. The reason that there is no modern word or phrase for it in English is that it is not a concept our society much discusses or cares about. It is, however, central to Confucius' thought and to those who followed him. It is not surprising that they emphasized filial piety, given that, in their time, sons were rebelling against fathers and family relations were often deadly – certainly in the families of rulers. Confucius saw filial piety as an antidote to his times.

A version of the concept of filial piety existed before Confucius.[1] It was based on the authority of the ancestors that, among the living, rested with the head of the family. The family was organized according to the rites of ancestral veneration. That is, the rules that decided who, in one generation, was the head of the family were the same rules that were applied to the direct line of inheritance and rank. So, while the practice of filial piety, as respect for ancestors, elders, and parents, existed in the past, its implications were not developed.

When asked about filial piety, Confucius answered tersely, "Do not disobey." When asked to explain, Confucius said that filial piety has three parts: "Parents, when alive, should be served with ritual; when dead, parents should be buried according to ritual; they should be sacrificed to according to ritual."[2] The living and the dead deserve the same respect and sincere behavior. We find service to the living and the dead always linked together in descriptions of filial behavior. The *Classic of Filial Piety* says,

> Confucius says, "A filial son serves his parents in the following ways: he offers them the utmost respect when at home; he serves them so as to give them the greatest joy; if they are ill, he feels the greatest anxiety; he is completely devastated at their funerals; when he sacrifices to them (as ancestors), he is completely reverent. If he can do these five things, we can say that he is able to serve his parents."[3]

These are the required ways to show filial piety: service and respect while parents are alive, the provision of funerals, and the veneration of the dead.

Filial piety, which had originally centered around ancestral rites and temples, became a moral concept in Confucius' hands. Confucius did not emphasize filial piety as having to do primarily with ancestral rites. He changed the focus of the concept to talk more about service to the living.

Confucius was very much concerned with the neglect of parents, especially when they became older and were no longer influential and active in the family's affairs. As part of emphasizing service to the living, he criticized those who carried out elaborate funerals but neglected their parents when they were alive.

Confucians argue that the bond between parent and child is the most fundamental of human relationships. Filial piety plays an important role in philosophical discussions, but filial piety is not an intellectual abstraction. It is the natural love felt toward parents and it could be found in everyone's heart: small children naturally love their parents. The natural ties of affection that children have for their parents are based, the *Classic of Filial Piety* says, on gratitude for one's life: "It is parents who give life; what could be greater?"[4] In the *Analects* Confucius makes the argument that the requirement of three years of mourning for parents is based on the three years of complete helplessness through which parents nourish their children.[5] The three years of mourning are a reflection of this debt. We owe our parents for the gift of our life and nothing we can do could ever repay that. Parents care for us when we are helpless; as we grow older we must repay that care.

Did Confucius mean that filial piety should be absolute? Does it require complete obedience? One of the passages in the *Analects* has been a focus for this question. In it, someone told Confucius, with some pride, that in his part of the country there are men so upright that, in one case, when a father stole a sheep, the son turned the father in to the authorities. Confucius responded, "Where I come from, upright people are not like that. Fathers cover up for their sons and sons cover up for their fathers. Uprightness is found in doing that."[6] Confucius is saying that the relationship between father and son must trump all other considerations, even laws and justice. Does this mean that one is required to practice filial piety, no matter what criminal behavior one's parents are involved in? Some later commentators have said that, if the practice of filial piety requires immoral behavior, like lying, this would be taking filial piety too far. Filial piety should not be blind. Filial piety should be checked by moral propriety: parents and children should act properly and, if parents do not, children are not bound by filial piety. However, this was not the way the notion of filial piety was understood in history and in practice.[7] In the classical texts, we never see Confucius talking about any limits to filial piety.

There are many times when what Confucius says seems reasonable and logical. Then, there are times when what we read seems terribly foreign to us. Unconditional obedience based in filial piety is one of the ideas that strike most twenty-first-century Westerners as unreasonable, or, at best, quaint. Most of us think that we should grow up to become an individual, our own person. Filial piety is set in a different context. There the ideal is to become a person who works effectively in a context, in this case one's family. Even knowing this, unconditional filial piety is one Confucian idea that is difficult to accept.

While Confucius did not talk about any limits to filial piety, he did talk about the possibility of criticizing or suggesting alternatives – to "remonstrate," as it is often translated. So he says, "When serving your father and mother, remonstrate gently. If they do not accept your criticisms, remain respectful, do not act against their wishes, and follow their lead without resentment."[8] If he sees his parents doing something he disapproves of, or disagrees with, a son can point this out. But if his suggestions are not accepted, the son has to go along with his parents, however much he may disagree. In a much quoted passage from the *Book of Rites*, a son can remonstrate more often and even more forcefully than the *Analects* suggests. The result may not, however, be to the son's liking:

> If a mother or father has a fault, the son should quietly, with a gentle voice and a blank expression, point out the problem. If this has no effect, the son should increase his reverence and filial piety. Later, the son can repeat his point. If the parents are displeased, the son should strongly state his point, rather than let them do something wrong in the neighborhood or countryside. If they are even more angry and more displeased, and, even if the parents beat the son till the blood flows, the son should not dare be angry or resentful, but instead should increase his reverence and filial piety.[9]

So, while one can disagree with one's parents, and one can, respectfully, say so, a filial son must, in the end, go along with whatever the parents are doing. This, says Confucius, should continue even after the death of one's parents: "Anyone who does not change his father's way for three years after his father's death can be called 'filial.'"[10]

However, it is the moral duty of the son to intervene when his father is doing something not right, just as it is for a government minister when his ruler is acting badly. The *Classic of Filial Piety* says, "So, when facing behavior that is not right, a son has no option but to remonstrate with his father, just as a government minister has no choice but to remonstrate with his ruler. Thus to remonstrate is the only response one can have to what is not right. To just follow a father's commands, how can this be seen as filial piety?"[11] On the one hand, a son must intervene when he sees something not right; on the other, should his father insist, a son, after remonstrating, must follow. This attitude may be difficult to accept, but one has to remember the behavior of many sons in the Warring States era.

Serving one's living parents was understood to be difficult. Confucius says that doing things for one's parents is not the problem; the main difficulty is controlling the expression on one's face.[12] Later, in texts like the

Book of Rites, the instructions for serving parents were made even more minute and even more difficult:

> In order to serve their parents, as soon as the rooster crows in the morning, sons should wash their hands, rinse out their mouths, comb their hair ... [and get dressed].
>
> Wives should serve their parents-in-law as they served their own parents. At the first sound of the rooster, they should wash their hands, rinse their mouths, comb their hair ... [and get dressed].
>
> Now that they are dressed, the son and his wife should go to their parents and parents-in-law. When they arrive, they should ask in a quiet and gentle voice if the parents' clothes are too warm or too cold, whether they are ill, have any pain, or any discomfort. If that be the case, the young people should then reverently massage the place.
>
> The young people similarly should help and support their parents in leaving or entering rooms, either by going before them or by supporting them. When they bring in the basin for them to wash, the younger will carry the wash stand and the older the water. The children will ask to be allowed to pour out the water; when the parents have finished washing, the children will hand them a towel. ...
>
> They will ask if their parents want anything and bring it respectfully. All of this must be done with a pleasant expression so that the parents will feel comfortable.
>
> Both parents, at their regular morning and evening meals, must be encouraged to eat everything by the eldest son and his wife who will eat whatever is left over. If the father is dead, and the mother still alive, the eldest son should wait upon her at her meals. ...
>
> Whenever they are with their parents, the sons and their wives should immediately answer any call and reverently proceed to do whatever they are asked. ... They should be careful and serious; while going out or coming in, while bowing or walking, they should not presume to belch, sneeze, cough, yawn or stretch themselves. They are not to stand on one foot, to lean against anything, or to look annoyed. They should not dare to spit, nor, if it is cold, to put on more clothes, nor, if they itch anywhere, to scratch. ...[13]

The practice of filial piety is not for wimps. These kinds of rules would apply to upper-class households and are set out as an ideal. It is unlikely that most people carried out this kind of non-stop display of filial piety. But as ritual became understood more and more as sets of rules and regulations, this kind of behavior was expected.

A lack of filial piety and respect for one's elders does not bode well for one's future. A young man once came to see Confucius and sat very casually, with his legs sprawled out, waiting. When Confucius saw the young man, he said that it was clear that this fellow had no respect for his elders and would have nothing to contribute to society as he grew up. Becoming an adult and then aging, he would be nothing but a burden to all those around him. Confucius then used his staff to rap the youth on the shin.[14]

The effects of filial piety are not just in the family. Filial piety in the home develops into the virtue of dutifulness or loyalty outside of the home. The *Analects* argues that if a young man is filial toward his parents and respectful to his older brothers, he will rarely become the kind of man who will defy his superiors or stir up rebellion.[15] The Confucian gentleman learns loyalty to his ruler by learning filial piety at home.

Much of the discussion is couched in terms of the relationship between father and son. Daughters too were expected to practice filial piety toward their parents and, once married, toward their in-laws. We will look at the status of women in Confucian thought in chapters 3 and 13, but here we can note that not only were daughters expected to be filial, but sons owed filial duty to their mothers as well. Because of filial piety, women had authority over sons and grandsons, but how much authority often depended on the times and the circumstances.

Filial piety was understood as central to all the basic human relationships. Later Confucians posited five basic human relationships: father and son; elder brother and younger brother; husband and wife; ruler and government minister; friend and friend.[16] Any other human relationship could be seen as some variation of one of these five. Our roles are based on how we relate to one another – as a father or as a younger brother. In each case, our behavior and our duty will be different, depending on what our role is in that relationship.

We should note a few things about the five relationships. First, it is clear that the family is the centre of life and that the state is modeled on the family. Second, the relationship of father and son is primary and is a model for the others. Third, women play a role in only one of these relationships. Finally, Confucians argued that each of these relationships was reciprocal: a father cared for, and educated, his son; in return the son showed filial piety and respect to the father. Each side of each relationship has mutual responsibilities. The difficulty is that, in real life, the first side of each of the first four relationships is the one with the power. One ought not to be surprised that, given human nature, over time all the privileges flowed to the first member of the relationships – father, older brother, husband, and ruler – and responsibilities flowed to the second member – son, younger brother, wife, government minister.

Ideally, the family is the first place we are taught how to behave and the place where moral cultivation begins. By practicing filial piety we learn to put others' interests before our own. This is why Confucius says that filial piety is the root of all the other virtues.[17] The family is not just the place where we are children; as we grow, deal with siblings and relatives, marry, have children, and care for aging parents, we have the chance to expand our moral abilities. Relations with our family teach us how to deal with other people and how to respect other people. Throughout the Confucian tradition the family plays a crucial role in the development of ethical virtues.

Confucian discussions of filial piety took on a cosmic aspect in later texts: "A humane person does not overstep anything, nor does a filial son. When a humane person serves his parents, it is like serving heaven; when he serves heaven, it is like serving his parents. This, therefore, is the perfection of a filial son."[18] The *Classic of Filial Piety* moves the concept of filial piety into a larger realm. Here we find the argument that there is nothing greater than filial piety and it is the basis of all teaching and virtue. Filial piety acts as a tie between heaven and earth, not only because when one serves one's parents one serves heaven, but also because "Filial piety is as the constant in heaven, as rightness on earth, and the path of human beings."[19] There is no moral behavior greater than filial piety.

The concept of filial piety is central to Confucian thought and we will see how it spread through the entire culture. Historians have pointed out that filial piety has shaped nearly every aspect of Chinese social life: attitudes toward authority, where and how people lived, concepts of self, marriage practices, gender preferences, emotional life, religious worship, and social relations. During the imperial age, good behavior was defined in terms of whether or not one was a good son or daughter. Many scholars have claimed it is the basis of Chinese culture.[20]

Dutifulness or Loyalty

The virtue of dutifulness or loyalty is implied in filial piety. A man's first duty is played out in his family. Reverence and respect, first for one's father and older brother, extend to other elder members of the family. For Confucius, this should then extend to one's superiors and one's ruler. So we find discussions of duty are usually linked to political relationships where one is to do one's duty to one's superiors.

Confucius described a government minister as "dutiful" because, when the minister was dismissed from his position three times, he showed no resentment and fully briefed his successor on the affairs of his office.[21] By doing so, the dutiful minister subordinated his own ambitions and desires to the orders of the ruler – he did his duty.

Edward Slingerland notes that there is debate about just what "dutifulness" or "loyalty" means. Traditional Chinese commentators defined the Chinese term *zhong* as "doing one's utmost." In the *Analects* it is used in passages discussing attention to one's ritual duties, especially in a political context, and so should be thought of as "dutiful" – fulfilling one's obligations and duties as set out in one's hierarchical role.[22] As we shall see, the term has come to mean "loyalty," and often implies an expectation of blind loyalty rather than its original emphasis on doing one's duty.

Like filial piety, discussions of dutifulness were meant as antidotes to people's behavior at the time. The reverence and respect due to one's feudal lord, with the loyalty that implied, had broken down with the decline of feudal relations. The great lords of the time paid their followers in money or in land. Government ministers were paid a salary. In many cases, a monetary relationship had replaced duty.

Dutifulness, like filial piety, was meant to teach people to put the interests of their superior, whether father or ruler, before their own. Private ambitions must be subordinated to the loyalty one feels. Like filial piety, loyalty could include criticism. Confucius argued that it is one's duty to object if a ruler is wrong. He said that if one is really loyal, really doing one's duty, "how could you not instruct your ruler?"[23] As we have seen with filial piety above, criticism is permitted, if done reverently, though the results may be hard on the son or government minister. In a later text, the *Book of Ritual*, it is noted that a filial son may speak up to criticize his parents three times, but, if ignored, he is to follow their wishes. Similarly, it says, a government minister should speak to his ruler and offer advice and criticism. If after three attempts the ruler continues to ignore the minister, the minister should resign.[24] The son cannot escape his relation to his parents, but a government minister is not related by blood to the ruler and so is permitted to leave the relationship if his advice is not taken.

Doing one's duty in a serious and proper manner is an extension of filial piety and has to do more with relations outside the home, especially political relations.

Honesty and Sincerity

Other virtues that Confucius emphasized are honesty and sincerity. Honesty is more than telling the truth, though that, of course, is required. Honesty is living up to what one says one will do. It means keeping your promises. This means not boasting or making sweeping promises. We should only speak when we are capable of delivering what we say we will do.

Sincerity, or integrity,[25] is closely allied to honesty. It means there should be no distance between what we think, what we say, and what we do. In many situations we can find ourselves busy analyzing a situation and what we are looking for is how this situation will harm or benefit ourselves. While we are thinking of how to benefit ourselves, we may say things or do things that do not reflect what we are really thinking. A sincere person does not have this split. Rather, they think, say, and do, the same thing, not calculating their own advantage.

Rightness and Knowledge

To be sincere, we need to know what is right. Rightness (in older texts translated as "righteousness") is knowing what is proper, what is right, what is moral. This, like loyalty, is based on one's duty in a situation and that, of course, is based on one's status. Rightness is what is appropriate. As we will see, Confucius did not teach rule-based behavior, so what is right is based on one's status, one's role, and the specifics of the situation.

Rightness is the standard of moral behavior, dependent on the situation. This standard is not determined by our desires or fears in that situation, but stands above them. It is contrasted with self-interest, with profiting oneself, and with gain.[26] We can know whether we are really performing properly, or merely deceiving ourselves, by looking to the standard of rightness.

Rightness, the standard of behavior, requires knowledge. Knowledge or wisdom is something that we may not be born with, but, for Confucius, it is always something that we can work to achieve. "People who are born with knowledge are the highest level; second are those who attain knowledge by studying; third are people who continue to study even though they find it difficult; at the bottom are those who find study difficult and do not even try to learn."[27] Confucius often describes himself as being in the second or third level, saying that he was not born with knowledge, but, because of his fondness for antiquity, was keen to learn; he says that he looked for the good in what he studied and tried to retain it.[28]

Wisdom begins with learning about things; Confucius' students learned about history, poetry, and ritual. This learning should, over time, lead to wisdom. What wisdom should bring us to is knowledge of ourselves and the knowledge of how to deal with the people in the world around us.[29] When asked to define wisdom, Confucius said, "Know other people."[30] Being a good judge of character is important in being morally effective. If you understand the character of the people you are dealing with, you can deal with them properly.

Knowing ourselves means being honest about ourselves: "To say you know when you do know, and to say that you do not know when you do not know – this is wisdom."[31] Knowledge then is related to honesty and sincerity: we should know that what we say is honest because it is something we can do.

Courage

It is all very well to have knowledge, practice filial piety, be loyal, dutiful, honest, and sincere, and know what is right, but in order to act on these virtues, we must have courage.

Courage had been talked about a great deal in the early Zhou dynasty: the nobles were warriors and spent their time in hunting or war. The strutting warriors of the time based their reputations on their physical courage. By the time of Confucius, war was waged more and more by big battalions than by battling heroes. The audacious warrior who disobeyed orders to show his courage had become a problem, not an asset. Still, courage was associated generally with physical courage, bravado, and honor.

Confucius took the concept of courage, made it a virtue, and put it in the service of moral behavior. "To see what is right, but not to do it, this shows a lack of courage."[32] For Confucius, courage is moral courage, and it was as difficult to find in Confucius' time as it is in ours. People worry about their status, their paycheck, their reputation, their family, and their future, and this leads to moral cowardice, just as Confucius said it would. As a result, civil servants and government ministers do not argue with their ruler – prime minister or president – when it is clear that government policy is wrong or immoral. Executives of corporations do not blow the whistle about wrongdoing in their companies; workers pour toxic waste into farmers' fields in the dead of night. These people, by and large, have the knowledge that what is going on is not right, but they are too self-interested and too cowardly to do anything.

Real moral behavior in the real world requires courage. But courage, when not guided by moral behavior, simply allows the wicked to be more wicked. Confucius said that a noble who is courageous, but who does not know what is right, will create political trouble, while a lower-class man who is courageous, but does not know what is right, will become a criminal.[33] Courage by itself is no guarantee of moral behavior; courage in the service of morality generates the energy to carry out that moral behavior.

Understanding, Sympathy, Compassion

The virtues we have looked at so far are very much "inner" virtues. But, in Confucius' thought, virtues are not cultivated for our private amusement or heavenly salvation. Moral virtues are meant to act out into the world; morality is not merely a private achievement. The last virtue on our list moves us outside of our private universe and has to do directly with dealing with other people.

Confucius startled his students one day by saying that all his teachings could be hung together on a single thread. Zengzi, one of his brighter students, explained to the others that this thread consisted of two things: loyalty/dutifulness and understanding/sympathy/compassion.[34] In other passages, Confucius defines what he means by the term *shu*, which we translate as "understanding," "sympathy," or "compassion." It means, Confucius says, "not doing to others what one does not want done to oneself."[35] This may sound familiar: it is often called the "negative golden rule." The positive golden rule would be given by Jesus in another context about five hundred years later as "Do unto others as you would have them do unto you." Scholars, naturally enough, have debated which version, the positive or negative golden rule, is the most effective, but for our purposes we can see that both of them mean that we should put ourselves in another's shoes.

For Confucius, the message is simple: treat the other person as you yourself would like to be treated.[36] With the knowledge of others that we have cultivated, we can understand another person's situation. Knowing that, we imagine ourselves in their place and try to act as we would want others to act toward us. This is especially important for the times we are in positions of authority, as a teacher or employer, for example. We can remember how we were treated, and, if we were treated badly, we should not do the same to those we now have power over.

In other situations, sympathy is just imagining the other person's situation: if the woman has three screaming kids in the car, give her the parking space. If someone drops all their papers on the floor, help them pick them up. If someone is passed out on the sidewalk, do something about it. We should imagine ourselves in another person's shoes not because we hope they will do the same for us, nor should we do it because it will be, in some way, to our advantage. Understanding or sympathy takes us outside of ourselves and beyond our personal inclinations and greed.

Sympathy works with all the other moral values. We can express filial piety not just by following certain rules, but by putting ourselves in a parent's place and anticipating what they would like. Sympathy works with honesty in tempering our honest response so that we do not hurt someone's feelings. Sympathy is often the catalyst that brings out the other moral virtues.

There can be too much of a good thing. Any virtue, taken to an extreme, can be dangerous. Courage can be excessive and, when it is, become recklessness. When someone asks how you like their new Hummer and you respond that it is an ugly gas-guzzling vehicle displaying the owner's self-indulgence, this may be honest, but certainly not polite. Too much honesty, without regard to the situation, can work against moral behavior. Too much loyalty, to the point where it is blind loyalty – my country, right or wrong – may well mean that one is ignoring other responsibilities like wisdom and moral courage. Too much of a search for knowledge could lead to a bookishness that does not act out into the world. Too much insistence on a standard of right and wrong, especially when these are not important issues, can lead to inflexibility and officiousness. Ji Wenzi, a minister in the state of Lu, was well known for his meticulous attention to his duty. When told that Ji Wenzi thought about things three times before he acted,

Confucius sarcastically responded, "Twice would be enough."[37] Too much wisdom can be misused. Expressing too much sympathy, without good judgment, can lead to us being taken advantage of. All the virtues can be taken to extremes, and when they are they become not virtues, but faults.

These virtues should be understood as dependent on one another and working together. We have seen how filial piety leads to dutifulness or loyalty, a love of learning leads to wisdom, honesty and sincerity mirror each other. Not only do we need all these virtues, but they work together. In introducing these virtues, I have arbitrarily separated them so we can look at each one in turn, but Confucian texts rarely talk about one virtue without another and never in the kind of shopping list that we have here.

Moral virtues of any kind are not something we develop instantly. Thinkers in classical China all talk about "cultivation." Just as one plants a seed in the ground, waters, and weeds, in order to cultivate a plant, so too moral behavior is built up over time. By studying the ancients and seeing good and evil behavior, one can see more clearly how one ought to behave.

Humanity

What we have seen of moral virtues so far sounds a bit like the Scout law: be thrifty, clean, and helpful. Confucius tells us to be filial, honest, sincere, dutiful, wise, courageous, sympathetic, and so on, but there seems nothing exceptional in this: many traditions say much the same. But for Confucius all of these virtues are just the building blocks to bring us to a moral attitude. This is *ren*. The word *ren* was originally used to mean something like "handsome," "manly," or a "man's man," and had nothing to do with morality.[38] Confucius reshaped the word to mean a moral, rather than macho, strength. The development of virtues and learning was meant to lead to this overarching attitude.

I have so far tried to avoid using Chinese terms, because they can be difficult for introductions: they can be found in the Glossary. A precise English translation of *ren*, however, is not easy. *Ren* has been translated as "benevolence," "humanity," "co-humanity," "love," "altruism," "goodness," "the Good," "authoritative person," and "self."[39] The choice of one of these English words as a translation will often depend on the interpretation the translator makes. I will use "humanity" as the translation for *ren* because it is the most common one and comes closest to expressing what we mean here.

Humanity is a moral attitude. Humanity is the umbrella that includes all the virtues – being honest, sincere, wise, courageous, practicing filial piety, and sympathy toward others. All of these moral building blocks bring us to the attitude of humanity. "Working your shopping list," as one of my students said, is how one develops the overarching attitude of humanity. Humanity is the pervasive moral attitude that we bring to the world we live in.

Having humanity requires that we overcome the greed and egocentricity of the self. Humanity is defined as the opposite of self-interest, profit, and looking for possessions.[40] Confucius said that if we could restrain our selfishness and return to practicing rituals, we would attain humanity. If we could manage to do it for an entire day, we could lead the whole world back to humanity.[41] This is not an easy thing to do, for, as Confucius says, he has yet to find a man who loves virtue as much as he loves female beauty.[42]

How do we become good people? "Focus your mind/heart solely on humanity and you will be entirely without evil," says Confucius.[43] If our aim in life is the cultivation of the building blocks of moral behavior so as to act out into the world with humanity, we will not be considering our self-interest nor putting greed for possessions or power first. No matter what is happening in our life, the attitude of humanity allows us to endure bad times and to be careful and generous in good times. An ideal person lives in a state of humanity.

Confucius' description of the building blocks of morality and the overarching attitude of morality allows us to see how he defined evil. Although he does not discuss evil as a concept, we can see what he meant by it by looking at the opposite of what Confucius defined as good. Evil is being rude; being careless; it is pride; it is the lack of self-reflection, self-awareness, and self-knowledge. Evil is deceit. Evil is greed for money, possessions, and power. Evil is a desperate need to be famous and to indulge in sensual pleasure. Confucius lived over 2,500 years ago and yet his relevance to the evils of our times is uncannily accurate.

The moral virtues and their culmination, humanity, are within us. But they must be practiced in social and political situations in the world. For Confucius, these inner moral values are expressed in ritual, and that is what we will look at next.

Ritual

Nowadays when we use the word "ritual," we use it in three ways. First, we talk about religious ritual – baptism or funeral rituals, for example. Second, we often use the word "ritual" in place of the word "habit": so it is my morning ritual to first drink a cup of coffee before I do anything else. Here it is a habit, something I do every morning. No prayer or incense need be involved. Finally, we often say something is just "empty ritual," meaning that the form has no content. For example, when someone asks how we are, we ritually respond and say that we are fine. We may not be fine at all, but we will, nevertheless, make the ritual response. Most of us tend to think that this kind of empty ritual is insincere and has no real meaning. As Confucius will show us, we are wrong to think that.

In the stories about Confucius' life, we have seen that he closely associated with ritual. As a child he was said to have played with ritual utensils and, as he grew, he studied with the masters of ritual. These rituals were of two kinds: first the religious rituals of the time, such as ancestral veneration, and, second, the rituals of noble etiquette and proper behavior.

There were many rituals involving supernatural powers carried out in Warring States China. The rituals of ancestral veneration, for example, are described at length in ancient texts, like *The Book of Poetry*. The ancestors, present in their ancestral tablets, were offered food in proper bowls and cups; jade discs and scepters were also placed on the altar. The texts describe the laying out of grain and wine, the invitations to the ancestors, and the impersonator of the dead. The impersonator of the dead, a descendent of the ancestor, took the place of the deceased and was thought to be possessed by the ancestor's spirit. The impersonator announced when the spirits had drunk their fill and when the spirits returned to their place.

Ritual specialists would need to know the proper utensils, their placement, the times to make offerings, when to bow, and who stood where. These were all things Confucius studied and taught. His students might then have gotten jobs as ritual specialists at court, managing the ancestral rituals, noble marriages, and funerals.

Confucius would also have taught all the proper forms of noble etiquette: that a lord enters a room before a duke; proper salutations from one rank to another; how to carry on diplomatic negotiations with another state, and so on.[44]

These were the two forms of ritual that Confucius grew up with. Confucius combined these two senses of ritual, religious ritual and noble etiquette, and then expanded on them for his definition of ritual. He noted that carrying out rituals requires reverence, for the ancestors, for example, and respect, for a duke or lord, and then expanded this to explain ritual as reverence and respect for all the people one deals with in social situations. Confucius concluded that ritual is a moral action that ensures a proper, civilized society.

This definition may be surprising, but when we think about it, it should not be. Let us look at some everyday examples. You meet a friend, you say, "Hi, how are you?" and the friend replies, "Fine. And you?" or words to that effect. Your first question, "How are you?" is not really a question about your friend's health. If the response you get is something like, "Oh, last night I couldn't sleep because I had a headache, but by this morning it was gone, though I'm still experiencing back pains from the pickup basketball game," then you know that your friend didn't really understand the question. Your "Hi, how are you?" is an acknowledgement of the other person and offers respect.

We notice this more when the ritual breaks down. If our friend ignores our question or refuses to answer, we will be hurt or insulted because, by not participating in the ritual, the friend is saying that he or she does not respect or value us. If, as commonly happens now, the friend responds only by saying "I'm fine," but not asking you how you are, the ritual is unbalanced and your friend has clearly been rude.

Meeting someone and offering to shake their hand works in the same way. If a hand is not offered in response to yours, the person has been rude and you feel like an idiot standing there with your hand in the air.

We practice rituals all the time, mostly not noticing them until they break down. The next time you feel annoyed at someone's behavior, try to think what your expectations were. The person who butts into line, for example, is ignoring ritual and disrespecting everyone else in the line. We are annoyed by this because this person has not followed the proper ritual.

When we were young, our parents spent a lot of time and effort to teach us the very basic rituals of "please" (what's the magic word?) and "thank you." We were taught to wait our turn, to share our toys, and not have a tantrum when we did not get our way. While it is true that today many people seem not to have been taught these basic rituals, our society is still based on the expectation that people will follow them.

We perform rituals all the time, whenever we interact with others. Because we do so many rituals every day, we tend not to notice them at all. Take the example of going to a lecture. We are going into a room where the chances are that we know no one there, yet, generally, we do not go in fear of our life. That is because people come in and take their places. They are relatively quiet and they set out paper and pens – all proper ritual indicating that they too have come for the lecture and not a fight. People do not usually dance on the desks, mug someone, or pull out a submachine gun. If they did, you would feel uncomfortable, or, in the latter cases, you would flee. The lecturer appears and, when it looks like the lecturer is ready to begin, people stop talking to each other and look toward the lecturer. If some people continue to talk to each other, even though the lecture has begun, the lecturer has to stop and say something to them. This is embarrassing to most of the people in the room – though often not to those who want to continue their conversation – because we should not have to be reminded of the proper ritual. The fact that we can go to theaters, classrooms, or meetings full of strangers and not be afraid is because everyone practices ritual when they come into the room and during the show, class, or meeting.

In times of war, or in places where ritual has broken down, we cannot trust strangers to behave in predictable and courteous ways and so become afraid. Ritual is essential for a civilized society and it is a moral action where one party shows respect for the other, whether this is saying hello, standing in line, or bowing to the Queen.

There are a few things to note when it comes to ritual. First, rituals are almost always balanced: even when one person is superior, they are required to play some part in the ritual for it to work. If one is introduced to the Queen, one bows or curtseys, and the Queen acknowledges the introduction in some way.

Second, ritual is learned. Our parents spent time teaching us the rituals of our culture; we were not born knowing them. This also means that ritual will vary from culture to culture: some shaking hands when meeting, others bowing.

Third, ritual teaches us proper behavior: for Confucius, rituals have less to do with the power of the spirits than with forms that instruct us in morality. In other countries and in other times in history, people have understood rituals as something that dealt with supernatural powers and that had to be acted out with each word spoken correctly, down to the most minute action and pronunciation. Confucius does not look at ritual like that: he sees rituals as the ways in which we practice civilized behavior.[45]

Finally, rituals are actions outside of us. We can carry on a ritual even when we do not like the ritual, do not like the person we are being polite to, and desperately wish we were somewhere else and not visiting great-uncle Henry. Ritual is an exterior action and does not, in itself, require any internal commitment. Confucius argues that ritual should not be morally empty; ritual should be an external expression of an inward morality. In turn, ritual should teach us how to cultivate internal ethical attitudes.

Later Confucians will also argue that ritual functions as a way to restrain our selfishness and channel our emotions. Even though we may be tired from a long day, ritual tells us not to be selfish: give up your seat on the bus to someone who needs it.

Ritual channels our emotions too. Funeral rituals are ways we express grief. They allow our grief a channel, a socially acceptable way to be expressed. At the same time, they limit our emotional expression so that we do not, for example, throw ourselves into the grave during the burial.

When we learn rituals and perform them properly, with inner moral intent, we become better people. The respect expressed in the ritual becomes the outer form of an inner moral world. So Confucius wanted the practice of ritual to be a constant in our lives. He said, "Do not look at anything contrary to ritual; do not listen to anything contrary to ritual; do not say anything contrary to ritual; do not move in any way contrary to ritual."[46] Everything we do must be an expression of ritual, not because it allows us just to play an empty socially acceptable role, but because ritual is a moral action that ensures a proper, civilized society.

Confucius demanded ritual behavior, first, because it is the basis of tradition; that tradition had, in the past, led to good behavior, good government, and a unified China. We inherit rituals from the past and the people in the past had good reasons for setting them up. Second, ritual is the web of social and political relationships. So, when ritual is practiced with moral intentions, individuals and society benefit. If we all treat each other with respect by performing the proper rituals, it is not just the individuals involved who benefit, but, in a ripple effect, all of society. We will see how ritual works into moral behavior, society, and government as we go on.

With his reinterpretation of ritual, we see once again that Confucius has taken a traditional term and redefined it to suit his own ideas. He reshaped the traditional usage of the word ritual to refer to religious ritual and noble etiquette into a broader definition of ritual as a moral action expressing respect for others. The practice of proper ritual will lead to a civilized society.

For Confucius, ritual is the external expression of an inner morality. Ritual gives us socially acceptable ways of behaving well. But ritual is not performed just for ritual's sake: there must be an inner moral component.

The inner moral world must meet the exterior ritual world. Carrying out rituals requires reverence, for the ancestors, for example, but expands to the requirements to respect and be humane to the people one meets. Doing a ritual properly teaches a person to cultivate the attitude of humanity. Ritual acts as the exterior guide for humanity. In turn, carrying out the proper ritual with the proper attitude reinforces both. Moral actions mesh with ritual.

For example, your friend is in hospital; proper humanity tells you that he or she is in pain and worried – you can imagine yourself in such a situation. The proper ritual is to visit and offer comfort. Humanity and ritual work together.

Both external action – ritual – and internal attitude – humanity – are required. If you just express your humanity, thinking about your poor friend, how ill and worried he or she may be – putting yourself in their place – you have been successful in humanity. If you do nothing further, you are not a moral person because humanity has to be expressed. All the sympathy in the world does not make you a good person if you do nothing about it. You may have good intentions, meaning to phone your aunt who lives alone, but it you do not actually do it, you have failed to act morally.

On the other hand, if you go to visit your friend in the hospital, you are doing the proper ritual. But if you spend your visit complaining about your health or talking about how busy you are, you are also not a moral person. You have not been sincere and you have not expressed humanity. To do the ritual without any real meaning behind it is hypocritical. You expect to be applauded for good behavior, but you did not have any moral intention.

The moral attitude of humanity works together with ritual, but we need to make sure that people are not hurt by the mechanical application of either a moral rule or a ritual rule. Again, this is why we want to treat the other person as we ourselves would like to be treated.

There is a wonderful, though probably apocryphal, story about Queen Victoria (r. 1837–1901) – a stickler for proper ritual if there ever was one. One night her dinner guests were ordinary people, not the upper-class people who were usually invited to dine with the Queen. When the footmen brought around the fingerbowls, these guests, not knowing any better, lifted the bowls and drank from them. The Queen could have followed proper ritual and rinsed her fingers with the water, but she followed humanity and, not wanting to embarrass her guests, she too drank from her finger-bowl. Had the Queen insisted on following proper ritual, she would have embarrassed her guests. Adjusting her behavior to the situation and putting herself in their place, she ignored the proper ritual. Ritual and humanity work together, but must deal with each situation as it arises.

Ritual directs our expression of humanity; the expression of humanity animates ritual. This reciprocal relationship can be seen with humanity and ritual, but applies to all the other virtues and ritual as well. Confucius said that too much respectfulness without ritual expression leads to a dithering person who is simply exasperating; too much carefulness without proper ritual leads to a timid person; too much courage without proper ritual leads to an obnoxious person; too much rightness without proper ritual expression makes us inflexible.[47] So all the internal virtues must be tempered and expressed through ritual. On the other hand, ritual with no moral foundation is empty and hypocritical.

Confucius never gives us a set of rules such as the Ten Commandments or the Buddhist Five Precepts. The rule "do not kill" is a very good rule. But there are situations where we may have to break the rule. A child is being abducted; you are armed and are the only thing standing between the abductor and the child. Can you shoot him? If you have to obey the moral rule "do not kill" at all times, you cannot. This is why Confucius did not deal in rules.

Each situation we encounter will be different; the people in that situation will be different. Moral behavior in one situation may be disastrous in another. Applying rules mechanically does not take into account what Confucius called "timeliness." Times, places, people, and circumstances all change, sometimes dramatically. Behavior must accord with timeliness, not a set of rules.

However, Confucius is not talking about some sloppy, "go with the flow" situational morality where we just do what we feel like.

Each situation and each person is different and we must use our knowledge of others and our knowledge of ourselves to lead us to a decision about

Figure 2.1 The Apricot Pavilion where Confucius is said to have taught

what to do. Added to that is our sense of sympathy or understanding – putting ourselves in their shoes. This leads to flexibility in the situation. On the other hand, there is no flexibility when it comes to the ethical demands on us. We need to be honest and to act with moral courage. We need to do our duty and act according to the standard of right and wrong. There are ritual rules. So, moral behavior is not just how you happen to feel at the time. While we may be flexible in a situation, we cannot be flexible about the standard of moral behavior that we are required to practice.

Life is difficult. This is especially true when we have to make decisions. Often we do not have all the information we would want and often we must make decisions quickly and may not have a lot of time to think. This is when the process of cultivation is most helpful. If we have practiced sincerity or honesty or moral courage in small things and, at all times, worked on the cultivation of humanity, we are more likely to act properly when something major happens. Humanity is cultivated over a lifetime. Confucius believed that, just like any habit, if we put virtues into practice and express them through rituals, over time they become stronger and more automatic. No one can do this perfectly the first time – moral cultivation, just like growing a plant, takes work and time. The proper behavior of a morally trained adult is not based on tastes or on our feelings at the moment: the moral attitude – humanity – cultivated properly, is based on a standard of right and wrong.

The insights Confucius had about humanity and ritual put him in the top ranks of moral philosophers, but Confucius is not finished yet. He still has much more to say about the ideal we must try to live up to and how that will affect society and government.

The Gentleman

Qu Yuan (c.340–278 BCE) was a poet and statesman. He advised his ruler, the king of the state of Chu, against an alliance with the state of Qin. He was accused of treason and banished. When Qin captured the capital city of Chu, Qu Yuan was in such despair that he committed suicide, drowning himself in the Miluo River.

The Dragon Boat Festival, held on the fifth day of the fifth month, includes making "zongzi," rice wrapped around a filling, to feed the fish lest they eat Qu Yuan's body, and also the dragon boat races as a symbolic attempt to save this most loyal and honest official.[48]

A person who can practice both humanity and ritual is called a "gentleman."[49] Originally this was a title of nobility referring to the younger sons of a lord. They would have been part of the noble, warring, class. "Gentleman" was a title based on birth, not merit.

Confucius, however, redefined the word "gentleman" to make it a goal one wants to reach. A gentleman is someone with ethical and ritual training and a good education, and is an example of moral behavior. A gentleman is what one should be; he is the paradigm, the model or standard, of what we should become.[50] To unify China and bring back the peace and good government of the early Zhou dynasty, government needed to be led by gentlemen, chosen for their moral character, not their noble birth.

With Confucius' redefinition, the status of gentleman is not achieved by birth. To become a gentleman one must be trained and educated, and practice morality.

The gentleman is usually described in opposition to the small or petty man. The small man concentrates on possessions; the gentleman concentrates on virtue.[51] The gentleman helps others build up their good points; the petty man encourages the bad in others.[52] The gentleman corrects his ruler; the petty man agrees with whatever the ruler says.[53] The gentleman is hard to please – things must accord with morality; the petty man is easy to please because he does not care if things are done morally; the gentleman is easy to serve because he understands people's abilities; the petty man is difficult to serve because he demands things beyond people's abilities.[54] The gentleman is grand, but never arrogant; the petty man is arrogant, but never grand.[55] The gentleman understands higher things; the petty man does not.[56] A gentleman never does things for his own benefit, but only does things that are right. A gentleman is not afraid, but ready to give his own life. A gentleman never forgets his promises.[57] In sum, the gentleman works at overcoming his own selfishness and at helping others become better people; the petty man is motivated by his own greed and desires.

Once we set our minds to becoming gentlemen, we are told not to worry if we are not recognized as gentlemen, but to worry only that we do not have the ability of gentlemen.[58] Being poor, having shabby clothes, or being hungry is not what a gentleman worries about: "The gentleman is not interested in a full stomach or comfortable housing. He is careful in his actions and his words, seeking out those who know the Way and being put straight by them. This is what it means to be eager to learn."[59] Getting a good job with a high salary is not the goal.

If a gentleman does become wealthy and famous, and achieves an important position in government, he accepts these things only when they accord with humanity and ritual. The moment they do not, a gentleman has enough self-respect to simply give them up.

One can learn to become a gentleman just as one learns moral behavior and ritual – through education. One is to become reverent and respectful when dealing with others.[60] Confucius says a gentleman cultivates himself to become respectful, to bring peace to others, and finally to bring peace to everyone – something even the sage-kings could not do.[61] By studying history, we can see how moral and immoral behavior had an impact on the world; by studying literature we learn the great aspirations of the ancients; by learning ritual we learn how to behave properly. Education is not meant to teach particular things, but to prepare us to deal with any situation. The aim of this education is not professional accreditation; the aim of education is to teach us to develop humanity and to act in the world. We are told that a gentleman never abandons humanity even for as long as it takes to eat a meal and is never in such a state of distress or trouble that he lets go of humanity.[62] Humanity gives the gentleman a sense of tranquility, no matter what his troubles.

Cultivating the self means growing the virtues within. It also means that, if there is a problem, we are to look within ourselves first to see if there is a fault in us that has brought this on. If we look within and find no fault, then the gentleman is neither anxious nor afraid.[63]

Confucius expected the gentleman to do two things. First, to serve in government, providing moral advice and education to the ruler. A gentleman as a government official should lead rulers to practice proper moral behavior and to rule well. Becoming involved in politics is the way the gentleman expresses his personal cultivation.[64] A gentleman who cultivates himself does not do so as a private exercise, looking for some kind of inner enlightenment, but rather to make the world a better place to live in.

While it is possible that a gentleman might achieve high office, it was not necessarily the case that virtue would be rewarded. Perhaps the gentleman, like Confucius himself, would not be able to find a job; it could be that, as a government bureaucrat, his ruler might not listen to his advice. Confucius expected that a gentleman in such circumstances should retire from government and become a teacher, educating the younger generation – much as Confucius had done.

Whether one becomes a government minister or a teacher, being a gentleman is a life-long process of cultivating virtues, examining oneself for faults, and acting in the world.

Along with the "gentleman," another exemplary person is the "sage." Confucian texts refer to the sage-kings of ancient times and to heroes like the founders of the early Zhou dynasty, Kings Wen and Wu, and the Duke of Zhou. A perfectly moral person would be a sage. While Confucius mentions the idea of a sage, he does so only in the negative, saying, modestly, that he has never met a sage and that he could never dare claim to be either a sage or to have humanity; rather, all that could be said of him is that he worked tirelessly and encouraged others to do so.[65]

Over time we can learn about virtues and practice them, building up the moral attitude of humanity and putting ourselves in another person's shoes. We can learn rituals and see how they allow us to respect others and maintain a civilized society. Doing these things makes us gentlemen. Gentlemen are not necessarily perfect in every situation, but do work hard at both humanity and ritual. This allows the gentleman to act in the world, either improving government or as a teacher. How we can improve our society and our government is what we will look at next.

3

Confucius' Teachings II: The Foundation of a Good Society and Other Topics

If the Dao, the Way, is being followed in the world then show your-self; if it is not, then retire in seclusion. In a state that has the Way, to be poor and of low status is a reason for you to be ashamed; in a state that does not follow the Way, to be rich and famous is equally a cause for being ashamed of yourself.[1]

One consistent thing we have seen so far is that, despite his reputation as a conservative old fogy, Confucius radically restructured many of the terms current in his time to fit with his own ideas. He himself said that he transmitted the wisdom of the past and did not create anything new. This is an odd thing for him to say, given that, as we have seen, he has redefined ritual, filial piety, courage, humanity, and the role of the gentleman. He may have been giving himself some cover for his innovative ideas by saying that these things all existed in the past.

To recap, there are many moral virtues we need to cultivate: filial piety, dutifulness, honesty, sincerity, rightness, wisdom, moral courage, and understanding or compassion. Cultivating these virtues leads us to a general attitude of humanity. Confucius redefined ritual to include religious rituals, and noble etiquette to mean ritual as moral actions that lead to a proper and civilized society. Ritual is the way we act in a web of social and political relationships; ritual, when practiced with moral intentions, benefits individuals and society. Working on the basis of moral virtues, with the attitude of humanity, and practicing rituals, can make us gentlemen – or, if we become perfected in them, a sage. Cultivating moral virtues requires an education, not just in learning facts, but in understanding moral behavior. This cultivation and education is a life-long process.

When Confucius explained this to the rulers of his time, there was nothing much that they would have objected to. Even if they had no intention of carrying out any of this cultivation, and even if they were the most depraved of characters, it is likely that they would have gone along with this, if only to make themselves look good. So why could Confucius not get an important government job? Why, if we are to believe tradition, was there an attempt to assassinate him?

The reason Confucius could not get a government job in any of the states of his time was not because of what he had to say about morality and ritual. It was because of his political ideas. Confucius had a subversive idea, distasteful to rulers then as it is now: Confucius believed that government exists for the benefit of the people.

Setting Words Right

Government needed to be reformed, or not just reformed, but overhauled from top to bottom. But before any reforms to government could be made, there was something that needed to be done first.

One of Confucius' students, Zilu, asked Confucius what he would do first if he was offered a job in government. Confucius replied that his first priority would be "to set words right."[2] Zilu was, as the reader may be, unimpressed. Zilu wondered aloud how Confucius could be so far off the mark as to want to start with a trivial thing like setting words right.

Confucius means two related things when he talks about setting words right. First, we must all name things by their proper names; we must all use the correct word when we discuss something. So, "downsizing" is not a proper word; it is merely bafflegab. It means "firing people." "Collateral damage" is not the proper phrase for what is happening; "killing civilians" is the proper phrase. Similarly, "enhanced interrogation" sounds innocent, but it is still "torture." The person on the phone in the call center is not a "customer satisfaction specialist" until they satisfy their customer – and even then they may or may not be a specialist.[3]

This jargon, buzzword, or bafflegab is not merely annoying. It is a lie. When government departments refer to me as a "client" or a "customer," they are lying about our real relationship. I am not a client or a customer, I am a citizen. If they can convince me that the relationship is a consumer relationship, then they are simply offering a product and I can choose to buy or not. But our real relationship is that I pay taxes that support the government and I can vote to keep or get rid of that government. That is not the same relationship I have with Wal-Mart.

Telling lies by using the wrong word allows for bigger lies. Phone a "customer support centre" and you will be told, by a recorded message, that "Your call is important to us." That is clearly not true; if it was, they would answer the phone. Labeling people as "terrorists" who possess weapons of mass destruction leads to war and the death of tens of thousands. In terms of "putting words right," there is no difference between these two examples. Misusing words leads to lies, whether it is our cable company or our governments. When words have been debased, big lies are even easier.

The difficulty in dealing with this phenomenon is that you have to go back to the basics and call things by their proper names and use accurate words before you can even get to the issues involved. Governments in particular are happy to keep the waters as muddied as possible.

This sort of thing was happening in Confucius' time too. Rulers of small states were calling themselves kings, though they had no right to the title. A noble family in Confucius' own state of Lu offered sacrifices at Mount Tai, something only the emperor was meant to do. Bafflegab, misdirection, and lies were as prevalent in his time as in ours. It is not easy to decide if that is comforting or distressing.

Confucius meant a second, and related, thing by "setting words right." If we need a table, that table can be made of wood, plastic, steel, or any other material; it can have four legs, two legs, or a single pedestal leg; it can be of any color. The only expectation we have around the word "table" is that it will have some sort of flat surface.

This is not how other words work: some words come with expectations about behavior. If someone is a father or mother, then we expect behavior that cares for children. If someone is a teacher, we expect teaching. Words like "father," "mother," and "teacher" come with expectations about behavior.

If parents neglect or abuse their children, they are not acting according to the expectations we have for "parents." If teachers do not bother to teach their students, they are not living up to the behavior we expect from their title. Using the principle of setting words right, if these people do not act as fathers, mothers, or teachers, then, says Confucius, they do not deserve these titles and should not be called by those names. People have to act virtuously and responsibly before they can properly be called parents or teachers – the words must correspond to real behavior.

We can apply the principle to parents and teachers, but "setting words right" applies to rulers as well. If a ruler does not rule virtuously, then he is not a proper ruler and does not deserve the title. This idea has serious political consequences: if a ruler is not a proper ruler, can he be disobeyed? Can he be overthrown?

It is not clear that Confucius wanted to go that far. He used the idea of "setting words right" as a judgment rather than a call for revolution. After Confucius, Mencius (see chapter 6) will argue that, if an unworthy man becomes ruler and is overthrown, it is not a ruler who is overthrown, but merely an unworthy man.

The idea of "setting words right" demands that people live up to the expectations we have when we give them particular titles. When Duke Jing of the state of Qi asked Confucius about the principles of government, Confucius said, "Let the ruler be a ruler, the minister a minister, the father a father, the son a son."[4] This cryptic saying is perfectly understandable in light of "setting words right": a proper ruler should rule as a proper ruler in order to have the title; a proper minister should be loyal and dedicated in order to be a minister; a father should raise, educate, and care for his son; and a son should have filial piety in order to be a proper son.

When Confucius' student, Zilu, complained that "setting words right" was a trivial way to begin to govern, Confucius corrected him and said, "If words are not set straight and names do not match reality, then nothing can be done successfully [... and] the common people will not know what to do or how to behave."[5] Confucius wanted to begin any reform of government with "setting words right" for the simple reason that, without it, we cannot talk to each other honestly and we cannot perform our roles properly.

When we, and our governments, use the proper word to describe something, we can speak honestly and accurately about it. When people fulfill the expectations that their roles have, whether as parents or rulers, we are behaving properly and honestly. We will know what to do and how to behave.

For the Benefit of the People

Confucius maintained that government exists for the benefit of the people. The first, and necessary, step in good government is to put words straight so that everyone knows what is going on and how to behave.

Caring for the common people meant ensuring that basic needs, like food and clothing, were met. It is crucial that the economy allow people to make a decent living. Taxes should not be punishing. When a ruler complained that the harvest had been a poor one and the tax money he got that year was hardly sufficient to cover his expenses, he was told that, instead of taxing at the 20% rate, he should reduce his tax to 10%. After all, if times were tough, taxes should be lowered so that the people would have enough to live on. Once the people have enough to live on, the ruler should be happy with that.[6]

When asked about government, Confucius said that the ruler should make sure that there was enough food and enough weapons, and that the ruler had the trust of the common people. If a ruler had to do without one of these three, he could give up the weapons. If he then had to choose between enough food and the trust of the common people, he should give up the food. This is because a government cannot stand once it has lost the people's trust.[7]

When people see themselves as part of a common whole, sharing good times and bad times with their ruler, they are more likely to trust their ruler. If people believe in their government, they will put up with all sorts of hardships. It is the ruler's job to build that trust. He does that by cultivating his virtues and being a gentleman. As the people see his behavior, they will model themselves on it. The ideal situation would be a ruler who was actually a sage – a perfectly moral human being. Confucius thinks that this is why the sage-kings of the past were so successful: they combined humanity and ritual in such a way that ordinary people followed them willingly.

Even if a ruler is not a sage, he can appoint wise ministers, Confucian gentlemen, who will give him good advice and serve him loyally. For their part, cultivated gentlemen should take office in states where they have a chance of influencing the ruler for the good or in states where the ruler was already good. To accept a salary from a bad ruler is a shameful thing[8] and gentlemen were to stay away from states that were so badly ruled that they were about to collapse. Real power should be given to educated, trained gentlemen who would be government ministers. They would care for the common people and advise the ruler wisely. They are the ones who will guide ordinary people and establish good government.

Ordinary people cannot manage on their own. We have already seen Confucius say that common people can be led so as to follow a path, but not so that they understand it.[9] Care and guidance must be given by government to bring people into the right path, and that is why the gentleman as government minister is so important. When Confucius talked about government for the benefit of the people, he was not talking about democracy. His view of government is a paternal kind of government: the government acts toward the common people as a father acts toward his children, guiding, caring, and disciplining. As far as Confucius is concerned, only the educated elite really understand the moral, social, and political objectives involved – they are "inner-directed"; that is, they are able to maintain their moral stance in good times or bad. Ordinary people, on the other hand, need a good environment, with good models and a good economy, before they can act properly; they are "outer-directed," changing according to good or bad times.

Laws

It is also important that these gentlemen-ministers are models of virtue so that ordinary people can follow them. Simply enacting laws does not provide that kind of guidance. Laws may be necessary for those who, no matter what kind of government is in place, will never behave. But laws and punishments do not teach people virtue. Instead, Confucius says, laws and punishments only make people learn how to avoid being caught. Confucius believed that if only laws and punishments are applied, people may follow the laws or find ways of evading them, but they will never develop a sense of shame.[10]

That is because we may obey a law only because we fear getting caught and punished. However, the law teaches us nothing in moral terms: it is simply a barrier. If, on the other hand, virtue and ritual are taught to people, then people will develop an inner sense of shame and behave themselves.[11]

The difference here is the difference between driving over the speed limit and being caught with child pornography. In the first case, the law sets a speed limit on a highway and, if I see no police cars, I may speed anyway. If I get caught, I have simply lost a cat and mouse game with the police, but I'm unlikely to be ashamed of speeding, possibly just embarrassed at being caught. In the second case, not only is possessing child pornography against the law, but it is considered shameful in our society. We have set up standards of virtuous conduct that exclude this behavior, so if one is caught, one is ashamed.[12] The speed limit law is external to me; the disgust at child pornography has become an internal moral judgment. This is why Confucius argued that ritual is better than law. You will always have to have laws to deal with the incorrigible, but ritual and virtue help develop people's inner moral sense. Once you have done that, a government does not need a policeman on every corner.

Models

This view of law and government is based on an insight Confucius had about "models." With a law, people obey for fear of being caught; once they follow ritual and a moral ruler, they obey out of inclination. Confucius believed strongly that models change people's behavior, and that once people saw moral gentlemen in the government, they too would tend toward moral behavior.

Think about our times, our models – the people we talk about and see on the news and in the magazines. They are politicians, actors, entertainers, and sports celebrities. Is it any surprise that, if ordinary people see bad behavior from these models, they feel free to do the same?

Only a handful of people today would know the name of Dr. Paul Farmer, who founded Partners in Health, establishing no-fee hospitals in Haiti, Rwanda, Peru, and other poor countries, but most people know who Tom Cruise is and about his domestic squabbles. There are good people around us, but we choose not to talk about them. The models we have often confirm, and encourage, our worst behavior.

On the other hand, sit back for a moment and imagine the following. Imagine that you live in a place where the people working in all levels of government are good people. They are trying very hard to solve problems. They are honest and conscientious, and they work hard. They answer their own phones. They may not always be successful, but they continue to try to deal with people carefully and respectfully. Would you feel differently in a society like that? Would you mind paying taxes? Would people led by that kind of government value education and government service? Would they be more moral? more polite?

Confucius is convinced that government officials act as models for the people. If people saw their sincere and honest hard work, ordinary people would become sincere, honest, and hard-working. He says, "The virtue of the gentleman is like the wind and the virtue of the common people is like the grass: when the wind moves, the grass is sure to bend."[13] Ordinary people will move in the direction that the gentleman leads them. This also applies to bad behavior. If the ruler and government ministers are corrupt, so will the people be. When a government official in the state of Lu complained to Confucius about the rising number of robbers, Confucius told him that if he got rid of his own desires for luxury, ordinary people would not steal, even if they were paid to do it.[14] By desiring the finer things in life, the official has shown his people that these things are valuable and so they steal them. If the official was honest and hard-working, the people would be too.

Confucius' ideal government is a government that rules through moral example and moral power rather than through laws, punishments, and coercion. This is government by morality, not government by force.

Good government can earn the trust and support of the common people. Should war come, ordinary people would be willing to fight for it. Given that Confucius lived in a time of war, we would expect that he would talk about it. Instead, we are told that when Duke Ling of the state of Wei asked Confucius about military matters, Confucius said that while he knew about ritual matters, he knew nothing of military ones. Confucius left the state the next day.[15] Confucius does say that it is the responsibility of the government to train the common people as soldiers and not just throw them into battle. This training, even under the government of gentlemen, could take a number of years.[16] But Confucius does not offer advice about military matters in his discussions of government. He believed that it was good government, not success in war, that would bring success to a ruler.

A state, run on moral lines, caring for the people, would be so attractive that people would flock to it, just as they ran from evil governments. There is a traditional story that, on his travels, he met a poor woman and her children who lived in an area infested with tigers. When Confucius asked her why she did not take her children and move, she said that the tigers were not as dangerous as life under the corrupt ruler of the neighboring state. Just as people naturally avoid evil rulers, so too they would be anxious to live in the state of a good ruler.

Confucius criticized the leaders of his time. They were interested only in themselves, in the latest luxuries, in displaying wealth and status. Their greedy ambitions led them to act only in their own self-interest and, as a consequence, to wage war. All of this was paid for, in one way or another, by ordinary people. They were heavily taxed and dragged into army service to fight wars that had nothing to do with them.

The ideal government that Confucius proposed would not work like that. If gentlemen staffed the government, they would not be looking out for their own self-interest. They would not be interested in luxury or display. They would not have ambitions to conquer others. The lives of ordinary people would improve, in the first instance, simply because the government would get off their backs.

Confucius' ideal government and society are based on ritual and morality.[17] A person cultivates moral virtues and learns ritual, first in the family, and then through education. Families, ideally, both teach proper behavior and are the primary place where proper behavior is expressed. A gentleman is educated in the lessons and arts of the past and this enables him to cultivate himself, learn ritual, and learn the standard of right and wrong. It is the gentleman's responsibility to take action in the world, especially, if possible, in government.

A ruler, ideally a sage or gentleman, should surround himself with other Confucian gentlemen in government who will not only relieve the burdens on the people, but provide a state where people can make a decent living and gradually internalize the morality that the gentleman models. The government would work hard at benefiting the people; and the people, in turn, would trust the government. That is the ideal picture, but in life things are rarely so easy or clear-cut. Confucius had opportunities to serve in government and found himself caught between his great desire to serve and help reform the state and his dread of not being effective and, in the end, abetting a corrupt ruler.

In one conversation reported in the *Analects*, Yang Huo, the steward to the Ji family in Lu, tempted Confucius. The Ji family was the great power in Lu, the power behind the nominal duke, and the Ji family carried on as if they were royalty. Confucius criticized their arrogant behavior a number of times. Yang Huo offered Confucius an office in the government of Lu.

Yang Huo asked Confucius why he continued to keep his talent hidden away. He asked further if a man could be defined as wise when he repeatedly missed opportunities to serve. Finally, Yang Huo pointed out that time was passing and Confucius was getting old without having taken the chance and taken political office. Clearly Confucius is a wise man and would be an asset to any government, yet he has continually refused government positions. How long could Confucius take the moral high road, claiming to be able to reform government and yet always refusing a place in it?[18]

In the end, Confucius refused the offer. Throughout the *Analects* we see Confucius desperate to act, but then withdrawing, remaining loyal to his ideals. This raises the question of when we should act. If there is a chance to benefit society, when should Confucius, or a gentleman, or any of us, lower our standards to take the position? How much corruption should we put up with? Can one serve even bad rulers, if there is a chance of influencing them? If no state is following the Way, how can we ever find a government to serve in? A gentleman should "speak truth to power," but what happens when he is ignored or, given the Warring States era, killed for doing so?

If we take a position in a government or support a government in some way, are we simply becoming part of the corruption we oppose? On the other hand, standing on the sidelines and not getting our hands dirty may make us morally superior, but hardly effective. Ideally we should have enough knowledge to be able to judge the timeliness of acting or not acting, but life was messy for Confucius as it is for us.

Another problem in Confucius' ideal of government has to do with the choice of Heaven. No state in the Warring States era could claim to have the choice of Heaven: if they had had it, they would have conquered all the others. Confucius opposes government by force, but the idea of the choice of Heaven implies the use of force to overthrow the old dynasty. This leaves Confucius in a quandary about his loyalty to the old Zhou dynasty and the choice of Heaven that would require one of the states to overthrow it. Later Confucians in the Warring States period will withdraw their loyalty to the old dynasty and opt for the idea that the choice of Heaven will come to whichever state becomes a moral proper state and so overthrows the Zhou.

There are those who say that Confucius' ideas would work only in the small states of his time and cannot be applied to the large nation-states of today. It is true that the government structure Confucius envisions is the structure he was used to seeing: a ruler, his noble ministers, and the common people. Confucius did not contemplate anything like a modern state or a democracy. But some of his ideas about politics could be applied. It might be interesting, and certainly refreshing, to see what a moral government would look like.

To summarize, Confucius' political ideas are based on the notion that government exists for the benefit of the people. A government run by Confucian gentlemen or sages would begin by putting words right. They would care for the people by providing a good economy, not overtaxing the people, and not throwing their lives away in battle. The people would trust such a government and, as the government provided models for behavior, the government would educate people in ritual and morality. Governments should rule through moral power and moral example, not through laws, punishments, and force. Moral cultivation in the individual must have social and political expression. Whether in our family, among our friends and co-workers, or in government, the moral virtues we cultivate will lead to a better society and a better government. Confucius, the "conservative old fogy," calls for a thoroughgoing reformation of the individual and of the state. We are to become educated, moral, and politically active. The state is to provide good government that will, in turn, promote morality. "Putting words right" and government by moral gentlemen, guiding the people, providing for them, and acting as models, all make society and government better.

Much of what we have looked at so far is interpreted by different scholars in different ways. For example, you may find different under-standings of humanity and of ritual in other texts and other transla-tions. The next sections describe some of the more contentious areas of Confucius' thought. First, we will look at his ideas of education. Education, in itself, is not the problem; the problem is who it is that Confucius thought could, or should, be educated, and that brings us to Confucius' attitude toward women. Second, we will look at Confucius' attitude toward the supernatural – the gods, the spirits of the dead, Heaven, and the idea of fate.

Education without Distinction

If you go to the Confucian temple in Taipei, the capital of Taiwan, in the main section you will see an enormous plaque with a quotation from Confucius that says, "Education without distinction." People will tell you that this means that education is open to everyone and that Confucius was the first to offer education to all.

It is not actually that clear that this is what the passage means. We find this saying in the *Analects* where Confucius says, "In education there are no different kinds."[19] There are problems around what is meant by "different kinds." Some argue that this has nothing to do with public education, but is simply Confucius saying that, no matter if one is a bit slow or almost a sage, we must all start out to be educated in the same way.

Others read this passage as saying that there are no different kinds of people when it comes to who can be taught. Confucius was open to teach-ing everyone, no matter who they were in terms of social class or wealth.

Confucius often talks about how poor some of his students were, especially his favorite student, Yan Hui (or Yan Yuan). Confucius was not impressed by rich students arriving in their carriages and offering substantial school fees, saying that even if a student came on foot and offered only a package of dried meat, he should be taught.

What we know about Confucius' students, however, is that they were all upper-class: some of them, like Confucius and Yan Hui, were relatively poor, but we do not know of any of Confucius' students who were from the common people. It would be surprising to find commoners among Confucius' students. At that time, ordinary men had only a very limited opportunity to become literate. Without basic literacy, it would have been impossible to study any texts that Confucius taught, like *The Book of Poetry*. As well, we find Confucius saying things like: while one can lead the common people in the right direction, it is not possible to make them understand it.[20] So it is not clear that Confucius believed education should be extended to all classes.

Women

Nor is it evident that he wanted education to be extended to women. Confucius rarely had anything to say about women in the *Analects*, and that may be just as well. The one time he says anything about women, he says, "It is always difficult to deal with women and servants: if you are too close to them, they become insolent; if you keep them at too great a distance, they complain."[21] Confucius also said that he had yet to meet a man who is as fond of virtue as he is of beautiful women, and Confucius' students were warned to guard themselves against female beauty when young.

The only woman named in the *Analects* is Nanzi. She was the wife of the Duke of Wei and, according to the sources, both politically powerful and promiscuous. Confucius is said to have met and spoken with her, something his students disapproved of. Confucius had to defend himself against their criticisms, saying he had done nothing wrong.[22] Like many passages in the *Analects*, there is no context here to tell us what Nanzi or Confucius said in the conversation or why he was talking to her.

All Confucius' students were male. Confucius' concerns are male concerns: getting a post in government, being a filial son, and so on. Women also do not figure in what we know about the lives and conversations of Confucius' students.[23]

Texts from Confucius' time and later Confucian texts were especially critical of women in positions of power. Wives and concubines were seen as the source of political troubles. *The Book of Poetry* says,

> A clever man builds city walls,
> A clever woman overthrows them ...
> Women with long tongues
> Are just cruel and violent.
> Chaos is not sent down from Heaven.
> It originates in women ...
> Women should have nothing to do with public affairs,
> But keep to spinning their silk.[24]

These characterizations of women as bringing disaster to governments and families can be found throughout the histories of the time.

We saw an example of this in chapter 1 in the story of the Duke of Wei who had two sons with his daughter-in-law and was part of her evil plot to kill her husband. In the histories especially we find a number of stories modeled in the same ways. In them, the evil, sexually attractive woman, the wife or concubine of the ruler, seduces him into making fatal mistakes in government. The loyal minister warns the ruler of the terrible consequences but the minister is not listened to, is fired, or is even executed. The ruler, in his besotted state of mind, rules badly and the state is conquered by another.

During the Warring States period, the status of women continued to decline. While some upper-class women were wealthy and politically powerful, inheritance had become almost entirely patrilineal. This meant that many women were less in charge of their own wealth and did not inherit equally with their brothers. The secondary status of women is seen most clearly in a passage from *The Book of Poetry*:

> When a boy is born,
> He is laid on a bed,
> Robed in a gown ...
> Lords or princes come from this family.
>
> When a girl is born,
> She is laid on the floor,
> Robed in rags ...
> She will do nothing bad,
> Nor anything good either.
> All she does is to carry wine and plates of food,
> And is no trouble to her father and mother.[25]

This attitude can be found echoed in later Confucian texts. Confucian ritual texts contain regulations for men and women: they are not to sit on the same mat, or to use the same rack for clothes, or to touch when handing one another something.[26] This lack of direct contact was meant to lessen the possibility of sexual arousal. To further this aim, the ritual texts also contain rules for the separation of the sexes: "Ritual begins with the correct relations between man and wife. ... In the home, there is a division between outside and inside; the man lives in the outer, the woman in the inner"; and "men should not speak about what belongs to the inside of the house, nor women to what is outside."[27]

Women were to provide a harmonious household, while the man's role was outside the home. Men dealt with the public issues and everything outside of the household, while women were to deal with the domestic and the private.[28]

Rules for domestic rituals, such as ancestral veneration, included women. When a woman married, she left her parents' house and went to live with her husband's family. In the ancestral veneration ceremonies, the first wife of the primary descendent of the ancestors (the eldest son) led the other women of the household, just as her husband led the other men. Both participated in the rituals. This has led some commentators to argue that women and men had complementary responsibilities. They point out that women are not labeled as the source of all evil, as they are in other traditions. They quote from the *Book of Rites* to argue that women were as valued as men: "The emperor and empress are necessary to one another, and through their interdependence they are able to complete all things."[29]

Others point out that however balanced the ritual of ancestral veneration may be between the actions of men and women, the ancestors being venerated are the man's ancestors and the children who carry on the family are his sons.[30]

Given this background and later Confucian texts, it is not at all clear that Confucius meant to extend education to women or to lower-class men. While the scope of his beliefs about education is not clear, it is clear that he believed that one should be educated, and not just educated to get a good job. Education was important because it had moral, social, and political goals.

The Gods, the Spirits of the Dead, and the Afterlife

> *The Annals of the Warring States* tells the story of the widow of the Duke of Qin who wanted her lover, a man from Wei, to be buried alive with her when she died. Her lover argued against her plan, pointing out to her that she did not believe in an afterlife and so his accompanying her to the grave would do her no good. If, however, it should turn out to be true that there is an afterlife, the Duke, her husband, would not be at all pleased with her arriving with her lover.[31]

Most of what we hear from Confucius is teachings about morality, social and political behavior, and the reform of both the individual and the government. Confucius never refers to gods, like the gods of rain, thunder, the earth, and so on. He is never described as praying to them. Given his times, this is remarkable. Most of the people of his day would have believed in the power of the gods, the spirits, and the ancestors; they would have tried various methods to find lucky days to do things; they lived in a world saturated with the supernatural. There was a wide belief in the power of ghosts – spirits of the dead who received no sacrifices – to do harm to the living, causing misfortune and bad luck. Supernatural powers were credited with causing everything from droughts to illness.

When Confucius does talk about the gods, it is not always clear what he means. For example, when Confucius was very ill, Zilu, one of his students, asked permission to pray, quoting a text that says, "We pray for you above and below to the gods of heaven and the gods of earth." Confucius replied, "In that case, I have been praying for a long time." What are we to make of this? Does it mean that Confucius has been praying to the gods all his life? Commentators have generally interpreted this passage as meaning that Confucius' whole life has been a prayer and so he did not need to pray to the gods. They base this interpretation on other things Confucius said about the supernatural. As well, his students tell us that Confucius never talked about strange prodigies, feats of strength, disorder, or the gods.[32] Nor does he seem to have been very interested in talking about the spirits of the dead.

Confucius would, of course, have been well versed in the rituals of ancestral veneration and taught the rituals to his students. The culture at large believed in the power of ancestors to bless and punish the living. However, Confucius rarely refers to the spirits of the dead, and when he does so, he is not willing to discuss or describe them at length. He says, "To work hard to ensure rightness among the people, and, while respecting the spirits, to keep away from them, this may be called wisdom."[33] So we should show the spirits respect, but not get close to them. In another comment Confucius makes, the emphasis is on a reverent attitude, not the spirits themselves. He says, "Sacrifice to the spirits as if they were present."[34] This seems to mean that, whether the spirits exist or not, one should be reverent in performing ritual.

As to whether or not there is an afterlife, Confucius' only comment in the *Analects* shows him as unwilling to discuss that either: when a student asked about the spirits of the dead, Confucius said, "You are still not able to do your duty to people, how can you do your duty to the ghosts and spirits?" and when the student asked further about death, Confucius replied, "You do not understand life, how can you understand death?"[35] While these statements do not dismiss a belief in an afterlife, or the existence of the dead in another place, or the existence of the gods, they do show us that Confucius did not consider these issues useful topics for his teachings.

Even though Confucius had little to say about the supernatural or an afterlife, later commentators would interpret what little he does say in radically different ways (see chapters 12 and 13). Whether these comments show Confucius as a religious person, a person with a spiritual nature, or a skeptic remains a subject of debate.

The Choice of Heaven and Heaven

The idea of the choice of Heaven or the command of Heaven developed in the early Zhou dynasty (see chapter 1) to explain why the Zhou dynasty had conquered the Shang. A virtuous ruler was chosen by Heaven to be the ruler of a unified China. The choice of Heaven continued to be used as a tool to make political power legitimate, but by the time of the Warring States, it was clear that no one had been chosen by Heaven to be the sole ruler of China. The idea of the choice of Heaven, by Confucius' time, had been broadened to apply to individuals who were chosen, or ordered, by Heaven to live up to what Heaven required of them. Confucius uses the term "choice of Heaven" in that way, saying that "at the age of 50, I understood the choice of Heaven."[36] After decades of study and self-cultivation, he was able to understand what it was that Heaven wanted him to do. This was a serious responsibility and one that should be carried out with reverence and with all the energy one has: the choice of Heaven is one of the few things, Confucius says, that a gentleman stands in awe of.[37]

In one passage where Confucius refers to Heaven, he says, "Does Heaven speak? Yet the four seasons move in their cycle and all things receive life from Heaven. Does Heaven say anything?"[38] Here Confucius refers to Heaven as nature, neither knowing nor caring what human beings do. Confucius' students said that Confucius never talked about the Way of Heaven.[39]

In other places, Heaven is obviously understood as acting in this world. When his favorite student, Yan Hui died, Confucius cried out in grief, "It is Heaven that has taken him! It is Heaven!"[40] This seems to fit with other references Confucius makes to a Heaven that has given him a mission. When threatened with death by Huan Tui in the state of Song, Confucius said, "It is Heaven that has given birth to the virtue that is in me. What can Huan Tui do to me?"[41] As long as he had the commands of Heaven, no human being would be able to stop him. During his travels, he was again threatened with death in Kuang. Confucius refers to King Wen, a hero to Confucius, and founder of the Zhou dynasty. "King Wen is long dead; does not our culture rest in me? If Heaven wanted our culture to die, why would those of us after King Wen have it? If

Heaven does not want our culture to die, what can the men of Kuang do to me?"[42] Confucius understood himself as having a commission from Heaven. An official once offered an explanation to Confucius' students as to why Confucius had not been able to obtain an important government office, saying, "Why should you students be worried about Confucius not having government office? The world has not followed the Way (see below) for a very long time and Heaven plans on using Confucius like the wooden clapper of a bell."[43] That the world does not follow the Way is fate; that Confucius will be used by Heaven to wake the world up is Heaven's command.

This command from Heaven may imply a close relationship between Heaven and Confucius. When Confucius complained that no one knew him, he says, "I do not grumble at Heaven nor blame human beings. I study what is around me so as to follow what is above. It is only Heaven that knows me."[44] And, while it is not clear that he prayed to the gods, he says, "A man who offends against Heaven has nowhere to pray."[45] Heaven has given Confucius a mission and it is only Heaven who truly knows him. But Confucius does not discuss what kind of Heaven this is nor how it works.

Fate

Confucius also uses the term *ming* – "choice," "mandate," or "fate" – by itself. Originally, *ming* referred to the length of one's life. We find it with that meaning in *The Book of History* and *The Book of Poetry*: "Heaven inspects those below and its standard is rightness. Heaven sends down a long life or not. Thus, it is not heaven that makes people die young, it is people who sever their life (*ming*)."[46] The length of one's life depends on ethical behavior that is rewarded by heaven. In Western Zhou bronzes, *ming* is used in the senses of "life span" and, as well, "endowment from heaven."[47]

Meaning "fate," *ming* has the sense of all the things that could happen to us. There are things over which we have no control: they are chosen or fated by Heaven. So we cannot control our life span, our health, or the times we are born into. If the society we are born into is corrupt, if it does not follow the Way, we can try to fix it, but may not succeed; this is fate. Similarly, if the ruler, who the gentleman serves, refuses good advice, the gentleman can do nothing other than continue to offer good advice. The reason Confucius was unable to achieve real political influence in his time was fate. Fate is decided by Heaven and, if Heaven wills a world in which the right Way prevails, that is what will happen; if Heaven does not will it, the world will be without the Way.[48]

The Way

Some people are surprised to find Confucius using the term "Dao," the "Way," assuming that is a word only used by the Daoist school. The term was widely used by all sorts of people throughout the period. However, when people used the word "Way," they did not always mean the same thing by it. When Confucius talks about the Way, he does not mean the natural and spontaneous Dao of the Daoist school (see chapter 5); he means a Dao that is an ethical, political, and civilized order. He says, "I set my heart on the Way, base myself on virtue, lean on humanity."[49]

The Way that Confucius has set his heart on is the natural inclination of human beings toward civilization, and that is what Confucius is talking about when he says, "A man has not wasted his life who, on the day he dies, learns about the Dao."[50] The natural human tendency toward civilization was expressed in the past by the sage-kings and the early rulers of the Zhou dynasty. It is also a moral Way, commanded by Heaven, that rulers, governments, and individuals must come to understand and to follow. We can learn the workings of the Way by being educated; we practice the Way through ritual, moral behavior, and good government. It is interesting that Confucius says that it is human beings who expand the Way, not the Way that expands human beings.[51] There has been considerable debate over what he means here, but it may be that it is the responsibility of human beings to develop a moral and civilized Way rather than the Way's responsibility to command us.

The references in the *Analects* to the spirits of the dead, the gods, an afterlife, and even Heaven are relatively few, especially when compared to Confucius' favorite topics, humanity, the gentleman, and ritual. Many of these references are cryptic as well, so it is not always clear what Confucius meant. There is little in other Confucian texts to help us either.

When we think about the word "religion" we usually think of it as focused on our relationship to the supernatural, be that gods, the spirits of the dead, or some ultimate principle or being, like Heaven or God. Confucius sometimes implies that sort of relationship. He did not see himself living in an empty universe that had no relation to human beings.[52] However, most of Confucius' attention is focused on self-cultivation, morality, and the ways to build a proper society.

Given what we have from Confucius, almost everything he says about the supernatural can be interpreted in different ways. For example, take his remark about his student not knowing how to serve the living and so not being able to learn about serving the dead. Does this mean that the student would have to work harder before he learned how to serve the spirits of the dead? Does it mean that while the spirits of the dead exist, it is more important to serve the living? Does it mean that Confucius did not believe in an afterlife and wanted his students to move away from the topic?

Similarly, some scholars have understood what Confucius says about ritual as ritual that must be understood in a more religious context. Even when rituals are between people, they are religious acts performed with the same reverence.[53] Others have read what Confucius said about ritual and the supernatural and concluded that Confucius was an agnostic and not at all interested in the religious side of life.

The continuing debate as to whether Confucianism is a philosophy or a religion often includes interpretations of Confucius' remarks about Heaven and the Dao (see chapters 12 and 13). Here we should note the things Confucius does not talk about. There is no creator-god: this is true throughout early Chinese culture as well as in the thought of Confucius. Whatever Heaven may be, it is not credited with a conscious creation of the universe. We find no speculation about how the universe came to be and very little comment on how it is constituted. Second, Heaven is not a place. Confucius does not talk about an afterlife, nor does he offer a good afterlife as a reward for a good life. Third, there are no sanctions in Confucius' thought. We are to be good people because we should, not because we expect a reward in an afterlife or to be condemned in the next world. There are no hells, no devils, and no Devil. For Confucius, selfishness and self-interest are enough to explain evil; there is no need to resort to the supernatural.

Debate continues over just what Confucius meant about the scope of education, about his attitude toward women, and about his religious views – or lack of them. We will see how the Confucian tradition develops as we go along and how people today talk about these issues. We do know that Confucius provided a complete prescription for the reform of the individual, society, and the state. As individuals, we encourage our moral virtues through education and self-cultivation, striving for the attitude of humanity. This has social and political implications. Individuals, gentlemen, with humanity, can lead us to a society that is more polite and where people are respected. This involves a state where government officials use language properly and work hard to care for the people.

4

Terms, and Mozi

Problems with "Schools" and "-isms"

While we could not describe Confucius' life as easy, he did have an easier time of it than his followers in one respect: he did not have to deal with many opponents. After Confucius' death, his followers would have to debate other thinkers who had their own strategies to reform the time and who attacked the kinds of things Confucius had proposed. To a large extent, Confucius was spared this.

The Warring States era lasted from 403 to 221 BCE and ended when the state of Qin succeeded in conquering all the other states and unifying China. This dynasty did not last long and was succeeded by the Han dynasty, a much longer one, ruling from 206 BCE to 220 CE, approximately the same length of time as the Roman empire.

It was during the Han dynasty, about a hundred years or more after the thinkers of the Warring States era, that scholars looked back and began to categorize the thinkers and the texts of the Warring States into schools of thought.[1] They set up strict lines among various schools of thought in the Warring States period and classified thinkers as belonging to Confucian, Mohist, Daoist, Logician, or Strategist schools.

The difficulty is that the thinkers of the Warring States era did not, in many cases, see themselves as belonging to a school at all. Many of these thinkers, and their texts, include ideas from various sources and do not fit neatly into one school or another.

So, who were these people if they were not, in many cases, members of a "school"? One of the Chinese phrases to describe the many thinkers of the Warring States is the "hundred schools of thought." While there were not really a hundred schools, the phrase is meant to show the wide variety and the various voices of the time. The thinkers of the Warring States era were scholars and would-be bureaucrats, like Confucius. Like Confucius, they tried to get a government position where they could influence rulers and bring into practice their own ideas about statecraft and reform. The vast majority of the texts from the Warring States period were addressed to rulers, and talk about how to rule well, according to the viewpoint of the author.

As the numbers of these scholar-bureaucrats[2] grew after the death of Confucius and throughout the Warring States period, it became common for rulers to have these scholars as guests, listen to their advice, engage them in debate, and listen to them debate each other. For some, having scholars on the payroll became a sign of the rulers' wealth, status, and high culture.

For example, in the state of Qi, the Tian family had overthrown original rulers of state, and were known as a bloodthirsty lot. They wanted to establish themselves as proper rulers and enhance their reputation. From the 400s to the 300s BCE, they became patrons of scholars, setting up the Jixia Academy and inviting scholars from across China. The scholars were paid well, given pleasant living quarters, servants, and suitable lecture halls. These scholars were not necessarily meant to be part of the government, but they were invited there to discuss various theories and there was a real exchange of ideas. Many of the big names in scholarship visited, or lived in, the Jixia Academy.[3] This academy is the most famous one, but there were others as well.

The scholar-bureaucrats traveled from state to state to these academies, many with their cartloads of books, trying very hard to make their voices heard, to defeat their opponents in debate, and to reform the government of the time. Some of them did indeed get government jobs. They shared the same concerns Confucius had: the breakdown in central government might well lead to a loss of civilization itself; the times were dangerous and governments corrupt; the common people were in serious trouble while the upper classes and the rich lived in luxury. What they did not agree on was how to solve these problems.

When we look back at this period, we see an exciting and interesting time with people debating everything from the very nature of human beings to how a good government should work. For scholars of the time, these very debates were a sign of how bad things were. If the brightest minds of the country could not agree on how to fix things, how would China ever survive?

The scholar-bureaucrats were almost entirely upper-class men – though some, like Confucius, may not have been wealthy. They were educated, as Confucius' students had been, in the texts of the time, texts like *The Book of History* and *The Book of Poetry*. As the Warring States era progressed, more and more of these scholars would be taught by other scholar-bureaucrats and would study the books of that particular teacher, or the teacher of their teacher. Some students stayed with one teacher, defending and passing on those teachings; others were less committed, studying with various teachers. People were identified by, and identified themselves with, this teaching lineage. This student–teacher relationship is at the core of what, in some cases, will develop into identifiable groups.

Problems with the Term "Confucianism"

When the Chinese words *jia*, "school," and *jiao*, "teaching," are trans-lated into English as "ism," as in "Confucianism," this leads to some big problems.

When we use "-ism" in a word, like "Buddhism" or "communism," we assume a number of things. We assume that there is a shared creed or shared set of ideas. There may be, as in the case of Buddhism, an initiation where the believer proclaims his or her membership in the group. Buddhists share the same goals, many of the same texts, basic principles, and methods. Even when Buddhism splits into sub-groups these basics are still there. "Communism" works in much the same way: despite differences in inter-pretation, there is a shared goal, some shared texts, and basic principles.

Looking at the word "Confucianism" we tend to make the same assump-tions about it. This is when we run into trouble. Confucianism does not have a creed or an initiation. There is no membership card – in fact, there is no organization to be a member of. Actually, there is no such thing as "Confucianism."

Five hundred years ago, when Roman Catholic missionaries first went to China, they found an important person and tradition being talked about, especially by the upper classes and government officials. First they Latinized the name "Kongfuzi" to "Confucius." Then they assumed that Confucius was the founder of the tradition. They further assumed that all traditions are based on a founder, and so they called the tradition "Confucianism." The assumptions they made were based on their own religion: Christianity takes its name from its founder, Jesus Christ. All traditions, it was assumed, had a founder and a name that reflected that founder.[4]

"Confucianism" does not. In Chinese, the term is *"Ru"* or *"Ru jia"* (the *Ru* school) or *"Ru jiao"* (*Ru*-ist teachings) and there is no reference to Confucius, or even Kongzi, in the term. *"Ru"* assumes a long tradition, even before Confucius, going back to the sage-kings and the most ancient of texts.[5] However, we do not just have problems with the English word "Confucianism"; there are also problems with the Chinese term *"Ru."*

An opponent of Confucius, the philosopher Mozi (*c*.480 BCE, see the section "Mozi and Mohism" below) is the first to identify people as *"Ru,"* but he does not say where the name came from.[6] This means that the first use of the term to describe a certain loosely organized group is in the latter part of the Spring and Autumn period, probably shortly after Confucius' death.

While Xunzi (*c.*310–210 BCE, see chapter 7) was the first *Ru* to identify himself as a *Ru*, and while he distinguished various groups of *Ru* as false, base, or proper, he too gives no history of the name.[7] The Han dynasty historian, Ban Gu, claimed that the word "*Ru*" came from the office of educators whose job included assisting the ruler in understanding the changes of the yin and yang and in teaching the people. This would place the use of the term back into the early Zhou, prior to Confucius, and that is unlikely.[8]

There are two traditions about the origin of the word "*Ru*." In the first, it is said that the *Ru* were descendents of the Shang dynasty who had been overthrown by the Zhou. They taught that one should be pliable and they were experts in classical ritual. Confucius was said to have been a descendent of the Shang royal house. The second tradition claims that the *Ru* were minor members of the Zhou royal family who lost their positions in the breakdown of 770 BCE, and so had no choice but to make their living from their specialized knowledge of ancient texts and rituals. Neither of these traditions is verifiable.[9]

Attempts to trace the history of the word *Ru* by analyzing the character have not been successful either. In the 1920s, Hu Shi argued that *Ru* is related to *rou*, "pliable," and represented the resigned attitude of the Shang people who had been conquered by the Zhou; however, many other scholars disagree.[10] John Knoblock and others also understand the term *Ru* as related to "pliable" but say it was used to mean "weakling," or something close to our modern "nerd."[11] So the Chinese term "*Ru*" was likely first used by people shortly after Confucius' death, but we do not know the origin of the term or why it was used.

While it might be more accurate to use the terms *Ru*, *Ru jia*, and *Ru-ist*, they are awkward and difficult for non-Sinologists.[12] I will continue to use the terms "Confucian" and "Confucianism," but we must keep in mind that the *Ru* tradition refers to a time before Kongzi (Confucius) and, while Confucius is the sage *par excellence* of the tradition, he is not considered to be its founder.

The next problems are: was there a Confucian school? were there people who considered themselves Confucians (*Ru*)? how did they identify themselves?

The *Mozi* (see the section "Mozi and Mohism" below), written after the death of Confucius, has a chapter, "A Condemnation of Confucians." Mozi describes Confucians as a group with certain shared occupations and views; he says that they were associated with mourning rituals. He accuses them of not believing in an afterlife, yet carrying out funerals as if they did. He criticizes Confucians for believing in fate. He says Confucians promoted elaborate rituals and music and that they believed that a gentleman must wear the clothes of the past and speak with the speech of the past in order to be considered a proper gentleman. He complains that the rituals they practiced were so minute and complicated that one could spend a lifetime studying them and never know all of them; as well, one could have a fortune and still not be able to pay for the performance of all of their music. He says that they were fond of music and used it to corrupt people; Confucians attracted followers with the sounds of singing, drums, and dancing.[13]

These descriptions of Confucians come from an opponent: Mozi and his followers frequently debated the followers of Confucius and there was no love lost between them, so Mozi's criticisms of Confucian behavior and thought should not be taken at face value. However, at least in his descriptions of Confucian ideas and occupations, Mozi seems to be accurate.[14]

To take some of Mozi's descriptions one at a time, one way Confucians were identified was by their relation to a number of texts. These are texts like *The Book of History* and *The Book of Poetry* that we have seen before and that Confucians believed Confucius himself had either written or edited (see chapter 8). These texts were known to be earlier than Confucius and part of the heritage of the Zhou dynasty. The texts would, in the Han dynasty, become part of the Five Classics. A Warring State text describes the scholars associated with the state of Lu, Confucius' state, and the classics of Confucianism. It says that the laws and traditions of ancient times have been handed down and can be found in *The Book of History*, *The Book of Poetry*, the *Book of Rites*, and the *Classic of Music*. The scholars of the state of Lu, with their large sashes and writing tablets, are known for their understanding of these texts.[15]

Using these texts, Confucians discussed the virtue of filial piety, respect for and service to one's parents, elder brother, teacher, and ruler. They also discussed concepts like humanity, the gentleman, and good government that benefited the people. According to a number of their adversaries, Confucians believed in fate, and said that one's life was decided at birth. This charge has caused some difficulty because it is not a clear position in any of the Confucian texts. It may be that only some Confucians held this position and that their arguments were not included in the later Confucian canon (see chapter 8).

Confucians looked to the past, to the early sage-kings and cultural heroes like the Duke of Zhou, for patterns of behavior. We have seen Confucius do this and his followers continued the tradition. The past provides a model of what government and society should do in the present.[16]

Confucians had expert knowledge of ritual and music. As for funeral ritual, it may be that many Confucians earned their living performing funeral rituals for the nobility. They may also have had government jobs as Music Masters. Confucians were closely associated with both musical performance and music theory and this brought them into conflict with those who argued that music was useless and should be banned (see the section "Mozi and Mohism" below).

Confucians were also identified by their clothes and their way of talking. They are described as wearing clothes from ancient times – an antique hat, ornamented shoes, a large sash – and they carried tablets used by officials in court ceremonies.[17] To match their antique dress, they were said to have spoken in an antiquated manner. This was to indicate their allegiance to the past, and it would certainly have made them stand out, much as people would today if they wore doublets and hose from Elizabethan times and spoke the English of Shakespeare. It may be that only some Confucians dressed and spoke this way, but it was one of the ways they made themselves distinct.

Confucians were distinct in terms of texts, ideas, teachers, dress, and speech. While their enemies might make fun of them, Confucians had a view of themselves as an elite, as gentlemen or superior men. Their status, they believed, was based not solely on birth but on their professional and moral abilities. Along with this view of themselves came the tradition that, even though they might have the knowledge and ability to advise the ruler, the ruler did not often listen to them. The counsel that Confucian officials gave their lords was, according to the Confucians, often overlooked in favor of short-term gain or extravagance. Rulers might not even recognize worthy officials and might not bring them to their court. Confucians often portray themselves as neglected advisors, and, in the Confucian classics, again and again rulers find themselves facing disaster for not following Confucian advice.

Confucius' students wanted to become government officials: they were already qualified on the basis of birth, and they worked for the second qualification – education. We are told that Confucius had three thousand students; but those who knew the "six accomplishments" numbered only 72. His students scattered after his death: some did attain office, becoming advisors and high officials in governments in Lu and in other states, while others became teachers.[18]

The students of these teachers taught others in turn until, by 300 BCE, there were from five to eight different groups of Confucians. Han Feizi says that by his time, about 250 BCE, there were eight groups of Confucians and each claimed to have the traditional teaching of Confucius. While there might have been differences among these groups, they all understood themselves to be Confucians – though some considered their *Ru* tradition better than others. Xunzi, a Confucian, for example, criticized those Confucians he described as "vulgar." He described these "lesser" Confucians as claiming loyalty to the early kings, Confucius, and a Confucian lineage, but, he said, they were not "proper": they followed Confucius' teachings in a partial or distorted way.[19]

It may be that the term "Confucian" was applied to a large number of people, and meant something more general like "literati." Of these literati, only some were strict followers of Confucius and stayed closely associated with his teachings. Others may have studied with "Confucian" teachers, but went their own way.[20]

To sum up, the term "Confucianism" can indeed be misleading if it is understood as an organized group with a structured ideology that all "Confucians" were required to follow. Confucians, or *Ru*, belonged neither to an organized party that had a required party line nor to an organized religion with a set creed and an initiation. They did, though, follow teaching lineages that drew their authority from Confucius and the ancient sage-kings.

In terms of identifying Confucians prior to the Han dynasty, it is clear that there was a basic core of shared ideas and teaching lineages that do provide some basis for an "-ism." There was also, however, a fluidity to interpretations and practices. These sub-schools of Confucianism may have dressed and spoken in much the same antique style. They handled the same lore of antiquity, though probably different versions of it, and educated their students in particular interpretations that were tied to teaching lineages.

Though loosely formed, the Confucians were a group identified as "*Ru*" by their enemies. They also used the term "*Ru*" to describe themselves. We have seen that Confucians were identified by their allegiance to the past, to the ideals of humanity, good government, rituals, and music, and also identifiable by their dress and manner. No matter how fierce the infighting may have been among Confucian groups, they all seem to have agreed on a basic set of ideas and practices.

Mozi and Mohism

> Confucians established their complex rituals and music to delude people. With their false grief at their long funerals, they fool the family. They say that all is fated and ignore the poverty around them. They are exceedingly arrogant and proud. They ignore what is essential and enjoy being lazy and overbearing. They love their food, but are too lazy to work.[21]

We have already seen one of the opponents of Confucians, the philosopher Mozi. Traditionally, he was said to have lived from 479 to 301 BCE. There is a long tradition that Mozi was from the lower classes, possibly a craftsman. He was assumed to be a contemporary of Confucius, and, like Confucius' family, according to tradition, from the state of Song. Mozi's dedication can be seen in the story that, in order to try to prevent a war, he walked from one end of the China of the time to the other, arriving with his feet bloody and swollen.

Modern scholarship rejects these traditions and says that he was born about 480 BCE, just after the death of Confucius, which would make Mozi a contemporary of the Greek philosopher Socrates (469–399 BCE). Like Confucius, Mozi was probably also a minor noble and clearly identified himself with the scholar-bureaucrats of the upper classes. There is a book named after him, the *Mozi*, and, even though most of it was written after his time, it still accurately describes Mozi's thought, because we find it repeated both by his enemies and in the later works of his followers.[22]

Mozi is a fine example of the passion that the problems of the era produced, and he conveys a real sense of urgency in his thought. To provide the basics of life for everyone, everyone's energies must immediately be put to work simply to provide food, shelter, clothing, and peace. There is no time to waste, especially if it is being wasted in frivolous, useless things. Mozi's thinking is straightforward: we must do useful things that will profit us; we should practice self-interest; we should obey our superiors completely; and, if we do this, Heaven and the gods will bless us. Mozi is important too for his contributions to argumentation in the Warring States era. He begins the discussion of how logic and rational argument work, the necessity of establishing definitions, and how to argue properly.

Mozi uses two main terms: profit and usefulness.[23] He argues that if something is useful then it is profitable or benefits us. In its simplest terms: what is profitable is useful; what is useful is profitable. So how do we define "profit" for the people? If something helps to build up the wealth of the state or increase the population of the state, it is profitable. So useful and profitable things include food, clothing, shelter, enriching the state, increasing the population, ending conflict among people, preventing war, and getting blessings from the gods.

Unprofitable and useless things include anything that wastes money, that wastes time, that does not benefit most people, that does not increase the population, and that may lead to war. Elaborate funerals, for example, keep people from doing their jobs, waste time, and waste money. Music is useless, transitory, wastes time, and wastes money. War is unprofitable and useless. Money is wasted on armaments; people's lives are wasted in battles. If the state wins, it has destroyed the territory it invaded; if it loses, it loses everything. However, Mozi allowed for defensive wars because the state needs to be able to defend itself. His followers' texts include chapters on military technology, focusing on defensive engineering and tactics.

Mozi sees the world in black and white. Useful, profitable things are good things; useless, wasteful things are bad things. Most of the things that Mozi classifies as useful are either basic necessities, like food and shelter, or quantifiable in terms of money, like enriching the state.

Mozi also argued that we naturally love ourselves and what motivates us is self-interest. Self-interest should lead us to want to profit ourselves. The way to profit ourselves the most is to have a society where the greatest happiness of the greatest number is established. So, we should practice universal love.[24]

Do not get too excited by the phrase "universal love." Mozi does not mean anything emotional or spiritual by it. Universal love is based on self-interest and reciprocity: you love me, I love you back. This love is not an emotion, but a way to bring one's own self-interest together with the self-interest of others. If we help out our neighbor, we do it because we want our neighbor to help us out. Friendship does not enter into it: helping your neighbor is based on our own self-interest. Universal love is a means to get us what we want.

A major problem of the time was conflict among people as individuals and as groups, whether classes or states. If everyone loved one another – followed their real self-interest – then people would feed, clothe, and care for one another. Large states would not attack small ones and the rich would not take advantage of the poor. Mozi argued that universal love existed in the past, under the sage-kings, but now that civilization has collapsed we can see only fragments of it, in love of family, for example.

Before civilization was established, Mozi says, everything was chaos and no one could agree on anything. Then people chose a ruler who had the choice of Heaven, ultimate control, and decided on right and wrong. The emperor is the only one who can speak with Heaven, and, as the only channel of communication, the emperor alone judges right and wrong. Heaven's will and the ruler's are the same. Things will go well only when the ruler respects Heaven and the gods and spirits. The power of the choice of Heaven flows downward from the emperor to his ministers and to the common people.

From the emperor down, superiors are always right and should be obeyed. When inferiors do something right, they should be rewarded; if they do something wrong, then they should be punished. Mozi called this "agreement with the superior." Social and political peace is only possible when this agreement is maintained. Agreement and obedience are the responsibilities of the inferior who must always obey his or her superior. Agreeing with one's superior would put an end to the infinite number of opinions coming from everyone. It is these opinions that lead to arguments, fights, and wars. Agreeing with one's superior means that there is only one opinion in the world.[25]

Religious arguments in Mozi are very cool: there is no religious fervor or devotional language. Mozi simply says that Heaven, the gods, and the spirits bless and reward those who practice universal love and punish those who do not. He uses examples from antiquity to show how some sage-kings were blessed, while tyrants, who were overthrown, were not. If we are successful, it is because we have practiced universal love and enlightened self-interest, and done useful and profitable things. This is not fate; we are responsible for what happens to us. There is no discussion of where Heaven comes from, the nature of the gods and spirits, or their origins and powers.

If we do all the *Mozi* recommends – practice universal love, and pursue what is useful and beneficial – we can return to the great civilization of the past.[26]

As you can imagine, with a point of view like this, Mozi was enraged by Confucians. As we have seen, one chapter in the *Mozi* is the "Condemnation of Confucians." Almost everything Confucians do and believe is wrong, Mozi says.

> Confucians are arrogant and pompous and so they are not suitable to teach other people. They adore music and use it to corrupt others. They cannot be trusted to teach others to manage government. They think everything is fated so they see no reason to work. They emphasize funerals and long periods of grief and so cannot teach others how to take care of the people. ... Confucius had an imposing appearance and was knowledgeable, but he used this to delude people ... all of his wide learning did nothing to help; his complex thought did not help the people.[27]

Confucians, for Mozi, were a wasteful and useless bunch who encouraged useless things like funerals and music. Confucians talked about filial piety and love in the family, running counter to universal love. They insisted on long periods of mourning for family members, wasting time and productivity.[28] As ritual masters, they organized wasteful funerals. Rulers were buried with gold, jewelry, fine clothes, and expensive utensils. The waste horrified Mozi. To make it worse, while wasting money on funerals, Confucians seemed not to believe in a life after death or the spirits of the dead. It is not clear where Mozi gets this idea about Confucians, as nothing in the Confucian classics indicates a lack of belief in an afterlife (little confirms such a belief either), but there must have been some Confucians of Mozi's time who argued against an afterlife.

Similarly, Mozi says that Confucians believe that everything in life is fated, but we do not find that in the Confucian texts – even though it was clearly a belief of some Confucians who Mozi encountered.[29] Mozi says that it was not fate that kept Confucius from receiving Heaven's choice and founding a new dynasty: Confucius was not successful because Confucius was wrong.

The *Mozi* also contains a chapter condemning music. Mozi says that the three things people want are food, clothes, and rest: playing music gives no one the money to get these things. Musical performances are only for the amusement of the upper classes, who waste their time instead of governing, and music gives nothing at all to ordinary people. Music, as it was often performed for the wealthy of his time, wasted money. Musicians, orchestras, dancers, and musical instruments had to be brought together and paid for. All of this expense gave only a transitory pleasure. Mozi says that music, in itself, is pleasant enough, but not worth the time and money wasted on it. Music is a private pleasure, enjoyed by the few at the expense of the many. He says that the ancient sages established government, palaces, clothes, and so on that were sufficient and economical; only later were luxuries like music invented. Mozi equates music and luxury.[30]

As Music Masters in some of the courts and as scholars trained in music as part of their education, Confucians then had to defend music against Mozi and his followers.

The Mohist[31] school became the largest school of the Warring States period. Like Confucians, they would have stood out because of their dress, but in the case of the Mohists, their clothing was simple and inexpensive. Unlike some other schools, the Mohists were indeed an organized group. The Mohists were not only organized, but clearly hierarchical: the leader of the Mohists, beginning with Mozi, was called a Supreme Master (there were three after Mozi). The Supreme Master had the power to execute anyone in the group who violated Mohist rules. There were many rules and regulations for the members and total obedience was demanded. This was based on Mozi's "agreement with the superior" ideas. The school was organized as a quasi-military group. Despite this, or perhaps because of it, over time the Mohist school split into three sub-groups.

Even though they made up the largest school of the Warring States era, the Mohists never achieved their aims. Their ideas were too radical for an upper class that enjoyed its luxury. Their religious sanctions did not scare rulers or the upper class. The great achievement of the Mohists was the way in which they changed the rules of debate, discussing the nature of language, setting up rules of logic, and making all other thinkers argue for their positions.

Mozi and his followers talked a lot about disputation or argumentation as a way to arrive at the truth. This is the beginning of not only rational argumentation, but also the self-conscious notion that one is arguing and that there are proper ways to do it. Argument became a mode of combat used to convince rulers of the right way to act and to defeat one's intellectual enemies. Later Mohists would continue to pursue these issues and would influence the form of argumentation to come.

After the death of Confucius we see a number of scholars or would-be bureaucrats, each with their own approach to solving the problems of the time. The followers of Confucius formed groups based on teachers and continued to support Confucius' teachings. They were described as distinctive because of their allegiance to Confucius and association with certain texts.

Mozi had his own ideas of how to solve the problems of the Warring States era. Work on practical things, he said, things like food, clothes, and shelter. End war, luxury, and waste. If we all want to act in our own self-interest, we should practice universal love. Heaven and the gods will bless us. Mozi condemned Confucius for being wrong about almost everything. More criticism from other thinkers was aimed at Confucius and that is what we will look at next.

5

Opponents

When Confucius arrived Lao Lai-tzu [Lao Laizi] said to him, "Get rid of your proud bearing and that knowing look on your face and you can become a gentleman. ... You can't bear to watch the sufferings of one age and so you go make trouble for ten thousand ages to come! Are you just naturally a boor?"[1]

Daoism

Confucians were attacked by Mozi and his followers for practicing useless things like ritual and music, for spending time talking about morality, for making money from useless, elaborate funerals, and for not paying attention to the real things in life, like the bottom line. Deep as this disagreement was, the most profound attack against Confucius came from another direction. This attack is found both in a text called the *Laozi* or the *Dao De Jing* and from a thinker named Zhuangzi (*c.*399–285 BCE, a contemporary of the Greek philosopher Plato) and the text named after him, the *Zhuangzi*. Later, in the Han dynasty, these two texts and thinkers, along with some others, were categorized as the Daoist school, though none of these people understood themselves as belonging to a school and, as we will see, organizing Daoists would be as difficult as herding cats.

The first text, the *Laozi*, was traditionally thought to have been written by a philosopher, Laozi, who was a contemporary of Confucius. There are some problems with this. First, Laozi is not a person's name. The "zi" means "teacher" or "master," as we have seen with Mozi, for example, but the "Lao" of Laozi in this case is not a family name.[2] "Lao" means "old" or "venerable." So "Laozi" means the "venerable teacher." Second, modern scholarship has shown that there is no one author of the text, but there are multiple authors, probably from different times.[3]

The second text, the *Zhuangzi*, seems to have been written after the *Laozi* as it refers to the *Laozi*. We know little about its author, Zhuangzi. He may have been called Zhuang Zhou[4] and had an official post. There are stories about Zhuang Zhou in the *Zhuangzi* but, like most of the stories in the text, they are too humorous in intent to be useful in a biography.

As you might guess, the Daoists talk about the Dao. But their view of the Dao is quite different from Confucius'. The Dao pointed to in the *Laozi* is natural and spontaneous. We cannot hear, see, or touch it.

Language is not capable of accurately describing the Dao, so the authors of the *Laozi* can only point to it, suggest images for it, and describe it through analogy. One of the reasons that the text is so terse and difficult is that the authors are trying to talk about something that cannot, in the end, be talked about. The word "Dao," meaning "Way" or "road," is only a shorthand reference for something language cannot really adequately talk about.

The ambiguous language and phrases in the text, plus the idea that human language is not able to adequately talk about the Dao, has led many readers to see the text as "mystical." This view is reinforced by the text's identification of the Dao with non-being. Daoists see the workings of the Dao as the interaction of being and non-being, and given that human language, and indeed human thought, are inadequate to capture the Dao, Daoists prefer to talk about the Dao in negative terms. This does not necessarily make the text "mystical."[5]

The Dao gives birth to all the things in the universe. While these things pass in and out of existence, the Dao is eternal. The Dao itself is not a thing – it is a process, a process of birth, death, movement, and stillness.

The Dao is described as weak, non-contending, not acting, and without an ego. The Dao will not argue with you, it does not have rules, it does not have plans. It acts naturally and spontaneously. But, if you are foolish enough to decide to row across an ocean with no experience, no equipment, and no regard for the weather, the Dao will kill you. That will happen, not because the Dao hates you – the Dao has no emotions – but just from the natural course of events. Everything that goes against the Dao dies. A creature who plans to work against the natural actions of the Dao will not be successful – or at least not successful in the long term.

One of the images the *Laozi* uses to describe the Dao is the image of water. Water is weak: you can easily put your hand under cool water flowing from a tap and not be harmed. Water flows naturally to the lowest place: like the Dao, it does not show off. Water, however, in the right circumstances, can drown people, smash roads and bridges, and obliterate whole cities. Water does not plan on doing any of these things; it does so naturally and spontaneously. We can die from disregarding the power of water.

The Dao is also compared to a baby who is supple, because the child is still natural, and a baby, unlike adults, can cry all day and not become hoarse. Another image is that of a woman who is quiet, passive, and non-contending – apparently the authors of the *Laozi* had never actually met a woman.[6]

The *Laozi* often says that the Dao does not act;[7] what it means is that the Dao does not ego-act. Natural and spontaneous action is not directed by an ego; an ego sets up plans and lists, fighting for what it wants and imposing its will. The Dao does not do that. Human beings, if we want to behave properly and successfully, should behave like the Dao. Our aggressive and assertive behavior and our desires keep us fighting each other and the Dao. A fight with the Dao is one we cannot ever win.

Instead of being like the Dao, human society and human behavior are dedicated to asserting our will over nature. Civilization is an artificial imposition of our will on the world. We spend a lot of our time fighting the erosion of our plans. Much of home ownership, for example, involves the maintenance of the house against the forces of the Dao – gravity, water, and weather. We keep having to repave roads, rebuild bridges and sidewalks and, not having learned our lesson, then we pave more roads and build more sidewalks.

We spend a lot of time doing things that are artificial, like education. Zhuangzi points out that there are two ways of knowing things. We can learn how to ride a bicycle or to swim. Even if we have not ridden a bicycle for years, we will still know how. We learn it and it becomes a part of us. On the other hand, we can take a first year psychology course and, if tested on the course ten years later, we will discover that we remember next to nothing. That is because this sort of learning is artificial – that is why it is so hard to learn and so easy to forget. Education of this kind is artificial and unnatural.

Forgetting, says Zhuangzi, is something we should do more of. We should forget all the artificial knowledge that has been pumped into us since we were children. He says, "You forget your feet, when shoes are comfortable. You forget your waist when your belt is comfortable. Understanding forgets right and wrong when the mind is comfortable."[8] We forget when things are not an irritant, when they do not catch our attention, when we are not filling our minds with artificial things. All the ritual and all the education we have learned have simply taught us to be unnatural and we should forget them.

Like the Confucians, Daoists talk about the sage, but given the wide range of authors it is not surprising that we find a wide range of pictures of what a Daoist sage would look like.

Chapters in the *Laozi* describe a control sage. He is a ruler who is said to be "not kind" and "treats the people like straw dogs,"[9] that is, as something that can be thrown away. Because this sage is one with the Dao, he attracts and controls other people. He gets rid of any cause of desires among the people, "strengthening their bones and weakening their wills."[10] In doing so he returns everyone to a simpler and less ego-driven time. This picture of the sage, however, has seemed to some readers to be too active and ego-driven to be a Daoist sage.

A sage might also be immortal. He has no "place of death in him"[11] by virtue of being one with the Dao. There are portraits of a Perfect Man in the *Zhuangzi* that show the sage as being able to ascend to the heavens and ride dragons. How much of this is exaggeration and how much should be taken seriously is still debated.[12]

Another description of the Daoist sage is of a person who is simple and unknown. He has no desires, does not ego-act, is not aggressive or proud. Should this kind of sage be a ruler, the people will become one with the Dao but will not notice how it happened.

A sage may also be a hermit or recluse. This is a picture of someone who has withdrawn from politics and society and cares nothing for the honors of nobility and riches. He may live in a cave or do the work of a commoner. He lives on very little and is unknown even to the people around him. The aim of this sage is not immortality, but survival. As the *Laozi* says, "He who lives out his days has lived a long life."[13] Because this sage has no desires, he does not get entangled in things; because he does not care about his honor, he does not die in duels or battles. He lives out his natural life span.

The *Laozi*, like almost all the other texts from the Warring States era, is written as advice to the ruler. The *Laozi* criticizes the upper class of the time:

> Those at court are corrupt:
> While the fields are full of weeds,
> And the granaries are empty;
> Still they are dressed in fine clothes,
> Equipped with swords at their sides,
> Stuffed with food and drink,
> And with far too much money.
> This is called being the leading robbers,
> And has nothing at all to do with the Dao.[14]

Like Mozi, the authors of the *Laozi* were repulsed by the extravagance and corruption of the rich.

The *Laozi*'s advice to rulers begins by explaining that their rigid and violent policies do not work. The more they try to impose their will on their subjects, the more the people will learn to evade the laws; the more they try to be aggressive toward their neighboring states, the more they are unbalanced. Governing a state, says the *Laozi*, is like "cooking small fish."[15] To cook them best, one should leave them alone. Be like the Dao and rule by doing nothing that comes from one's ego.

In the past, when things were better, there was nothing we think of as "civilization." That does not mean there was no society – Daoists are not proposing we go back to living in trees – but society was quite different. The *Zhuangzi* says:

> Long ago ... [in the times of the sage-kings], the people knotted cords and used them. They relished their food, admired their clothing, enjoyed their customs and were content with their houses. Though neighboring states were within sight of each other, and could hear the cries of each other's dogs and chickens, the people grew old and died without ever traveling beyond their own borders. At a time such as this, there was nothing but the most perfect order.[16]

In this golden age there are no big governments, no bureaucrats, no wars. The past, and recommended future age, is perfectly ordered: the state is small; there is little in the way of technology; records are kept by knots on ropes rather than by writing; and, most importantly, the people have no, or few, desires. Human beings lived this way successfully, the Daoists say, until disaster struck. Then the sage came along with

> the crouchings and bendings of the rites and music, which were intended to reform the bodies of the world; with the reaching-for-a-dangled-prize of benevolence [humanity] and righteousness [rightness], which was intended to comfort the hearts of the world. Then for the first time people learned to stand on tiptoe and covet knowledge, to fight to the death over profit, and there was no stopping them. This in the end was the fault of the sage.[17]

The Daoists say that when Confucius came along, standing on tiptoe, he searched for right and wrong and caused an uproar. It was Confucius who disturbed a harmonious society and caused others to have desires. Then, when the Dao began to be lost, Confucius began to talk about humanity, rightness, and filial piety – all of which had been practiced perfectly before without discussion – but now that they were lost, people had to talk about them.

Zhuangzi is alone, however, in not being interested in politics or in giving advice to the ruler. The *Zhuangzi* is not written as advice for a ruler, but is a text full of stories and jokes that takes much of what is in the *Laozi* and develops it further.

One of Zhuangzi's major criticisms of Confucians is that they insist there is a definable right and wrong. Zhuangzi argues that right and wrong are simply a matter of point of view: what is right for you develops from your point of view, which I may or may not share. Definitions of right, wrong, proper, improper, good, bad, ugly, and beautiful are a matter of taste, and Confucians are wrong to think otherwise. Confucians, like the rest of us, use their egos and try to impose their wills. Confucians, and most of the rest of us, think they can define right and wrong. Confucians teach artificiality and unnatural behavior, like ritual and education. They are convinced that they know what they are doing and that everyone should follow them.

Zhuangzi saw the Confucians as marvelous targets for jokes and stories. He made up all sorts of stories about Confucius, Confucians, and things that they did. One of the stories in the *Zhuangzi* shows Confucians robbing graves, while using all the proper ritual to do so. "The big Confucian announces to his underlings: 'The east grows light. How is the matter proceeding?' The little Confucians say, 'We haven't got the graveclothes off him yet, but there's a pearl in his mouth!'" They go on to quote ancient texts until they finally manage to steal all the treasures in the coffin.[18] Zhuangzi's more serious point is that Confucian notions of ritual and proper behavior can be used to justify all sorts of bad behavior in the hands of those with no conscience.

One of the axioms of Confucianism is that human beings are social creatures and that we will naturally tend toward the building of civilization. Daoists argue that we have had dozens of civilizations and, whether they were kingships, theocracies, autocracies, or democracies, the one thing we know about all of them is that all of them fail. This is because, Daoists argue, civilization cannot succeed. It is an artificial and unnatural thing. Everything that goes against the Dao dies. Civilization cannot be fixed, as the Confucians believe. Civilization is the problem.

Confucians are wrong on two important counts: there is no standard of right and wrong, and civilization cannot be fixed – it is doomed by definition.

The Strategists

While Mohists may have constituted the largest group in the Warring States era, followed by Confucians, neither were the most popular. In a time of constant warfare, it is no wonder that the most popular thinkers and texts had to do with the military. One military text that has survived is the *Sunzi Bingfa*, known in the West as *The Art of War*.[19] This was one of a large number of military texts written during the Warring States period and these texts were the most widely read and the most talked about.

Later Chinese scholars looked down on things military and so these texts were not included in the later categories as a school of thought. However, during the Warring States era, as one might imagine, they were extremely important to an upper class trained in both literary and military accomplishments.

Sunzi's *Art of War* is thought to be a combination of other military and strategic texts. Like all the Strategists, Sunzi argues that any method, moral or immoral, can be used to win. Lately in the West it has been read, predictably enough, as a way for corporations to win out over their competition.

For Warring States rulers, war was a serious business: either one won a war or one was wiped out. So the text begins its advice to a ruler long before a war is underway. Warfare, for Sunzi, includes diplomacy, economic measures, and the use of spies. For the Strategists, the point is not only to use these methods, but to do so with methodical planning.

Sunzi talks a lot about planning in order to manipulate a situation until it is to your advantage. One needs to begin with information, which is why spies are so important. Then one must go on to weigh the situation and to make plans.

The use of spies and deceit to deal with one's enemy was essential. "The reason that a farsighted ruler and his commander are able to conquer an enemy is that they know things first. This does not come from consulting the gods or the ancestors, but from spies who learn the enemy's situation."[20] Sunzi devotes a chapter to the effective use of spies of all sorts. Using the information a ruler can get from spies, a ruler might be able to sow dissension in another state, to encourage sons to rebel against their father, or to finance a noble family's bid to oust the ruling family.

The best victories have nothing to do with winning a battle and killing all your enemies. The best victory is to win a war without going to war at all. If you can bring about the downfall of the enemy state without a battle, then you have not only not risked your own state, but you have won another.

If you must go to war, you are already on shaky ground. In that case, Sunzi's advice is to never enter a battle that one might lose. The ruler must be certain of victory before committing his forces. Again, using spies and encouraging deserters from the other side will allow the ruler, or his general, to calculate when to fight and when to retreat. Sunzi says,

> Warfare is the Way of dishonesty. So, when you are able to act, make it look like you cannot. When you are ready to attack, make it look like you are not ready. When you are near your enemy, make it seem like you are far away; when you are far away, make it look like you are nearby ... if your enemy is united, sow disharmony among them. Attack only when they are not prepared. Be where they will not expect you.[21]

The Way that a successful ruler must follow is the Way of dishonesty. Strategists were not interested in morality, ritual, or argument. Success, by any means, was all that mattered.

The Logicians[22]

The Logicians were certainly not a unified group; in fact, aside from later Mohists, they were not a group at all. The label "Logician" was applied to a number of people in the Warring States era who tended to focus on issues of argument, logic, and language. They were despised by Confucians, Daoists, and ordinary people who sat through their mind-numbing arguments about logic and language. Unlike many other thinkers of the time, Logicians were not interested in looking to the past to discover what was right and wrong – they ignored the sage-kings – instead they used argument to decide things.

Some Logicians were perfectly happy to argue any side of a question and to teach others to do the same. These men were much like the Greek Sophists, arguing for pay or entertainment, with no commitment to right or wrong, just like a modern lawyer who will defend anyone if paid enough. To their credit, Logicians insisted on logic, even if they did not believe what they were saying.

Others, like the later Mohists, examined how one could make arguments and what was logical and what was not. The Mohists were also interested in looking at how one comes to know anything. They talked about how sense information is transformed into abstract thought. Abstract thought is a higher form of knowing things and does not always depend on sense information. Knowing time, past, present, future, for example, is not dependent on the senses. This means that when we know something we are doing more than just experiencing it. Later Mohists looked at how this works and how we come to think about things. Logical thought is possible, they concluded, and gradually this leads us to the knowledge of right and wrong.[23]

One Logician, Hui Shi,[24] is someone we know about only from references to him in other texts like the *Zhuangzi*, where he seems to have been a good friend of Zhuangzi's. We have few of Hui Shi's arguments, but what we have are set out in a series of paradoxes. They seem to depend on point of view: for example, "the heavens are as low as the earth and the mountains only as high as the marshes," depending on where one is standing at the time. Other paradoxes depend on definitions and point of view: "the sun at noon is declining": the sun can reach no higher point than it does at noon. "A creature born is a creature dying": once a mortal creature is born it can only die.[25] There is nothing in these paradoxes to make us think that Hui Shi or other Logicians, aside from the Mohists, had any notion that there was a basic truth or a standard of right and wrong. They were interested only in how logical arguments work.

Other Logicians worked more with issues around language. What is the relationship between the thing and the name or word we have for it? Is "t-a-b-l-e" a table? If not, what is it? The most well-known of these Logicians was Gongsun Long.[26] He said that there are names/words for particular, concrete, things and for abstract things, but they do not work in the same way. His most famous statement is "a white horse is not a horse":

> The name/word "horse" points to a certain shape, while the name/word "white" points to a color. ... When a horse is needed, yellow and black ones will do, but when one needs a white horse, yellow or black horses will not do ... therefore yellow and black horses are separate kinds and can respond to the call for a horse, but not to the call for a white horse. ... A white horse is "horse" plus "white." "Horse" plus "white" is not "horse." Thus, a white horse is not a horse.[27]

Words/names like "white" are abstract,[28] what Gongsun Long calls an "idea," a "universal." You can show me white paint, white paper, white walls, but you cannot show me "white." "White" cannot exist by itself, but only as an abstract term that, when paired with another word, like "paper," becomes the concrete particular "white paper."

Concrete, particular things exist in time and space and we have words for them. Abstract words/names do not exist in time and space. "Horse" is another abstract word. It defines a certain genus and species, but does not refer to a particular horse. A white horse is a concrete, particular thing. A concrete white horse is not an abstract, so it is not a "horse." Thus a white horse is not a horse.[29]

Strategists like Sunzi, the Sophists, and Logicians like Hui Shi and Gongsun Long were not interested in talking about morality. They could argue about all sorts of things, but none of them were interested in committing themselves to moral behavior. Some, like Hui Shi, may have argued that morality was just a matter of taste, just as his friend Zhuangzi did.

Legalism

As the Warring States era drew to a close, a number of thinkers began to talk about government in a particular way. Again, this was a very diverse group and the label "Legalism" was applied by later Han organizers.

Most of the thinkers we will look at here assume a pain–pleasure model of human nature and, like Mozi, the idea that human nature is basically self-interested. Human beings want to maximize pleasure and minimize pain. Politically, this means that a government can use rewards and penalties to motivate people. Like the Mohists, Legalists present their ideas as utilitarian and logical, claiming that the result for rulers will be wealth and power. Because of this, they are sometimes, astonishingly, called "realists."

Shang Yang or Lord Shang (d.338 BCE) was a senior advisor to the ruler of the state of Qin and is said to have written a text called the *Book of Lord Shang*. To centralize power, he advocated a taxation system where all taxes are paid directly to the ruler. Military service should be required from all men and the military should use extreme penalties as punishments so that soldiers will find it less frightening to face the enemy than to face the punishments for running away. Like military service, the law should apply to all, no matter what their rank in society. Rank should be a reward either for military service or for service to the state. Erroneous learning and useless occupations should be banned. Whether in the military or in civil society, the ruler should use rewards and penalties because, as Shang Yang says, human beings will naturally tend to pursue self-interest. In short, the ruler should be in control of a society where people are anxious to serve him.[30]

Shen Buhai (d.337 BCE), an approximate contemporary of Aristotle (384–322), was a chancellor in the state of Han and interested in how government bureaucracy should work.[31] He discussed techniques of statecraft, bureaucracy, and government organization. He focused on how a ruler could control his officials. This was a problem, given that the ruler was related to many of his government officials, many rulers were easily flattered, and many were often not well educated. Shen Buhai says that one way to limit the power of officials is to encourage them to spy on one another. As well, if there are job descriptions, we can know if a job is being done or not, and promotion can be objectively decided. Shen Buhai was trying to solve practical problems in governing. His ideas and those of Shang Yang were picked up by later thinkers and woven into a new approach.

Han Feizi (*c*.280–233 BCE) studied with the Confucian teacher Xunzi (see chapter 7) and read both Shang Yang and Shen Buhai. He understood them as talking about the same sorts of things: government and law should apply to all, government and law should be impersonal, and government can control human behavior through rewards and punishments.

Han Feizi built on these ideas. He argued that power and authority must be centered in the hands of the ruler. Not only should the ruler run everything, but he should do so, ideally, in an automatic, unfeeling way so that not even the ruler's personality should be involved. From Daoist texts, Han Feizi borrowed the idea that the ruler should be hidden and mysterious. People should not know his likes or dislikes, so that they will obey his orders exactly and not try to do other things to curry favor.

Using fierce punishments, the ruler should ensure that people obey, not out of love or duty, but because they fear the ruler. Doting mothers produce spoiled sons; so, too, merciful rulers produce rebellious subjects. Even though there are good men in every state who do not need to be controlled, a ruler must control everyone and not base his rule on these exceptions. Everyone must come to fear the ruler.[32]

Looking to the past does not help us, because the sage-kings lived in different times. Now we need strong government to end the chaos of the time. One of the causes of this chaos is scholars and texts with different opinions. Scholars just waste food, says Han Feizi, and should get a real job. Han Feizi says, "In a state with a wise ruler there are no books – only the laws provide teachings."[33] Books are not useful and just confuse people by proposing different ideas.

The first of Han Feizi's principles of government was to centralize control in the hands of the ruler; the second principle is law. Law must apply to all and the punishment for breaking the law must be fierce. When this was put into practice, people could have their hands cut off for dumping ashes in the street. If the punishment for breaking small laws was so awful, people would not break any laws at all. The law must be strict; the law must be enforced. Law is an instrument that controls people.

The third principle of Han Feizi's thinking is power. Power is used to make others obey and is far more important than virtue or wisdom. Power must be centered in the hands of the ruler alone. The ruler chooses ministers on merit, offering them rewards and punishing them severely if they step out of line. Ministers have no power themselves; only the ruler does.[34]

Confucians argued that those in government ought to be models for people. If the law is the model, then why have governors? If laws are just formulae, then people will simply get smarter at getting around them; people will not learn to act morally. Confucians continued to argue with Legalists that making people fear does not work in the long run and that one has to make people internalize morality for society to work. Han Feizi believed that systems of behavior could be forced on people, and that would make them do what is best for society.

Others

The Mohists, the Daoists, the Logicians, and the Legalists were not the only people Confucians had to contend with. Although we do not have any of his writings, we hear about Yang Zhu (*c.*440–360 BCE), who advocated a "selfish love." If everyone simply followed self-interest, he seems to have said, society would benefit. He was also accused of hedonism and it was commonly reported that he said, "even if all the world would benefit, he would not pull a single hair from his leg."[35] That is, he argued that one should not harm oneself even if it meant saving everyone else. Yang Zhu seemed to have argued that it was every man for himself.

There were other voices too. Some argued that if everyone, including the ruler, went back to being a farmer, society would immediately become more equitable and peaceful. Others were fascinated with finding ways to become immortal. Some advocated breathing exercises, others special diets; others looked for chemical compounds that, when eaten or drunk, would make one immortal.

All of these views, some more systematic than others, made up the cacophony of the Warring States era. Confucius' followers were promoting only one view among many. A number of thinkers, like the ones we have seen in this chapter, argued that morality is simply a matter of point of view. Others said morality was irrelevant: people act from their own self-interest and nothing more. Attacks from other thinkers and the increasing demand for logical argumentation shaped the interpretations of Confucius' thought as the era went on.

6

Mencius

So, when Heaven is about to send down great responsibilities on you, it will first send sufferings to test your will and hard work to test your flesh and bones. It will have you suffer from hunger and poverty. It will frustrate all your plans. In this way it will move your mind, toughen your nature, and make up for anything you lack.[1]

The first great interpreter of Confucius' thought is Mencius (371–289 BCE). Mencius was considered to be the best interpreter of Confucius from the 1100s on. When the Catholic missionaries arrived in China, they found that Mencius was honored above all other followers of Confucius and so he too got a Latin name. In Chinese, his name is Mengzi, Master Meng.[2] Mencius' title is the "Second Sage," second only to the premier sage, Confucius.

Many stories have been told about Mencius' childhood and about his remarkable mother, Mother Meng. When her husband died while Mencius was still young, she worked very hard to provide her son with the best education and taught him the ancient classics. She saw that his behavior was being influenced by the neighborhood they lived in: when they lived beside a store, he played at buying, selling, and making a profit. She moved a number of times until she finally found a neighborhood where Mencius could pursue his studies. She could not afford school fees, so little Mencius sat outside the school's window, soaking up knowledge. Finally the teacher recognized Mencius' love of learning and admitted him. Mencius found school too easy and he began to cut classes. Mother Meng saw him playing truant one day and, when Mencius returned home, she asked him what he had done in school that day. In the eternal manner of all children when asked that by their parents, Mencius replied, "Nothing." Mother Meng picked up a knife and sliced the cloth on the loom right across. She said that she had spent months weaving this cloth to support Mencius, but now it was ruined. So too, breaking off from study ruins the student. Mencius

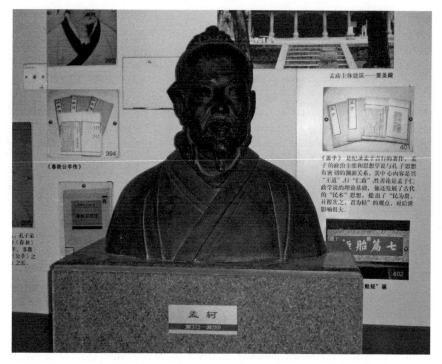

Figure 6.1 Statue of Mencius

reformed himself. These are charming stories meant to show Mencius' promise, even as a child. But, like the stories around Confucius, we should probably take them with a grain of salt.[3]

The later Han dynasty history, the *Records of the Historian*, contains a biography of Mencius, saying he was born in the small state of Zou, on the border of the state of Lu, near Confucius' home. He is said to have studied under Confucius' grandson, Zi Si. This tradition about studying with Zi Si is meant to indicate a direct teaching lineage from Confucius, to his son, to the grandson, and to Mencius. Like Confucius, Mencius wanted a government position and traveled about China trying to get a job. The later histories say that he attempted to advise the rulers of the states of Liang and Qi and may have held a position in the state of Qi, but Mencius was not able to persuade the ruler to follow his advice and retired to become a teacher and "transmit the teachings of Confucius." He may have had some minor positions, but Mencius, like Confucius, mostly taught. We have a book, the *Mencius*, parts of which might have been written by Mencius.

The bulk of the text, however, was written by his students, who based it on Mencius' teachings and conversations.

Mencius held Confucius in the highest esteem, saying, "Ever since human beings came into this world, there has never been anyone like Confucius!" Mencius' only wish was to follow the example of Confucius. In his later years, Mencius saw himself as the sole transmitter of Confucius' teachings, "Heaven does not yet want the world to have peace and order. If it wanted peace and order, who is there these days, except for me, who could bring it about?"[4] Mencius was aware that he had to transmit Confucius' teachings not as something people would just accept at face value, but that he was required to argue and convince people that what Confucius had taught was correct. After spending his whole life making arguments in defense of Confucius, Mencius makes a funny remark by saying, "It is not that I enjoy arguing, it is just that I have had no choice."[5] Even though Mencius pretended that he was pushed into arguments, he clearly understood the threats he faced and was able to come up with a good defense of Confucius' teachings.

In the hundred years since Confucius' death, society had begun to change. The old feudal system was shattered. Rulers were centralizing power more and more. War among states had increased. More rulers were influenced by ideas of rewards and punishments, based on the notion that human beings are merely self-interested.

Human Nature is Good

By Mencius' time, Confucius' teachings were just one of many competing teachings. Mencius revered Confucius and much of Mencius' thought can be understood as a replica of Confucius' – with an important difference. Mencius faced problems Confucius never had and was up against opponents Confucius never faced. The Mohists, the Daoists, the Logicians, the Strategists, and most of the other thinkers we have just looked at were in full cry by Mencius' time. They raised issues Confucius never had to face: What is the usefulness of rites and music? Is success more important than morality? What is the definition of goodness? Are human beings best understood as merely self-interested? Are right and wrong just words we apply to things depending on our point of view?

Mencius had to defend Confucius. For Mencius, the most profound attack came from the Daoists, and these were the criticisms that moral behavior is just a matter of taste; right and wrong merely depend on our point of view; and ethics is only something that we learn, but has no intrinsic reality. If moral behavior is just a matter of point of view, if it is "different strokes for different folks," then Confucius' teachings are one point of view. There is no reason to become educated in morality, to be a gentleman, or to practice humanity.

Mencius responded to all of this by saying that human nature is good.[6] Be careful with this statement. Mencius was not a fool; he lived in the world as we do, and he knew that there were many nasty people out there. What he is saying is that human nature is good, not that human beings are good. He says that human nature has within it the potential to grow into goodness, just as a fruit tree has the potential to grow fruit.

It is all very well to say that human nature is good, but, by Mencius' time, one would have to do more than just say it: Mencius had to prove it. Mencius uses a form of argument, common in his time, called analogical reasoning: using an analogy to make his point. As we shall see, he takes A, describes how it works, and compares it to B, arguing that B works in the same way.

Mencius backs up his claim that human nature is good by approaching the issue in five ways. First he talks about the four "sprouts" or beginnings. Human nature contains within it four sprouts. We are born with them.

> Everyone has a mind/heart that contains within it compassion, shame, respect, and the knowledge of right and wrong. A mind/heart with the sprout of compassion leads to humanity. A mind/heart with the sprout of shame leads to rightness. A mind/heart with the sprout of reverence and respect leads to ritual. A mind/heart with the sprout of right and wrong leads to wisdom. Humanity, rightness, ritual, and knowledge are not strapped on to us from the outside; we most certainly have them already.[7]

These sprouts or beginnings are: compassion, shame/dislike, modesty, and a sense of right and wrong. These sprouts are things we are born with and are part of our emotional reactions to the world. If we cultivate these sprouts, like a farmer growing a crop, they will develop into moral qualities. The first, compassion, is a natural sympathy towards others. If we nurture that, it will grow into the virtue of humanity – putting ourselves in the shoes of others. The second sprout or tendency is shame. When we do something wrong, we are ashamed of ourselves. If we nurture that, it will grow into rightness: knowing what is proper, what is right, and what is moral. We are born with a sprout of modesty that, if cultivated, becomes knowing what is proper, knowing ritual. Finally we are born with a sense of right and wrong and that, if tended, will become wisdom. These sprouts are the beginning of goodness.

Is Mencius right? Do we have these sprouts? Certainly small children do, at various stages, show a sense of compassion toward others. As well, we have all heard the child's cry, "It's not fair!" that presumes some sense of right and wrong. Modesty may be more culturally learned and it is difficult to decide about how much is learned and how much may be natural in a sense of shame. Sarah Blaffer Hrdy argues that during the evolution of human beings we adapted by developing ways to share food and involve ourselves in the care of children who are not our own. This was new and different. It was based, she argues, on the development of powers of engagement and sympathy with others. This is why even before the development of language, we know that babies recognize, interpret, and imitate expressions of people around them. In modern humans it has been shown that the pleasure centers of the brain are stimulated when we help others.[8]

Whether Mencius is right or wrong on the particulars, his argument is that, when we are born, we naturally contain within us certain tendencies that, if nourished by proper adult role models and by education, can lead us to moral behavior.

Mencius' definition of human nature is different from the common understanding of human nature. Most thinkers of Mencius' time saw human nature as made up of emotions and desires.[9] Mencius never argues against this, but says that our human natures also include natural tendencies toward goodness.

The second approach Mencius takes is to argue that we are all, basically, the same. The great sages of the past, and Confucius himself, were not freaks of nature, but were human beings just like us. There is no difference between us and a sage, except that a sage has cultivated the sprouts within. If sages are capable of cultivating their sprouts, so are we all. And, if sages are great moral examples, it is because they have the sprouts within them, and so do we all. Mencius uses the analogy of growing barley, a cereal grain.

> When it comes to growing barley, the seeds are sown and covered in soil. The soil is the same and the time when the seeds are planted is also the same. They grow rapidly, and soon are all ripened. If there are differences from one barley plant to another, these are because of the differences in the richness of the soil, the unevenness of the rain and differences in farming. So, things of the same kind are all similar. Why would we think that this did not apply to human beings alone? Sages and the rest of us are of the same kind.[10]

The analogy here is between the barley crop and human beings. Any differences among the barley are caused by external circumstances. In the same way, human beings are the same, just like the barley seeds: any differences among us are due to circumstances. Mencius goes on to argue that we have similar tastes in recognizing food and music and, while we may prefer some things over others, we all know what food is and we all know what sounds constitute music. Why then, he says, should we think that our minds' tastes would be that very different?

If we all begin with the same nature, if we all have within us the potential for humanity, rightness, ritual, and wisdom, why then do some of us
become sages while others do not? Mencius says that we simply do not
concentrate on the goodness within and cultivate it. Human beings are
alike: we are all born with the same capacities and, if those capacities reach
their potential, we can all become sages.

We can see this natural potential within us when we are surprised and
act without thinking about our self-interest. In his third approach, Mencius
says,

> Everyone has a mind/heart that is aware of the sufferings of others. ...
>
> Even in these days, if a man saw a young child about to fall into a
> well, he, like everyone else, would feel alarm and compassion as his first
> reaction. He would feel like this, not because he wanted to get in good
> with the child's parents, nor because he wanted to be famous among
> their neighbors and friends, nor because he hated the sounds of the child's
> cries.
>
> From this we can see that, if one does not have a mind/heart of compas-
> sion, then one is not a human being. Similarly, if one does not have a mind/
> heart that feels shame, one is not a human being. If one does not have a mind/
> heart that feels modesty, one is not a human being. If one does not have a
> mind/heart that knows right and wrong, one is not a human being.[11]

Humanity can be seen to be naturally present within us because, just as
when seeing a child about to fall into the well, even the worst of us will,
if surprised, feel a sense of alarm. When we have time to think about a
situation, we will often begin to figure out how this might work to our
advantage. We calculate the long-term implications; we remember past
slights. It is then that we behave badly. But, when surprised or in an
emergency, we are more like to behave well because all that is operating
is natural to us.

The fourth approach is to defend his theory that human nature is good
from those who point out that there are clearly evil people in the world.
Mencius says that, with the proper cultivation, the basic sprouts in human
nature develop into goodness in one's mind/heart. Without this, we lose
any connection to what is within us. He says,

> The trees of Ox Mountain were once beautiful. But because it bordered on a
> large city, people attacked the mountain with hatchets and axes. How could
> it remain beautiful? The trees were not attacked every day and did get some
> rest at night. And there was rain and dew, so it was not that there were no
> sprouts at all growing there. But then cattle and sheep were sent out to graze
> on the mountain and, after that, it was as if it were totally bald. People, seeing

it bald, believed that there had never been any trees on Ox Mountain. Was this really the nature of the mountain?

When we consider what is in people, could they really not have the mind/hearts of humanity and rightness? The way a person throws away their good mind/heart is just like the axes and the trees. With the mind/heart being attacked every day, how can it remain beautiful? With the rest it gets during the night and at times during the day, a person's likes and dislikes are sometimes close to those of others. But then what they do during the day once again attacks the mind/heart. If the attacks are constantly repeated, then even a night's rest is not enough to preserve the mind/heart. The result is a person not very different from a beast. When other people see his resemblance to a beast, they think that he never had any moral capacity. Is this really the nature of the man?[12]

We can lose our innate goodness to the point where it looks like we never had any to begin with, just as, in Mencius' analogy, the mountain has lost all its trees. This does not mean that our original goodness is not there; it means that we have cut and hacked at it to the point where it cannot be seen.

We can see Mencius' fifth approach in two related passages. The first is in his conversation with another thinker, Gaozi.[13] Gaozi used analogy in his argument too and argued that human nature is like water. Water will flow either east or west, whichever is more natural to it. So too, human nature is neutral: it does not know good or bad except as it may be moved in one direction or another.

Mencius replied that, while it is true that water may be made to flow east or west, depending on what is open to it, the nature of water is always to flow downwards. Like water that will always flow downhill, so, too, human nature will tend toward the good. And, just as water may be manipulated by the use of dams and dikes to flow in certain directions, so, too, human nature can be manipulated and people may behave badly. The nature of water is to flow downhill; the nature of human beings is to tend toward the good.

We can see this natural standard of goodness within us when we look at our attitudes toward life and death. Mencius says that, much as he loves his life, he would not do anything at all to stay alive. Similarly, death is something he hates, but he would not do anything at all to avoid death. The desire to live is basic to us all, but we will not use any means to stay alive. There are simply some things that are so horrible to us that we would not do them, even if it would save our lives. If faced with the choice of saving their own lives or the lives of their children, most parents would give up their lives. This means, he argues, that we have within us moral standards that are more important to us than even our life.[14]

Human nature is not just self-interest. There are points in life when we choose to do things, or not to do things, on an ethical basis. Human nature may be shaped by the family we grow up in or by external events to flow east or west, but it will always tend toward the good and we can see that when we look at decisions we make about life and death.

Mencius argues for his position that human nature is good by taking these five approaches to it. First, that human nature contains certain sprouts or tendencies that, if cultivated, can grow into moral qualities. The seeds in our human nature are what make human nature different from the nature of other animals. Second, he says that human beings are all alike in having these sprouts. The sages are not special in their morality; we are just like them. Sages are special because of their cultivation of the sprouts. The only reason we are not all sages is that we have not fully cultivated the tendencies to morality within us. Third, we can see signs of these sprouts whenever we are surprised and act naturally from them. Only when we have a chance to think about profiting ourselves do we behave badly. Fourth, if human nature is good, how can we explain evil people? Evil people exist, says Mencius. Their natural tendencies toward the good have been hacked down and covered over to such an extent that it is hard to believe that they ever had any goodness within them. Fifth, there are some things that we cannot bear to do. That is because there is a tendency toward the good: human nature flows toward the good as water flows downward. Mencius is arguing that our human nature cannot just be reduced to self-interest. There is a lot more in us that also provides motivations for our actions.[15]

So the foundation of moral behavior is internal. It is not welded onto us from the outside. Moral behavior is natural to human beings. Mencius says that human beings differ from other animals in very little and that difference is in the human potential for moral growth. We all love all the parts of ourselves, says Mencius. Those who nurture the goodness within are greater than those who emphasize their senses. The latter lose their "original mind/heart."

"Losing one's original mind/heart"[16] means we can lose our sense of morality when we let self-interest and greed guide us: a gentleman maintains his mind/heart by cultivating the goodness within and so is always in accord with humanity and ritual.[17] It is the mind/heart that thinks, decides, and focuses; we can lose it when we are ensnared by things outside us. The mind/heart works something like a rational faculty for Mencius, and it is deeply connected to our inner moral being and to our human nature. The mind/heart does not work like the ears or the eyes; the mind/heart can think about things and, unlike the senses, cannot be fooled as easily. However, if the mind/heart does not think about things, it can be fooled and left without understanding. Mencius says, "To completely develop one's mind/heart is to understand one's own nature; to know one's own nature is to know Heaven."[18] Our rationality, our inner moral tendencies, and Heaven are closely connected.

What makes a gentleman different from other people is that a gentleman preserves his mind/heart and does so through practicing humanity and ritual. Mencius said, "The difference between human beings and animals is very small. Ordinary people frequently give up this difference; a gentleman preserves it"[19] and "A great man does not lose his child-like mind/heart."[20] Preserving our original mind/heart depends on self-cultivation. This is a steady, daily growing of moral qualities within us. We do not suddenly become good people through enlightenment or salvation. Instead we need to be careful and thoughtful at all times, gradually becoming better in our actions. We need to reflect on the situation and on what we are doing. Self-interest conflicts with moral behavior and self-interest must be overcome. But, this growth must not be forced.

Mencius says that we must not be like the man from Song who was troubled because his plants were not growing and so pulled at them. "When he returned home he said to his family, 'I am tired today because I have been helping the crops to grow.' His son hurried to look and found that the seedlings were dead. There are some who do not 'help their crop to grow'; seeing no benefit in it, they do not weed their crop. Others 'help their crop to grow' by pulling at it. This is not only of no benefit, but actually harmful."[21] Expecting perfect results in all our actions, "helping the plants to grow," will lead to failure. And when we fail, we will give up.

Human Nature and Heaven

Mencius says that Heaven gives us humanity, dutifulness, conscientiousness, truthfulness to one's word, and unending delight in what is good. All that people can give us are honors like titles and high position.[22] Mencius carried his argument further by saying that our basic human nature contains the potential for good because of its relation to Heaven. Only human beings can reflect the goodness of Heaven. Heaven, for Mencius, is the metaphysical basis of morality. We already know Heaven is an ethical entity from the idea of the "choice of Heaven." Heaven bases its choices on moral considerations, choosing, for example, a moral man to be the ruler and rejecting the immoral one.

We will look more closely at what Mencius says about the relationship between Heaven and human beings below, but here we can see that he has argued for two, related, things. First, that morality is innate and unique to human beings. Second, Mencius has given morality a metaphysical basis. By arguing that human nature reflects the goodness of Heaven, Mencius puts morality on a foundation. Heaven itself is moral; human beings reflect that morality. So moral behavior is not a matter of taste or point of view, it is natural to human beings and is based in Heaven itself.

Government

Mencius understood himself as elaborating on Confucius' ideas. He believed that Confucius had taught that human nature is good. Mencius saw himself as fleshing out the implications of that. Mencius follows Confucius in his arguments about government as well. The bulk of the *Mencius* is devoted to discussions between Mencius and rulers, with Mencius advising the ruler on moral government or discussing ancient and Warring States politics. When we read descriptions of Mencius' conversations with rulers, it is perfectly clear why Mencius was so rarely employed:

> Mencius spoke to King Xuan of Qi, saying, "Imagine that one of your ministers entrusted his wife and children to his friend and traveled to the state of Chu. When he returned, he found that his friend had let his wife and children become cold and hungry – what should he do?"
> The King said, "Get rid of the friend."
> Mencius asked, "If the Chief Guard is not able to keep order among the guards, what should be done?"
> The King said, "Fire him."
> Mencius said, "If the whole state from border to border is not well governed, what should be done?" The King turned toward his servants and talked about something else.[23]

If Mencius talked to rulers like this, it is no wonder that they did not hire him.

Like Confucius, Mencius says that government exists for the benefit of the people. The ruler's job is to care for the people and so, says Mencius, a ruler is not actually very important: "The people are the most valuable part of a country; the spirits of the land and of the grain are second; the ruler is the least."[24] It is the ruler's job to look after the people, to put people first and himself last. Of course this did not go down well with rulers of the warring states.

As a model for the people and as someone who cares for the people, the ideal ruler is not authoritarian. Mencius defined a ruler who uses force to rule as a dictator; a real king rules so as to care for the people.

A ruler is placed in his position by Heaven, says Mencius. If a ruler does not care for the people, he is, according to the principle of "putting words right," not a ruler. If he is killed, it is not a ruler who has been killed:

> Someone who violates humanity is called a violator; someone who destroys rightness is called a criminal. A violator and a criminal is someone we call a low-class lout. I have heard that a low-class lout called Zhou [the last ruler of the Shang dynasty] was killed, but I have not heard of a ruler who was assassinated.[25]

While he may call himself "ruler," if his behavior is not proper, he is not a real ruler. He is just some "lout." Similarly, and even more radically, just because a ruler has a son, there is no reason why that son should inherit the position. Rulers should be chosen on the basis of their conduct, not on the basis of their father's. "If Heaven wishes to appoint a worthy man, the worthy man is appointed; if Heaven wishes to appoint the son, the son is appointed."[26] The choice of Heaven should produce a good ruler, not just the son of a ruler.

Does this mean that one can justifiably overthrow a bad ruler? If the ruler is not a real ruler, according to the principle of putting words right, is it permissible to rebel against him? Mencius does not go that far, but we can speculate that this could have been his conclusion. Instead, Mencius uses his arguments about government to evaluate rulers, not to suggest uprisings against them.[27]

Throughout the *Mencius* we can see the need for putting words right as Mencius visited the "king" of the state of Qi and the "king" of the state of Liang. Both were using a title that was not proper to who they were. When Mencius went to see one of these "kings," King Hui of the state of Liang, the king remarked that it was an honor that Mencius would come so far to "profit" his state. Mencius responded by seizing on the word "profit" and argued that, when the king thought of nothing but profit, so too would his government ministers. Seeing how his government ministers behaved, the common people too would only think about profit. Once "profit" was all anyone thought about, the only sure outcome would be competition among them all for their own self-interest.[28]

As we have seen in Confucius' thought, Mencius says that the ruler should act as a model for everyone in the state: "Treat the elderly in your family properly as elderly people should be treated and extend this to elderly people in other families; treat young people in your family properly as young people should be treated and extend this to young people in other families. If you do this, the empire will fit in your hand."[29] As the model for everyone in every station, it was up to the ruler to always behave properly. The ruler's example would be seen, and copied, by everyone. For Mencius, the ruler has an awesome responsibility in caring for the people. People should know that they had an upright ruler and develop confidence in his government. With the confidence of the people, a ruler will be successful. The ruler acts toward the people as a father does to his children. This is a paternal view of government, patterned on what we have seen in Confucius' thought.

Mencius says that we must all be given a chance to cultivate the goodness within. If we are raised by bad models and if we are never taught how to cultivate our goodness, we are unlikely to be able to cultivate goodness. A bad environment is one reason that many people do not develop what is within them. A bad economy is the second reason. Mencius said, "In years of plenty, most young men are quiet; in years of poverty, most young men are violent; it is not that the potential that Heaven has sent down to them changes. They become violent because of what traps and drowns their mind/hearts."[30] Mencius thought that we cannot expect people not to steal if they are starving. If people are forced to live in poverty they cannot be expected to develop moral behavior.

Mencius spent a lot of time talking about the economy. Poverty is the source of all moral and social evil; poverty among the people is the fault of selfish rulers. The ideal state should provide economic well-being for its people. This will allow everyone to share in the wealth and allow everyone to cultivate their inherent goodness. The government must not overtax the people. People must be allowed to provide for themselves and rulers should not be taking tax money from them so as to enjoy a luxury that the people cannot dream of.

Mencius proposed a new tax system where all the fields would be divided into nine sections. Individuals would farm their own fields and the crops from the center field, the ninth, would be given to the ruler in taxes.[31] This way a year of bad harvests would affect the ruler as much as the people. Mencius was also the first to call for environmental awareness, the preservation of forests and fishing, and for diversified farming as ways to protect and enhance people's livelihoods:

> If you want to put a government of humanity into effect, then simply return to the basics. Plant mulberry trees in every household of five fields; that way, fifty-year-olds can wear silk. If chickens, pigs, and dogs are raised, then seventy-year-olds can eat meat. If you do not disturb the work of planting and harvesting in each of one hundred fields, even a household that has eight mouths to feed will not go hungry. If you are careful about education, explaining the rightness of filial piety and respect for brothers, then the elderly will not be carrying loads on the roads. It has always been that, when the elderly are able to wear silk and eat meat, and when the Chinese people are not hungry nor cold, their ruler has become the emperor.[32]

A ruler who concentrates on enriching his people, improving the economy, and educating them in morality is well on his way to ruling all of China.

Mencius says that the government should respect all classes; the government should be loved and revered and provide models of good behavior. Governments should not be feared: the four evils of government are cruelty, oppression, injury, and meanness. The ruler must care for the people and be a model to the people. Any ruler who does not rule properly does not deserve the title "ruler." The ruler's primary concern must be the economy because ordinary people cannot be expected to behave well in bad times.

Mencius on Confucian Themes

Now that we have seen Mencius' theory of human nature and his ideas about society and government, we can look at how these ideas play out when Mencius develops other ideas from Confucius.

When King Xuan of Qi confessed that he felt sorry for an ox that was about to be slaughtered at a sacrifice, Mencius used the occasion to point out that the king was capable of kindness and compassion, but chose not to act that way when he ruled his people. The king's fault was not that he lacked the ability to rule well, but that he refused to rule well.[33] The compassion that the king felt should be developed into the virtue of humanity and extended to his people. The king was clearly capable of ruling well, but chose not to.

Mencius told the king to use humanity in governing his state. The result would be that he would attract talented ministers, ordinary people who would farm, and merchants who would want to do business. The king would be a model and his government would be successful. Mencius went on to say,

> To not have a constant means of income, but to be able to maintain a constant mind/heart – only a scholar is able to do that. As for the common people, if they do not have a constant means of income, they will not be able to maintain a constant mind/heart. Without a constant mind/heart, they will fall into sleaziness and evil. Once they have sunk into crime, to punish them is just to trap the people. How could a man of humanity entrap people?
>
> So an intelligent ruler regulates the people's livelihood to make sure that they have enough both to serve their father and mother and to manage for their wives and children. This way the people will have enough food when times are good and still not starve even when times are bad. This way they will quickly move toward goodness and follow it easily.[34]

Like Confucius, Mencius believed that ordinary people could only follow the example of their superiors. Only a gentleman can preserve his mind/heart in good times and bad. As for the people, they are like children who must be provided for and led to goodness.

In conclusion, Mencius tells the king that, should he rule morally, good advisors would be drawn to his government, farmers would be anxious to farm in his state, merchants would flock to his markets, and he would attract people from other states who cannot bear their rulers.

Mencius faced another issue that Confucius had also faced: should one take a job in a corrupt government? Mencius argues that one should not be blinded by money to either the way we are offered jobs nor the kinds of jobs we are offered:

A basket of food and a bowl of soup. If you get them, then you will live; if you do not get them, then you will die. But, if they are given to you with contempt, then even a homeless person will not take them. And if they are trampled in the dirt, then even a beggar won't take them.

But, when it comes to a high salary, then you think you can overlook ritual and rightness and accept them. What does a big salary add to me? Am I going to take it for the sake of living in a beautiful mansion? For the enjoyment of a wife and concubines? To have my poorer friends feel indebted to me? In the first case, even for the sake of one's own life, one could not accept what was offered. In the second case, for the sake of a beautiful mansion one does accept. ... this kind of thinking is called "losing one's original mind/heart."[35]

Accepting money and not paying any attention to the moral consequences of one's position is to "lose one's original mind/heart." Mencius refused to take government positions merely for power and money.

Talking to King Hui of Liang, Mencius criticized rulers who interrupt farmers in their busiest seasons by sending them to war. This resulted in families starving and scattering in their search for food. "These rulers," says Mencius, "push their people into pits and into water."[36] Like Confucius, Mencius did not discuss military matters, but he did say that the state must also protect people from invasion, so there needs to be an army, but the focus should not be on the army and the ruler should not invade other states. The people should not be bothered by military service in busy seasons of planting and harvest and they should not be sent to war untrained. Anyone advocating war or teaching the skills of warfare – Strategists presumably – Mencius viewed as evil, delighting in piling up corpses. Mencius said, "There are people who say 'I am good at military formations. I am good at waging war.' This is a great crime." "Death is not enough of a punishment for them."[37]

Morality can be found in ourselves and we should look to ourselves for a moral compass. Mencius articulates that admirable Confucian quality – examining oneself first in any situation. He says that if someone is nasty to you, first look to see if you have been practicing humanity and proper ritual. If you have, and the other person is still obnoxious, then look to see if you have been doing your duty. "If he examines himself and finds that he has done his duty, but the other person is still nasty, a gentleman says, 'This person is simply hopeless! There is no difference between a person like this and an animal. You cannot expect an animal to know how to behave.'"[38]

In the same vein, Mencius said, "If you love others, but they do not respond, then look inwardly at your own humanity. If you govern others, but they do not obey, then look inwardly at your own wisdom. If you are ritually polite and others do not return your courtesy, look inwardly at your own respect. Whenever you do not get a proper response, look for the solution first within yourself."[39] When we have problems, particularly with other

people, we are to stop first and look at our own behavior, examining ourselves before blaming others. This is an excellent, if difficult, habit of mind.

Like Confucius, Mencius saw filial piety as the basis for learning morality. Like Confucius too, Mencius had to defend the three-year mourning
period for parents. When King Xuan of Qi wanted to cut the mourning
period down to one year, one of Mencius' students asked him if this was
such a bad thing. At least the king would be observing a year of mourning,
which was better than none at all. Mencius responded, "This is the same as
saying to someone who is twisting their elder brother's arm – 'Do it gently.'
The king must be taught filial piety."[40]

Mencius was also sensitive to the problems surrounding the practice
of filial piety. When asked if a father should teach his own sons, Mencius
advised against it. After all, he said, a teacher must correct his students
and, if the student still does not learn, he may lose his temper. This ends
up hurting both father and son, as the son, in revenge, may say, "You
correct me, but you do not behave correctly yourself." Father and son, he
says, should not demand goodness from each other, for, if they do, they
may become estranged.[41]

During the time of Mencius, followers of Confucius were gradually developing discussions of ritual in two directions: first, there was an increase in
specific regulations dealing with everything from the proper wood allowed
for a casket depending on the rank of the deceased to regulations about
how one should eat (see chapter 8). Second, we find a stronger set of rules
dealing with the separation of men and women. Separation included separate living quarters in the home, separate spheres of activity, and detailed
regulations concerning the interaction of men and women, as we have seen
in chapter 3. This seems to have been widely discussed among Confucians
at this time and was the point of many debates. Mencius did not, so far as
we can tell, get involved in these arguments. But he did think that rituals
evolved from the expression of one's inner nature. He says that

> In ancient times, people did not bury their parents. When the parents died,
> they were thrown into the ditch. But, as the sons passed by them one day,
> they could see that the corpses were eaten by foxes and flies buzzed around.
> The sweat broke out on the sons' foreheads and they could not bear to look.
> Their sweat was not a show for others, but an expression of their inner hearts.
> Then, they went home for shovels and baskets and buried the bodies.[42]

Not throwing the bodies in a ditch is an expression of the mind/heart's
feeling of compassion and shame.

A rival thinker tried to trip Mencius up by asking about a Confucian
rule about ritual. This is the one we saw in chapter 3 that says that men
and women are not allowed to touch each other. If men and women are not
allowed to touch, what should you do when your sister-in-law is drowning?

Mencius immediately dismisses the ritual rule, saying that anyone who followed it when their sister-in-law was drowning would be a beast. Clearly this is an emergency and touching the woman is the proper response.[43]

The state must provide education, and, again, this would allow people to cultivate their inner morality. Like Confucius, Mencius was not specific about whether or not this would include lower-class men and women. The education Mencius talked about, however, is, like Confucius' idea of education, not just learning facts, but an education in morality. As it was for Confucius, education was crucial to Mencius. Education is the way in which one cultivates the goodness within. Mencius advocated learning the ways of antiquity, the sage-kings, the rulers of the early Zhou dynasty, and, of course, the teachings of Confucius. Education should lead to moral cultivation.

Like Confucius, Mencius had little to say about women, and that may be just as well. Mencius said, "When a daughter marries, her mother gives her advice. Sending her daughter off at the gate, the mother cautions her, 'When you go to your new family, you must be respectful, and you must be careful. Do not disobey your husband.' To be obedient is proper to the Way of a wife."[44] He agrees with Confucius and the Confucians of his time that women should be respectful and obedient.

Finally we come to about half a dozen passages in the *Mencius* that will be emphasized by later Confucians. We have seen that Mencius, like Confucius, believed that Heaven had endowed him with a mission. Mencius goes further in his statements about a connection to the cosmos. Mencius says, "Wherever the great gentleman passes there is transformation. Wherever he stays there is a spiritual influence flowing above and below with Heaven and Earth."[45] A great gentleman is part of the dynamic workings of "Heaven and Earth," a phrase often used to refer to the universe. Mencius also describes this in a passage where he talks about his "vast overflowing *qi*." When he was asked what his strong points were, Mencius said,

> I know words. I am good at nourishing my vast and overflowing *qi*. ... This *qi* is, in the highest degree, unlimited and unmoving. If it is nourished with integrity and is not harmed, it will fill the space between heaven and earth. This *qi* unites with rightness and the Way; without rightness and the Way, the *qi* will starve. This *qi* is born from accumulated rightness and not an occasional show of rightness. Action that is below the standard set in one's mind/heart will starve the *qi*.[46]

We will look more closely at the various meanings of the term *qi* in chapter 9, but here Mencius uses the term to mean the basic part of a person, the energy that animates us. It is like human nature and, like human nature, tends to the good if cultivated over time. This, Mencius says, is closely connected to rightness, the standard of good, and to the Confucian Way of morality and civilization.[47] The basics in human beings can unite with the universe – but only when we practice morality. Mencius makes the same sort of point when he says,

> Anyone who completely knows their own mind/heart, then, knows their human nature. When you know your human nature, you know Heaven. To keep your original mind/heart and nourish your nature, you serve Heaven.
>
> Neither an early death nor a long life should cause you any worry; instead you should cultivate your self and establish your own destiny.[48]

The connection between human beings and Heaven can be experienced if we practice morality and come to know ourselves. Finding, and keeping, our original mind/heart means behaving properly over time. We have seen Mencius say that the gentleman does not lose his original mind/heart and preserves the mind/heart as it was when he was a child. In this way, says Mencius, we can come to know Heaven.

Mencius also links human beings and Heaven together through the virtue of sincerity. Sincerity, as we have seen, means to think, act, and speak without any self-interest or "double-mindedness." Mencius uses a chain argument to talk about sincerity. He begins with the first link, which is understanding goodness. If a man can do this, then he is true to himself. This allows him to please his parents. If he can please his parents, his friends will trust him. If his friends trust him, his superiors will have confidence in him and he will be able to govern the people. Mencius concludes, "So, sincerity is the Way of Heaven; to think about sincerity the Way of man."[49] By being a truly ethical person, being sincere, we can share in Heaven's ethical character. This leads us to one of Mencius' most famous statements: "All things are complete within me. If one examines oneself and finds sincerity, there is no greater joy."[50] When Mencius says "all things" he means all the things of the universe. They find completion within us when we share in the universe's virtue of sincerity.

Just what Mencius meant by these kinds of statements is much debated. It looks like he believed that a properly cultivated person could, in some way, join together with the universe itself in its moral purposes. The difficulty is knowing just what to make of Mencius' statements. This is because what is missing is any description of Heaven or the moral universe, how it is constituted, how, exactly, it works, and all the other more "theological" points we would expect to find.

Summary

Like Confucius, Mencius begins with the individual. We have within us the potential for moral behavior. Moral behavior always has a social dimension: it must be acted out in our family, society, and state. Mencius' defense of Confucius' teachings grounds morality in human nature and in Heaven. He develops these new ideas of human nature and our relationship to Heaven in the context of Confucius' teachings. He also builds on, and amplifies, political ideas we saw in Confucius. Over a thousand years after his death, Mencius' ideas about our relationship to the universe were picked up and his reputation vaulted over all other Confucians to make Mencius the "Second Sage." Mencius was the first great interpreter of Confucius in the Warring States era, but he was not the only one.

7

Xunzi

Low-class Confucians loosely follow the ways of the ancient kings – just enough to cause confusion in our time. ... their methods are in error and they pick up knowledge from anywhere. ... their theories do not really differ from Mozi's. ... they use antiquity to cheat stupid people and make money from them.[1]

The second great interpreter of Confucius is Xunzi.[2] Born about 310 BCE, almost two hundred years after the death of Confucius, Xunzi would have been in his teens or early twenties when Mencius died. While the date of his death is not known, there is a long tradition that Xunzi lived to be almost a hundred years old. This would mean he died somewhere around 210 BCE.

Xunzi, Master Xun, does not have a Latinized name. This is because, while Xunzi's interpretation of Confucius was the dominant one from his time to the 1100s CE, after that Mencius was taken as the correct interpreter of Confucius (see chapter 6), and to this day, Mencius is still accepted as the proper successor to Confucius. As a result, when the Catholic missionaries came to China, they heard little about Xunzi, but a lot about Mencius, so Xunzi does not have a Latin name. Xunzi's lesser status continues and can be seen, for example, in the Confucian Museum and Research Center in Qufu. Mencius is portrayed there as a great Confucian worthy and honored with a bust, while Xunzi is merely represented by a picture of his portrait in a collage of pictures of texts and temples.

Though a native of the state of Zhao, in his mid-teens Xunzi traveled to the Jixia Academy in the state of Qi and was such an impressive scholar that he may well have become the head of the Jixia Academy in his 40s. Two of Xunzi's students, Han Fei and Li Si, went on to define the Legalist school.[3] Xunzi did not spend all of his time at the academy, but traveled to many other states, like other scholars, looking for a job. One firm date in Xunzi's life is 255 BCE when he was appointed to be the magistrate of

Lanling in the state of Chu. He was dismissed from that post and went to his native state of Zhao where he was given the rank of a senior minister. The government of Chu reconsidered and invited Xunzi back to Lanling where he remained a magistrate until the assassination of his government patron in 238. He never again took a government position and it is likely that he lived long enough to see the triumph of the Legalist state of Qin.

We have a text, predictably called the *Xunzi*, much of which is thought to have been written by Xunzi himself. This text, however, did not make it into later canons of Confucian classics. But the *Book of Rites* is part of the Confucian canon (see chapter 8), and parts of the *Xunzi* are repeated in the *Book of Rites*.[4] We can see the pervasive influence of the Mohists and Logicians in the text. While a strict Confucian, Xunzi felt obliged to supply definitions and logical arguments to back up his positions.

Xunzi was very serious in his reverence for Confucius and his thought. He says,

> Confucius possessed humanity, was wise, and was not blind. This is why his study of government was so great that he was the equal of the early kings. His teachings included all the ways of the Zhou dynasty and could be put into practice without any blindness to any point. Therefore his virtue was equal to the Duke of Zhou; his fame was on a par with that of the founders of the three dynasties. This was the blessing of being free from blindness.[5]

Xunzi describes blindness as obsession and a lack of clarity. Confucius was able to see the truth; unlike so many others, Confucius saw clearly and completely. As a result, Xunzi says, Confucius was able to teach the ways of the sage-kings and was so sincere that he was able to bring together different kinds of people and attract men of talent. Like Mencius, Xunzi saw Confucius as the ultimate teacher and Xunzi wanted nothing more than to defend the true thought of Confucius from all its enemies, both inside and outside the Confucian tradition. While Mencius had complained that there were thinkers he had to argue with, Xunzi was positively besieged not only by the Mohists and Daoists of Mencius' time, but by Logicians, Strategists, Legalists, and all the other Confucian groups with whom he disagreed. He was most irate at the pernicious teachings of Mencius.

Human Nature is Evil

Xunzi says that, as an interpreter of Confucius' thought, Mencius got almost everything wrong. Mencius' errors began with his views on human nature. It is clear, Xunzi claims, that human nature is evil and is based entirely on selfishness.[6] This is what Confucius really meant.

As with Mencius' claim that human nature is good, we have to be very careful with Xunzi's claim that human nature is evil. When we think of "evil," we may think of devils or the Devil, and that is not at all in Xunzi's use of the word. We may also think of ideas like the Christian idea of the Fall from grace; again, this is not what Xunzi has in mind. "Evil" is related to "ugly" and used to describe things that evoke a feeling of revulsion.[7] When he says that human nature is evil, Xunzi means that we are incapable of living in a civilized way with other human beings if we just follow what is natural to our human nature. He says,

> Mencius said that human nature is good. I say that this is not correct. From antiquity to the present day, what the world has called good is what is correct, ordered, peaceful, and well governed. What has been called evil is what is biased, disordered, perverse, and chaotic. This is the difference between good and evil.[8]

Goodness is the ability to live in a peaceful and well-ordered society and to behave correctly according to morality and ritual. Evil is self-interest, bias, disloyalty, and immorality.

Xunzi also carefully defines what he means by human nature: "Human nature is what is produced by nature; it is what is not learned; it is what needs no effort to be able to do."[9] As an example, he says, we are born able to hear and we do not need to be taught how to do it. Mencius, he says, did not carefully define human nature and this was one of the reasons Mencius did not know what he was talking about.

Human nature includes the emotions and desires, which are stirred by the senses. Xunzi lists as the emotions liking and disliking, happiness and anger, and sorrow and joy. These emotions are natural to us and, when we act on them, we will act badly.

> Now, the nature of man is that he is born with a love of profiting himself. Following this nature will cause aggression and greed to grow, while courtesy and deference are lost. Human beings are born with feelings of hate and envy. Following these causes violence and crime, while loyalty and trustworthiness are lost.

Desires develop when the senses tell us about things we want:

> Man is born with the desires of the ears and eyes so that we love sounds and colors. If we follow them, then sleaziness and chaos result, while ritual, rightness, civilization, and order are lost. Because of this, when we follow our human nature and our emotions, then we must develop aggression and greed, we must overturn social divisions, and bring chaos to order – all of this will end in violence.[10]

When emotions and desires rule our actions, we are led to evil. Simply following our nature will lead us to evil: envy, hatred, violence, crime, selfishness, disloyalty, and greed. Throughout his chapter "Human Nature is Evil" Xunzi lists the attributes of human nature as a love of profit, the emotions of envy and hate, the desire for what we see and hear, desires for food, warmth, and rest, prejudice or bias in our favor, and self-interest.

If we all act from our human nature, chaos results. No one would respect or consider anyone else; society would be impossible. We would all spend our time fighting each other for the many things we desire. From birth on, Xunzi says, we naturally love ourselves, follow our desires, and look to our own interests. If we follow these natural tendencies, we will grab everything we can. What is basic to all human beings is a nature that drives us to satisfy all of our desires. Human nature is indeed natural and spontaneous, as Daoists argued, but this means it is greedy, selfish, and evil.

The desires and emotions, says Xunzi, are the materials of human nature and react to external stimulation in a natural, if evil, way. The mind, Xunzi says, sits among the emotions and desires and chooses. When the mind chooses among our emotions and desires, we think. This Xunzi calls "conscious exertion." It is this alone that can save us from the rampaging emotions and desires based in our natures. When the mind makes decisions, this is thought. Desires and emotions cannot be eliminated, but they can be kept in check by the mind. When the mind thinks and acts properly, it develops "artificiality."[11] Artificiality is what is acquired; it is not natural to us. When artificiality, based on thought and training, is built up, we can control desires and emotions. If it is continually practiced, artificiality becomes "second nature." An acquired or artificial nature can be developed through education, teachers, models, and a great deal of effort.

Xunzi points out that we all want to eat, to be warm, and to rest. But we learn not to eat before our elders; we help our elders out with work when we would rather rest. We are courteous to them and we subordinate our needs to theirs. These actions run contrary to our inborn nature and we can only learn to do them through conscious effort and acquiring artificiality. Xunzi concludes by saying that

> to follow human nature and our true emotions means that we would not
> be courteous or deferent to others. To be courteous and deferent to others
> runs against our feelings and human nature. We can see from this that it is
> clear that human nature is evil and any good in human beings comes from
> conscious effort.[12]

Only conscious exertion, where the natural inclinations we have are held in check, allows us to act properly. This is "artificiality."

Building artificiality is something all human beings are capable of. Like Mencius, Xunzi argues that everyone can become a sage. A sage can follow humanity, morality, and rightness. We can too if we "engage in study, focus the mind/heart on this aim, unify our intentions, think about principles … and accumulate goodness without slacking off."[13] Sagehood is within our grasp, if we build up the artificial shell of morality. We can all become sages if we work hard enough at it.

Morality is Artificial

Mencius had argued that morality is basic to us, found in the sprouts of our human nature and given to us by a moral Heaven. Xunzi says that morality is not natural: it is an artificial construction. For Xunzi, morality is more like traffic laws. We decide to drive on the right side of the street or the left side of the street; we decide that red lights mean stop and green lights mean go. It does not matter if we drive on the left or right hand side of the street; what matters is that we all do it. Traffic laws are arbitrary, but, once agreed on, work for everyone. Similarly, for Xunzi, morality is a product of the human mind, set up by the sage-kings and crafted so that people could live together. When morality is applied to our evil human nature, we can change. We are changed by education as we learn artificiality. We learn ritual, we learn new habits and so morality becomes our second nature. Morality is the artificial product of culture and education. Xunzi happily accepts Laozi's criticism that morality is artificial. Of course morality is artificial, he says, and that is a good thing because what is natural to human beings is evil.

One of the first objections that comes to mind about all of this is to ask, if human beings have natures that are evil and spend their time satisfying their desires, where did morality come from in the first place? Xunzi's answer is that the sage-kings of the past created morality so as to bring order. But, where did the sage-kings get their morality? According to Xunzi, morality is not innate, so how did the sage-kings create it?

> Someone may ask, "If man's nature is evil, then how were rituals and rightness created?" I can say to them that ritual and rightness came from the sage-kings' artificiality. Ritual and rightness did not come from anything inherent in the sage-kings' nature. So too, when a potter shapes the clay to create the pot, the pot is the creation of the artificial and acquired nature of the potter and not the product of anything inherent in his nature. … The sage-kings accumulated thoughts and ideas; they practiced artificiality. That is how they developed ritual and rightness and raised the standard of government. Ritual and rightness were born from their artificiality, not the sage-kings' human nature.[14]

Xunzi argued that just because something is produced, like a pot, the pot was not innate in the potter who produced it. Similarly morality did not need to be innate in the sage-kings for them to produce moral rules.

The sage-kings realized the horror of human life in its natural state of "war of all against all." They wisely set up limits and rules to govern human behavior. They saw the social chaos that following our natures produced. In order to control it, they instituted ritual and moral rules, much like traffic laws. This is the foundation of civilization.

One of Xunzi's arguments against Mencius has to do with the sage-kings. Why would we have needed sage-kings, Xunzi asks, if human nature was good? Why would we need ritual and morality? Why we would need to learn anything? It can only be that human nature is evil. That is why we had to invent ritual and morality.

Now this is an unfair reading of Mencius who argued only that human nature contains sprouts of goodness that need to be cultivated, but Xunzi is convinced that civilized values are necessary only because human nature is evil. Xunzi had read the Daoists and agreed with them that civilization is artificial and unnatural. But, for Xunzi, the great achievement of civilization is precisely its artificiality.

Learning an artificially imposed morality will dramatically change us. Xunzi likens us to a warped piece of wood that has to be steamed, put in a press, and forced to bend its shape before it can be straight. Teachers must be obeyed and models must be studied:

> So it is that a warped piece of wood must first be pressed in a frame and then steamed in order to soften it. This allows its shape to be bent before it can become straight. A dull piece of metal must first be whetted on a grindstone before it can be made sharp.
>
> Now, human nature is evil. It must receive the instructions of a teacher and follow models and only then can it be put right. We must learn rituals and rightness before we can be orderly. These days, men have no teachers or models, so they are biased, wicked, and not properly behaved. Because they do not have rituals and rightness, they are wicked, rebellious, and disorderly.[15]

Teachers are absolutely essential and the *Xunzi* says that formal education under a master is a necessity. Education is the enormous task of controlling the desires of our nature and this can be done only by taking on board all of the culture of the past. Like all Confucians, Xunzi sees the process of becoming a better person as a process of self-cultivation that is possible only through education.

Ritual

For Xunzi, we live in a world of scarcity – there is just not enough to go around. Whether it is food or fame or power, there is not enough for everyone to have everything they want. If everyone vies for the same things, violence will result. Ritual was invented to control desires and to deal with the problem of scarcity. When we follow social rituals, we all get some of our desires met. Xunzi says that "Rituals trim what is too long and extend what is too short; rituals use up surplus and make up for what is lacking; rituals extend the civility of love and reverence; rituals gradually bring us to the beauty of rightness."[16] Ritual allows for the establishment, and acceptance, of institutions. We agree to live in a society where some get more than others. We respect social institutions, like a monarch, for example. The ruler gets more money and power than the rest of us, but we learn to respect this social division. When we respect the ways in which society works, we can live in an ordered way. Without rituals, desires would rule and there would be no division of resources or of labor.

Ritual also restrains, channels, and refines human emotions. Instead of losing our minds at the death of a loved one, ritual gives us something to do and ways of expressing our grief. It teaches us how to express that grief so that we are not excessive, but are able to express grief in socially acceptable ways. Ritual tempers our grief and allows us an appropriate way of expressing it. Similarly, wedding rituals allow us to express joy and affection and give us ritual ways to do so.

Rituals divide up scarce resources. They can control the ways we express our desires. Rituals teach us how to practice morality by showing us how to act. Rituals allow us to properly express our emotions. Rituals allow us to refine and decorate our actions.

One odd thing with Xunzi's arguments about ritual is that they seem, to some degree, to be trying to prove that ritual is useful. Xunzi says that ritual has both social and personal uses, negotiating scarce resources and channeling one's emotions. While Xunzi is still firmly in the Confucian tradition, it looks like he is trying to justify Confucian teachings on the grounds of their usefulness.

Government

Like Confucius and Mencius, Xunzi lays the blame for the current state of affairs solely on corrupt rulers. In his usual acerbic way, he is not shy about criticizing them:

> Rulers double the taxes on necessities like knives and spades in order to steal money from the common people; they double the taxes on the fields and meadows in order to steal food from the common people; they charge custom at border stations and taxes in marketplaces in order to make life difficult for people.

In their greed for money, rulers taxed people unmercifully. These taxes were not just on farmers' produce but on basic necessities. Rulers also interfered with trade and commerce by charging custom duties on goods as they came to the borders and by charging sales tax in markets. This was not the only problem:

> This was not enough for rulers. They also promoted spying and underhanded plots to get more power and begin rebellions in other states. By this they tried to overthrow other noble families, all of which leads to ruin and destruction. The Chinese people know perfectly clearly about the wickedness, violence, and anarchy of these kinds of rulers and they know that rulers like this will lead to dangers and ruin.
>
> Because of rulers like this, government ministers will assassinate their lords, subordinates will murder their superiors. Government officials will sell their own cities, turn their backs on principles, will not do their duty if that duty may be life-threatening. This whole thing has no other cause than the ruler, who has brought it about.[17]

Like other Confucians, Xunzi sees the ruler as acting as a model, and when the ruler plots, is violent, lives in luxury at the expense of the poor, and in general exhibits no moral principles, the rest of society will follow. The result is a society

> where the strong bully the weak and the clever intimidate the stupid, where the lower classes disobey their betters, and where young people insult their elders. Because morality is not the foundation of government, the old and weak grieve at having no means of support, while the stronger in society complain about division and conflict.[18]

This is a description of society that may sound familiar to us: the use of rudeness and bullying in social interactions, the lack of respect for others, the elderly living in poverty, and, in general, a contentious society.

Xunzi argues that class divisions are a necessary thing in order for there to be a division of labor and for rituals to work. Not everyone can be a ruler. In addition, there has to be a division of labor so that people can be skilled in one skill and do not need to learn how to do everything.

Xunzi is a Confucian and believes that the ruler is responsible for caring for the people, no matter what their class. The ruler must be a good model. The ruler must choose moral and upright ministers who will also be role models for the people. Government must not overtax the people. It should provide some education and defend the state from invasion. Many of the political ideas we have seen in Mencius we find in Xunzi as well.

Given his views, it is not surprising to find Xunzi arguing that building a good society based on ritual and morality will be a long-term project.

We are working against evil human natures. When we first start, we will need to reinforce ritual and morality with rewards and punishments.[19] As incentives, rewards and punishments will lead people toward a true practice of ritual and an understanding of morality.

When Xunzi visited the state of Qin, he reported on the government of Shang Yang (see chapter 5). He was horrified to see an orderly and prosperous state where people obeyed and feared their government and where there were no factions and no corruption. The government of Qin had accomplished this even though they had not promoted scholarship nor used Confucian methods. While he admired much of what he saw, he said that this kind of state had no moral base and predicted that it would not last long – especially, he said, as it had no Confucians in it.[20]

Xunzi did not immediately dismiss a dictatorial form of government as Mencius had.[21] Even dictators, ruling by force, were able to impose order and provide their people with a basic standard of living.[22] They unified their states and set up clear rules for government and laws. Their failure was their inability to win the hearts of the people. For Xunzi, these dictators were preferable to many of the rulers of his time who cared only for wealth, plotted against their subjects and their allies, and behaved treacherously to everyone. A dictator, though, is no equal to a true ruler who acts from morality, cares for the people, and follows Confucius' ideals.

Language

When it came to dealing with the various Logicians and their discussions of language, Xunzi maintained Confucius' principle of "putting words right." He had a practical view of language, arguing that the names of things are constructed by human beings for our convenience.[23] This way we know what the other person is referring to. Names for things are agreed upon and become custom. We come to know things by receiving sense information. The mind/heart sorts this information into categories of similar and dissimilar, giving things names and developing ideas. All human beings work this same way and so language is a reflection of a human understanding that we all share.[24]

Xunzi compares language to weights and measures, saying words must be the same for everyone or chaos will follow. The confusion about the meanings of words has extended to the words "right" and "wrong." People know what "right" means as a word, but no longer know what actions are right. If we put words right, then people will know what the word means and to what it applies. To obscure the meanings of words or use them in different and confusing ways will bring chaos to society. Xunzi wanted anyone who confused words, Logicians presumably, to be punished, just like those who cheat on weights and measures.[25]

Heaven

In the early Zhou dynasty and in some of Confucius' comments, we have seen Heaven referred to both as a moral entity and as nature. Xunzi uses the word "Heaven" to mean nature: Heaven is nature and Heaven is amoral. Xunzi's view of Heaven is close to the Daoists' view of the Dao. Heaven does not give us a good human nature. Heaven does not care about human behavior at all. He says that the actions of Heaven are natural and do not respond to the virtues of one ruler nor to the corruption of another ruler. Good fortune is the result of good government, wise planning, and moderate spending. This will make for a successful government and does not depend on any decision by Heaven. Heaven deals with all people equally, whether they are the greatest sage-king or the worst of rulers.

> If you answer nature's regular course with good government, you will have good fortune; if you respond to it with bad government, you will have misfortune. If you strengthen the basic things you need to do and regulate the ways you do things, nature cannot make you poor. If you plant and raise things properly and your actions are in harmony with the seasons, then nature cannot afflict you with anything bad. If you follow the Way and act rightly, then nature cannot bring you calamities. If you do this, then floods and droughts cannot cause famine, extremes of cold and heat cannot cause illness, and unlucky and freak events cannot cause misfortune.[26]

We should use the abundance nature gives and build up supplies of food and increase the wealth of the state.

Xunzi says that nature does not stop winter just because human beings dislike the cold.[27] Nature is impartial. Our concern is to respond intelligently to what nature does and this will give us successful economies and governments. So, Xunzi says, instead of singing hymns and glorifying Heaven, we should spend our time understanding how to farm according to the seasons.

In Xunzi's biography in the *Records of the Historian* it says that Xunzi hated evil rulers who focused on magic and prayers, believing in omens and luck. Instead of governing well, or even rationally, most rulers of Xunzi's time followed superstitious advice about lucky and unlucky days and planned according to them. They also used natural events, like storms and comets, as signs of good or bad luck. Xunzi argued that Heaven does not send omens to regulate human behavior:

> When there are comets or trees groan, everyone in the state is terrified. They ask what the cause of such things could be. I say, so what? When there is a change in the movements of Heaven and Earth or a change in the yin and

yang, there may be unusual events. It is all right to marvel at them, but not alright to fear them. Sometimes there are solar and lunar eclipses, sometimes the wind and rain are unseasonable, sometimes a new star suddenly appears – there has been no time when these kinds of things have not happened.

It is natural for all sorts of strange phenomena to occur. This is just nature, it is not a sign to us nor does it have any significance for us. Every age has experienced this kind of thing and none of these phenomena have had any meaning in terms of human activities. There are omens of a declining society and these, Xunzi goes on to say, are very easy to see:

> What we should be afraid of are man-made horrors. Plowing that is so bad that the harvest is lost; weeding so badly done that the crop is lost; government rules that are so bad the people are lost; fields that are so overgrown with weeds that the grain is lost; grain that is so expensive that the people starve; bodies of the dead scattered along the sides of the roads – these are called man-made horrors.[28]

There is no meaning in eclipses, great storms, falling stars, and other phenomena that we do not understand. The real omens are plain to see: bad government and starving people. These are omens that truly portend the end of a state. Heaven does not send us messages in response to human activity. There is no link between Heaven and human beings.

Prayer to the gods is all very well for the ignorant who think that it works, but an educated gentleman should see this as an occasion for a pleasant ceremony. Xunzi says,

> You prayed for rain and it rained – what do I think about that? I say, so what? If you had not prayed for rain, it would have rained anyway. When there is a solar or lunar eclipse, it is the custom for people to beat drums and make noise to save themselves; when there is a drought, we pray for rain; before we start any important project, we hold a ceremony to tell the future with bones and yarrow stalks [used in the *Book of Changes*]. We do not do these things because we think that they will produce the results we want, but because we want to decorate the occasions with ceremony. So, the gentleman thinks of these things as decorations, while ordinary people think they are supernatural. To think of them as decorations is what really brings luck; to think of them as supernatural is what really is unlucky.[29]

Xunzi is firmly in the skeptics' camp when it comes to ideas of omens, prayer, and what he would call "superstitions." Heaven is amoral and there is no union between human beings and Heaven: Heaven does what it does; human beings do what we do.

Xunzi was also a skeptic when it came to common superstitions of the time, like ghosts. He says,

Always when people see ghosts, it is only at times when they are startled and
excited; their sense is confused and blinded. So they claim that what does not
exist, actually does exist and what does exist, does not. And then they believe
they have settled the matter.[30]

It is all very well for the irrational and deluded to believe these things, but
a wise person does not.

Xunzi also argued against a common practice of his time: physiognomy.
This is the practice of telling a person's character and predicting their future
by signs on a person's face, lines on the hand, or the appearance of the
body. Xunzi argues that appearance tells us nothing about the inner moral
qualities of a person and there is no way we can predict a person's future
from their face.

Finally, Xunzi was especially critical of the various sub-groups of
Confucians in his time. He describes some of them as ignorant Confucians,
some as interested only at playing with ritual. Others, he said, believed
weird things. For Mencius and his followers Xunzi reserved a special
venom. Confucians, says Xunzi, should dress properly, have a proper teaching lineage, and agree with Xunzi.

Xunzi on Confucian Themes

Xunzi uses all the Confucian terms and ideas we have seen before. Xunzi
argues for a morality based on filial piety, humanity, sincerity, and so on,
just as all Confucians do. But, for Xunzi, this morality is arbitrary and artificial. It was made up in the past as a way to control the desires and emotions of our human nature. It is not given by Heaven, as Mencius argued.

Education is crucial for Xunzi. This is how we take on board all the
morality and ritual we need in order to develop our artificial second nature
and become civilized people. That is why education is difficult and why
students must have a teacher and must be obedient to that teacher. Without
education, we have no chance of overcoming what is natural to us.

Xunzi talks about becoming a gentleman and, as we have seen others
do, contrasts the gentleman with the small or petty man. In line with other
Confucian thinkers, Xunzi says that gentlemen must be educated, have
humanity, know ritual, and look within themselves to cultivate goodness.
Like Mencius, Xunzi argues that sages, the great models of moral behavior,
do not differ in any essential way from the rest of us. All of us, by establishing our artificial moral nature, are capable of becoming sages.

Like all Confucians, Xunzi recognizes the importance of ritual. For
Xunzi, ritual refines and directs our raw impulses. Ritual controls our
desires and allows us to express our emotions in a balanced and socially
acceptable way. Ritual also has the social and political function of appor-

tioning scarce resources so that we can all live with some of us getting more than others.

It is when he discusses government that Xunzi is most like Mencius. They both argue that rulers must care for the people, be a model to the people, provide education, and not overtax the people in order to live in luxury.

Xunzi uses Confucius' idea of putting words right and extends it to deal not just with governments, but with the debates over language. Words exist for our convenience. They must mean the same for all of us or else they become lies. Xunzi had little patience with those who played with words, whether they were corrupt rulers or Logicians.

When Xunzi talks about Heaven, we can see how different he is from Mencius. Mencius thought of Heaven as some sort of moral entity and he believed that human beings reflect or receive moral abilities from Heaven. Mencius also talked about human beings forming a relationship with Heaven.

Xunzi refuses all of what Mencius says about Heaven. He argues that Heaven is amoral, neither moral nor immoral, but indifferent. Xunzi's view of Heaven is like the Daoist view of the Dao: Heaven is natural, spontaneous, and has no intentions, one way or the other, toward us. We cannot form a relationship with Heaven. Heaven sends us no omens or signs. Xunzi is still in the Confucian tradition with this position: we have seen Confucius refer to Heaven as nature as well. Xunzi's defense of Confucius comes from a different direction.

Like other Confucians, Xunzi attacked competing schools of thought. When Mozi argued that we should love everyone without distinction, Xunzi responded by saying that any society must have social distinctions for it to work. Mozi argued that everyone should live as frugally as possible. Fine foods and embroidered silks were wasteful, merely decorative, and did not contribute to profiting the people or the state. Xunzi responded by saying that, while this might be true in times of famine or a poor economy, there are usually enough things in the world for us to enjoy. Moderation in spending is sufficient to avoid waste.

Xunzi also argued against Mozi's contention that music was useless and should be abolished. Music brings harmony to people. And, Xunzi says, if we gave up producing and doing all the things that Mozi defined as useless, the economy would collapse. If we had no distinctions among occupations and classes and no differences between ruler and subject, society would collapse. Nature provides us with what we need. Moderation and planning are required for a rich and successful country.[31]

Xunzi says that Mozi was obsessed, or blinded by, the idea of usefulness and so he did not understand proper human behavior. His theories would result in everyone being interested only in profiting themselves and fighting each other for their own self-interest.

Xunzi saw other thinkers as obsessed too. Logicians, he says, became obsessed with logical propositions and ignored the realities of life. The Daoists became obsessed with nature and forgot all about human beings. All these other thinkers were blinded by being obsessed with one, and only one, point.[32]

Summary

Mencius was completely wrong: human nature is not good. Human nature is evil and selfish. Left to our own devices, we will be envious, greedy, and violent. Because of this the sage-kings instituted morality, an artificial construction, and imposed it on society. To change our naturally evil nature to a moral nature, we need a long education, teachers, and models. We can learn rituals that offer respect to others, as Confucius taught. Rituals also channel and refine the emotions and help us deal with scarcity. Government must provide models of moral behavior, provide education, and, in general, care for the people. Part of government is, as Confucius said, putting words right and all the fancy discussion about language is useless: words mean what we decide they mean, and they allow us to communicate. The Confucian enterprise of leading people to morality through education, government models, and the practice of ritual is not based, as Mencius argued, on a moral Heaven. Heaven is nature and does not care what human beings do.

Xunzi and Mencius agree on many basics: the importance of education, morality, and ritual. They agree that government exists for the benefit of the people. But they explain the underlying reasons for Confucius' teachings in radically different ways.

Some of the acidity of Xunzi's arguments stems from a sense he seems to have had that all was lost. Confucians had broken up into small groups. The notion that human beings were merely self-interested and could be controlled by rewards and punishments had won the day. The rulers of the central states were especially incompetent and corrupt and the specter of the state of Qin haunted them. Xunzi may have lived long enough to see the triumph of the state of Qin and of his student, Li Si, as the prime minister of Qin.

Mencius and Xunzi were not the only Confucians of the Warring States era: we know that there were other groups of Confucians. We will look at what we know about those other Confucian groups and about Confucian texts in the next chapter.

8

Confucians, "Confucian" Texts, and the Qin Dynasty

Confucius said, "Do you think that advice from wise men will nec-essarily be used? Is it not true that Prince Bi Gan had his heart cut out? Do you think that men who are loyal will keep their jobs? Gong Longfeng was punished. Do you think that men who criticize their rulers are listened to? Didn't they cut up Wu Zixu's body and put it outside the Gusu gate? So we can see that there are many men who had no luck with their times. I am not the only one."[1]

Other Confucian Groups

As the Warring States era went on, we know that Confucians divided into sub-groups. Xunzi talks about various groups of Confucians and we have seen Xunzi's student, Han Feizi, say that by his time, about 250 BCE, there were eight groups of Confucians and each claimed to have the traditional teaching of Confucius.[2] While there was conflict among some of these groups, they all understood themselves to be Confucians – though some, like Xunzi, considered their Confucian tradition to be better than others.

In the later Han dynasty, we find a description of Confucian group-ings. The *Han Shu*, the Han history,[3] looked back at various states of the Warring States period and said that Confucians in the state of Qi "loved the classics and the accomplishments" and of those in the state of Lu that "they honored ritual and rightness." Qi Confucians discussed politics and government and argued that only the worthy should govern. Mencius was said to have been influenced by the Confucians of Qi and we have seen that Mencius does not much discuss rites and music. It is also said that the Qi school based much of its thinking on the yin-yang and five phases theories (see chapter 9) along with belief in omens.

The Confucians of Confucius' home state of Lu were said to have taken the study of ritual as their core; they were not as much interested in government as in rites and music. The Lu school was said to be less systematic in method, but was interested in morality, and later Confucian metaphysics was based on their thinking; they were somewhat more involved in methods of self-cultivation. It is not clear now what the differences were exactly, but debate between Confucians of Qi and of Lu was vigorous, probably over the interpretation of the classical tradition.

Xunzi did not describe groups geographically, associated with states. He listed groups of Confucians whom he described as "vulgar." He described lesser Confucians as claiming loyalty to the early kings, Confucius, and a Confucian lineage, but, he said, they were not "proper" Confucians: they followed the teachings in a partial or distorted way.[4]

According to the *Xunzi*, among these lesser Confucians were followers of Confucius' student, Zi Zhang.[5] Another group was made up of those who followed Zi Xia. He was a student of Confucius, a minister to the Marquis Wen of Wei, and well known for his teaching.[6] A third group that Xunzi describes are the followers of Confucius' student Zi You. Zi You held office in the time of Confucius; Confucius is said to have known that the area was well governed by the sound of its music. Zi You often appears in the *Analects* where he identified the Way with music and rites. The fourth group of Confucians whom Xunzi disliked were those who claimed to follow Zi Si, the grandson of Confucius; Mencius was Zi Si's student.[7]

Xunzi did approve of one of Confucius' students, Zigong, saying he transmitted the Confucian teachings of Confucius and the Duke of Zhou.[8] Other students of Confucius who were mentioned as the founding teachers of Confucian groups include Yan Hui from Lu; Yan Hui, as we have seen, was praised and mourned by Confucius. His group is said to have emphasized poetry. Another was Qi Diao. The *Han Shu* "Yi Wen Zhi" lists a book under his name, which is no longer extant. The *Han Feizi* says his group emphasized ritual. Zhong Liang, also from the state of Lu, is seen in the *Book of Rites* "Tang Gong" chapter discussing funeral ritual; his group was said to have emphasized music.[9]

It is not easy to trace all the Confucian groups or the points of debate among them and I must ask the reader's pardon for these partial descriptions. The difficulty of assigning the texts and traditions to any one of the groups listed in the *Xunzi*, the *Han Feizi*, and elsewhere should by now be clear.

Confucians, even though divided, were recognizable throughout the Warring States era. They were defined, and defined themselves, as loyal to Confucius' teachings. They followed Confucius, the ancient sage-kings, and their heroes, the early founders of the Zhou dynasty. They read and taught versions of certain texts. They talked about morality, ritual, being a gentleman, and government for the benefit of the people – even if they disagreed about the basis for these ideas.

Scholars in recent times have held very different opinions about the ways in which Confucians of the Warring States era operated. For example, Mark Csikszentmihalyi argues that Confucians were involved in independent traditions that each took their authority from Confucius. The outlook of each group significantly differed from all the rest and these differences were more than just differences in interpretation of a single teacher.[10] Nylan understands the term "Ru" to have referred not just to strict followers of Confucius, saying that the term applied to a number of professional "classicists" who had studied Confucius, but used that education to further their own ambitions or those of their state. This is in contrast to the smaller groups of "self-identified ethical followers of Confucius."[11]

There are wide differences in opinion. Some see Confucian groups as having similar concerns and vocabulary, but emphasizing one part of Confucius' teaching and drawing their authority from a teaching lineage. Others see Confucian groups as far more distinct from each other. Still others, like Nylan, argue that many of the figures we have called "Confucian" were scholars who were not necessarily committed to Confucius' teachings.

While the two great interpreters of Confucius' thought in the classical period are clearly Mencius and Xunzi, there were other Confucians with other points of view. There seem to have been some Confucians who believed everything in life was ordained by fate and others who denied the existence of an afterlife. Their enemies describe Confucians with these views, though no trace of them can be found in what would become the Confucian canon. Were their enemies wrong or exaggerating? Have their views been edited out of the texts? We can find some hints in the classics, particularly in the discussions of music, of Confucians who thought that human nature was neither basically good nor evil, but just natural. This would seem to be yet another Confucian interpretation.

The divisions we see among classical Confucians continued on through Chinese history as one thinker or another reinterpreted Confucius and came to an interpretation he thought was the correct one.

Confucius and "Confucian" Texts

One of the markers of following Confucius was the study of, and allegiance to, certain texts. The *Zhuangzi* says that Confucius went to the Zhou court to deposit his books. When he was asked to sum them up, Confucius said they rested on humanity and rightness. Zhuangzi's stories are made up, but they show the perception that Confucius and certain books were connected. These texts were tied to Confucius' thought and contained his teachings.

The *Zhuangzi* names six texts in another discussion where Confucius says he has studied six classics: the books of *Poetry* and *History,* the *Spring and Autumn Annals*, the *Book of Changes,* the *Book of Rites*, and the *Classic of Music*.[12]

When it comes to understanding these texts – how they are made up, and what they were – we need to be very careful. The problems around these texts are similar to problems around most early texts: what constituted a text? who wrote it and when? which version of, for example, *The Book of History* was Confucius, Mencius, or Xunzi referring to?

One of the problems in discussing these books is the way in which the books themselves were put together. The texts themselves were fluid in two senses. First, they were not "books," but a collection of chapters that could be combined in different ways. Second, many of the older texts, like *The Book of History*, were used by schools of both Confucians and Mohists, for example, but there were different versions. *The Book of History* is thought to have become a standardized text only by the time of Xunzi.[13]

Another problem involves the term "classic." In the *Analects*, Confucius does not refer to "classics." He says that texts are important, but it is later Confucians who describe them as essential. We have seen Confucius say that one should study *The Book of Poetry* and that it is important to do so, but only because it was useful, not because it was a classic.

Mencius talks about classics as the essential teaching of Confucius and the sage-kings. By the time of Xunzi, the texts were beginning to be recognized as a set. Many of these texts, like *The Book of Poetry*, were originally part of a common tradition. Confucians appropriated that tradition and claimed to speak for it. The reason Confucians appropriated these traditional texts was that they believed that Confucius had written, edited, or expurgated them.

The oldest texts are *The Book of Poetry* and *The Book of History*. *The Book of Poetry* is a collection of 305 poems and songs.[14] Parts may date back to early Zhou, while some poems may be as late as the Spring and Autumn period, that is from the tenth to the seventh centuries BCE. The poems include everything from praise of the early Zhou rulers to romantic love poems. Some of the poems are thought to be criticisms of rulers, couched in folk poetry. The text was meant to be read aloud, "chanted" as Mencius says. It was memorized by upper-class men who used poetical references from it when they spoke as a sign of their good breeding. These poems were shared by the culture at large. Confucius taught this poetry and his followers came to believe that the text was associated with his teaching. They believed that Confucius had selected each poem out of three thousand original poems and that *The Book of Poetry* had been edited by him.

The Book of History contains speeches and stories that claim to describe the history of events from the times of the sage-kings to the 600s BCE.[15]

The text's descriptions of early periods are considered quite unreliable. Even Mencius doubted their truthfulness and said, "It would be better if there had been no *Book of History* than to believe everything it says."[16] While most of the early material it covers is considered unreliable, reliability improves as it goes along. *The Book of History* does not just recount history, but describes a history that it understands as made up of moral lessons. Like *The Book of Poetry*, there were a number of versions of *The Book of History* circulating during the Warring States period. Confucius was said to have taught this text to his students, and it was believed that he had written or edited it.

During the Warring States period, each state kept its own annals. These were histories of the activities and events in the state, set out by ruler and subdivided into seasons. The *Spring and Autumn Annals* is a chronicle of the history of the state of Lu. Its full title is the *Spring–Summer–Autumn–Winter Annals*. In the city of Qufu, in the Confucian temple area, there is a bench said to be the one on which Confucius wrote this text. The *Spring and Autumn Annals* has traditionally received a great deal of attention as Confucius is reputed to have said, "If I am to gain recognition it is because of my work on the *Annals*, if I am to be condemned it is because of my work on the *Annals*." Mencius confirms the importance of the text by saying that when Confucius completed it, the *Spring and Autumn Annals* "struck terror into the hearts of rebellious subjects and sons who did not do their duty."[17]

The difficulty with this is that there is very little in the way of moral teachings in the text and often it is, frankly, boring. For example, the entry describing the 22nd year of the rule of Duke Zhuang says, "In his twenty-second year, in the spring, the Duke proclaimed a great amnesty. Our duchess Wen Jiang was buried in Guichou. The people of Chen killed their duke's son, Yu Kou. It was summer, the fifth month. In the seventh month, autumn, in Bing Shen, the duke made a treaty with Gao Hou of Ze in Fang. In the winter, the Duke went to Ze with offerings of silk for a marriage contract."[18] Most of the text is like this. Not only do we not find discussions of humanity and ritual, but the references the text makes to events and figures in other states are incomplete.

For this reason the *Spring and Autumn Annals* is usually read with its commentary, the *Zuo Zhuan*. A commentary is a book that explains, or in the case of the *Zuo Zhuan*, expands on, another book. The *Zuo Zhuan* is a much more lively account of what was happening to various states and their leaders. For the passage from the *Spring and Autumn Annals* above, the *Zuo Zhuan* tells us that the reason the duke proclaimed a great amnesty was to atone for the very bad behavior of his mother before her burial. It also tells us that it was not the people who killed Yu Kou, but a plot set up by Yu Kou's father. The duke's offer of a marriage contract, so soon

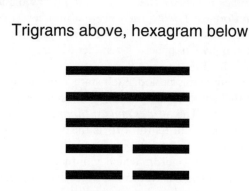

Trigrams above, hexagram below

Figure 8.1 Trigrams and hexagrams in the *Book of Changes*

after the death of his mother, was considered scandalous and the lady he became engaged to had as bad a reputation as his late mother. The *Zuo Zhuan* commentary has been dated to the fourth century BCE and is the work of a number of authors.

The *Book of Changes* or *Yi Jing* is a book of divination. You may be more familiar with the title in the Wade–Giles version, the *I Ching*.[19] *Yi* means "change," and the text is meant to be a description of the process of change. One learns how to avoid misfortune and how to take advantage of opportunities in that process of change. Divination is based on two lines, solid _____ and broken ___ ___. These lines are arranged in groups of three, trigrams, beginning with the two basic trigrams, one of which is three solid lines, the other three broken lines. The solid and broken lines can be interchanged to make a total of eight trigrams. These eight trigrams are then multiplied by themselves to make up the final 64 hexagrams or six-line symbols (see figure 8.1). Each of the 64 hexagrams is meant to represent some point in a constant, regular, cycle of change or progression in both the universe and human activity.[20]

The system of the basic eight trigrams was believed to have been invented by the sage-king Fu Xi. The hexagram system was said to have been set up by King Wen, the Confucian hero and founder of the Zhou dynasty. The "Ten Wings" and commentaries and explanations of the text were said to have been written by Confucius himself, but modern scholarship dates them to the early Han dynasty.

These explanations contain a great deal of moral advice and discussion, so this may be why Confucius was associated with them. The *Book of Changes* later became the basis for *feng shui*, the art of placement. It is still widely used today in divination, where one's situation in the process is described and advice given about love, business, and the future.

These texts existed in some form before Confucius, but, as you can see, all of them were believed to have been connected to him. Confucius' students, and those who followed them, believed that Confucius' thought could be seen in the moral lessons in the historical, poetical, and divination texts that he had handled and taught. Modern scholarship has debunked these beliefs and rejects the traditional association of Confucius and these texts.

Confucius taught his students the classical learning that included the things that Confucius himself had learned as a boy and young man: poetry, history, literature, ritual, and music. It is after Confucius that these areas of learning become associated with texts, like *The Book of History* and *The Book of Poetry*.

There are two more texts mentioned in Zhuangzi's description of Confucius' "classics." These are the *Book of Rites* and the *Classic of Music*. While Confucius certainly talked about ritual, the *Book of Rites* that we now have is not a text he used. It was written after Confucius.[21] The text contains everything from instructions for royal ceremonies to descriptions of rules about the kind of wood that can be used in coffins, depending on one's rank, to the ways in which wedding gifts should be exchanged. So there are parts that are more like manuals of rituals or instructions. Other parts of the text have philosophical discussions and this is where we find a great deal of material we can also find in the *Xunzi*. Two chapters of the *Book of Rites* would later go on to have a life of their own.

The first of these chapters is *The Great Learning*,[22] a work traditionally attributed to Confucius' grandson, Zi Si. It is a compact résumé of Confucian ethical and political philosophy. *The Great Learning* presents its arguments in "chain arguments." Once it establishes one link, it leads to another:

Once things are investigated, knowledge is complete. Once knowledge is complete, thought is sincere. Once thought is sincere, the mind/heart is put straight. When the mind/heart is put straight, the self is cultivated. When the self is cultivated, families can be regulated. When families are regulated, the country is governed well. Once the country is governed well, the whole world is at peace.

The basic idea is that we must begin with moral self-cultivation. We do that by investigating things, extending knowledge, being sincere in our thoughts, and rectifying the mind. Self-cultivation is the basis for a well-ordered family, a well-governed state and a harmonious world. The text solidly links ethics and politics. Later Confucians would give this chapter singular prominence (see chapter 11).

The second chapter from the *Book of Rites* that will later gain prominence is the *Doctrine of the Mean*.[23] It too was traditionally attributed to Confucius' grandson, Zi Si. It discusses the mean, the middle course. This mean, or balance, is also the harmony of the universe, so the text is one of the few texts that deal with the transcendent.

> To have no emotions of pleasure and anger, sorrow or joy surging up is called being in a state of balance/mean. To have these emotions surging up but all in due time is called being in a state of harmony. The state of balance is the supreme foundation of the world and the state of harmony is its universal path. Once balance and harmony are achieved, Heaven and Earth maintain their proper positions and all things are nourished.

Balance is found in going beyond the emotions; harmony in controlling the emotions. The human state of balance or harmony resonates with the universe.

We also find a discussion of the virtue of sincerity, which is brought to the forefront in the *Doctrine of the Mean*. This virtue has been described as having no distinction between what is internal to oneself and what one does. In this way we are completely without self-interest. Here sincerity is expanded to mean that one loses the distinction between what is oneself and what is other:

> Sincerity is the Way of Heaven, to become sincere is the Way of human beings. To be sincere is to hit the balance without effort, to possess it without the processes of thought, and to be centered in the Way with a natural ease – this is to be a sage. To be sincere is to choose the good and hold to it.

The *Doctrine of the Mean* will be used by later Confucians to give a transcendent element to their interpretation of Confucius' thought.

What is missing is the *Yue Jing*, the *Classic of Music*. There are references to it in Warring States texts like the *Xunzi* and the *Zhuangzi*. There was a *Yue Jing*, a *Classic of Music*, in the Han dynasty and this was understood by later Confucians to be the *Classic of Music*. However, this text cannot be the *Classic of Music* referred to in the Warring States period. In 136 BCE, the Han emperor Wu set up five seats of learning in the imperial academy for the study of the classics, but these did not include a seat for music. There was no *Yue Jing* until the reign of Wang Mang (8–23 CE) who had a *Yue Jing* written. As a usurper of the throne, his aim was to legitimize his rule and, like the Duke of Zhou, "establish the rites and set up music." So the text from the Han is not the real *Classic of Music*.

We do, however, have chapters in various texts that are devoted to philosophical discussions of music. The first is the *Yue Lun*, the *Discussion of Music*, a chapter found in the *Xunzi*. Much of the *Discussion of Music* from the *Xunzi* is quoted verbatim in the *Yue Ji*, the *Record of Music*, now a chapter in the *Book of Rites*. The third source is found in the *Shi Ji* and is the *Yue Ben*, the *Book of Music*. It repeats the *Record of Music*. The final source is sections on music in the *Lu Shi Chun Qiu* compiled about 240 BCE. A pre-Qin encyclopedic work, it is traditionally said to have been written by scholars of the Confucian, Mohist, and Daoist schools for Lu Buwei (d.235 BCE).[24] What remains unknown is whether any of these chapters were what was referred to as the *Classic of Music* in the Warring States period, or if that Warring States text has vanished.

During the Warring States era, various Confucian groups studied the group of texts, many of which, as we shall see, would come to form the Confucian canon. They also wrote texts. After the death of Confucius, we have the *Analects*; after the death of Mencius, we have the *Mencius*; while Xunzi may have written much of the *Xunzi*, it was compiled in its present form after his death. Confucians also wrote the *Classic of Filial Piety*, which describes the central Confucian virtue of filial piety (see chapter 2). It is a very short work that shows Confucius in conversation with one of his students on the topic of filial piety. The text is thought to be linked to a chapter in the *Book of Rites*, and may have been composed before 239 BCE because passages from it appear in the *Lu Shi Chunqiu*, a text from that date.[25] Confucians also wrote the *Book of Rites* and included much of Xunzi's thought. Others extended and commented on other texts like the *Zuo Zhuan* commentary for the *Spring and Autumn Annals*. Some commentary from various groups may have been incorporated into texts like *The Book of History* along with their interpretations of Confucius' teachings.

Throughout history, some of these texts, and the pictures that they present of Confucius, have been preferred to others. From the Warring States era on, various scholars have, at various times, emphasized certain texts as representative of Confucius and his thought. The Han dynasty established what are called the "Five Classics," *The Book of History*, *The Book of Poetry*, the *Spring and Autumn Annals*, the *Book of Rites*, and the *Book of Changes*. In the Middle Ages, Confucians chose "The Four

Books" – the *Analects*, the *Mencius*, the *Great Learning*, and the *Doctrine of the Mean* – as the most representative of Confucius' teachings. Texts have been preferred or neglected depending on how Confucius' thought has been interpreted.

The First Emperor and the Reunification of China

> In the past the empire was fragmented and in confusion. … Now your Majesty has unified all under heaven … yet these adherents of private theories band together to criticize the laws and directives … each one proceeds to discuss it in light of his private theories. At court they disapprove in their hearts; outside they debate on the street. They hold it a mark of fame to criticize the ruler, regard it as lofty to take a dissenting stance. … I request that all writings, *The Book of Poetry*, *The Book of History*, and all the sayings of the hundred schools of philosophy be discarded and done away with.[26]

The state of Qin, located in the west of Warring States China, had always been considered semi-barbaric, backward, and uncouth by people in the central states. In 361 BCE, the duke of the state of Qin hired Shang Yang, who put into practice his ideas about government (see chapter 5). The result was a strong, centralized government where noble families had little power. In a change that ended the old feudal system, taxes were paid directly to the ruler. Government was based on the military model and military leaders had, in many cases, risen through the ranks – following Shang Yang's idea of rewarding meritorious service. While the army was strong, taxes were high to maintain it. In Legalist fashion, people were encouraged to spy on one another, a legal code was established, and the laws were harsh and strictly enforced. Families were divided into groups of five or ten and each group was responsible for the behavior of the individuals in it: if one broke the law, they were all punished.[27]

One difficulty that Legalists found with Legalist thought, when put into practice, was that it made life uncertain for everyone, but especially for those at the top. People were concerned only with power and their own self-interest, intrigue and plots were common, and many of Qin's top officials, or those who wanted to be, died early and often gruesomely. When the Duke of Qin, who had hired Shang Yang, died, Shang Yang was killed by assassins employed by the new duke. Li Si, one of Xunzi's students, took over as prime minister and was likely the source of the orders to kill his fellow student, Han Feizi, when he visited Qin in 233 BCE.[28]

In the decade from 230 to 221 BCE, Qin conquered the last of its enemies, the states of Han, Zhao, Wei, Chu, Yan, and Qi. Some of the states in the central region had belatedly formed an alliance against Qin and sent assassins to try to kill the ruler of Qin. Following the Strategists' advice, Qin used bribery, assassins, and terror: they are reported to have once butchered an enemy army of, so it is said, 100,000 men who had surrendered. The aim was to terrify any enemy soldiers facing them in the next battle. The state of Qin finally conquered all of the China of the time in 221 BCE.

The ruler of the state of Qin was now the ruler of all of China and called himself "The First Emperor."[29] The same rules and Legalist philosophy of government that had governed Qin now governed all of China. Li Si continued as prime minister and devoted himself to centralizing government as he had in Qin. The old system where the nobility were given land in return for loyalty was rejected. Instead the territory was divided and governed by officials appointed by the central government. Civil and military authority were divided and both were controlled by the emperor. This system laid the foundation for the imperial period to come.

Now that one government ruled a unified country, weights and measures, which had been different in each small state, were made uniform. Similarly the writing system, which had many regional variants, was standardized. Even the size of carts was made uniform so that the tracks in mud roads would be the same for all.

Weapons were gathered from all over the country and wealthy, noble families were moved to the neighborhood of the capital so that the government could keep an eye on them. Spying and denunciation were encouraged.

The First Emperor joined together the many walls along the borders of northern states to begin what would become the Great Wall of China.[30] He also had a number of palaces built, along with an enormous tomb. Westerners know the First Emperor best through the discovery in 1974 of the thousands of terracotta soldiers that guard this tomb. The rows and rows of infantry, cavalry, archers, and generals, all made of clay, are considered one of the greatest archaeological finds of the twentieth century. All of this was expensive. Taxes were high and the walls and the palaces were built with forced labor. As the First Emperor expanded his territory, people were deported to these new areas.

Han dynasty historians hated the First Emperor and accused him of executing anyone who criticized him or his government. They also said that in 213 BCE the First Emperor ordered that all books, except those on medicine, divination, and agriculture, should be burned. Han Feizi was of the opinion that books are not good for the state because they encourage opinions; Li Si's rejected texts might glorify the past and use that past to criticize the present. Given this, the order to destroy books is not out of line with the First Emperor's thought. There are wonderful stories of brave scholars facing death rather than giving up their books and families that hid their texts in walls and roof thatch.[31] Over 400 scholars approached the emperor and appealed to him to save the books. It has always been thought

Figure 8.2 Wall where, it is said, the classics were hidden from the First Emperor

that most of these scholars would have been Confucians, as they were most closely tied to the texts. The First Emperor had the scholars buried alive in a pit and has been known ever since, in the Chinese phrase, as the one who "burned the books and buried the scholars."

This is a tremendous story, pitting the forces of culture and knowledge against the despotic power of ignorance. However, it is likely just a story. We now know that there were scholars of the classics appointed to the First Emperor's court as experts in *The Book of Poetry* and *The Book of History*. None of the texts used at court were subject to this ban. The real damage to the transmission of texts was when the Qin capital fell and the imperial library was burned.[32]

The First Emperor had reason to fear for his life: there were a number of assassination attempts. Because of this, and in line with the Legalist notion that the emperor should be unknown and mysterious, he was forced to travel secretly and to take a number of security precautions. The First Emperor did tour the country, ensuring that his orders were being carried out, and to search for immortality. He was convinced, as were many of his time, that by finding special foods or drinks he could become immortal. In the 11th year of his rule, while following up a report of a marvelous sea creature whose flesh could ensure immortality, the First Emperor died at the age of 49. Far away from the capital, his death was kept a secret by filling his carriage with salted fish so that the smell from his decaying body could not be identified. So it was that the First Emperor of China returned to his capital to be buried just outside of the present-day city of Xian. Li Si, still prime minister, engineered a coup against the First Emperor's oldest son and had another son crowned as his father's successor. This son, in turn, had Li Si executed.[33] Three years of civil war followed with the enemies of the Qin rulers breaking into the First Emperor's tomb and stealing weapons from the terracotta warrior statues that were meant to protect the First Emperor in the afterlife.

The Qin dynasty, which the First Emperor had proclaimed would last for ten thousand years, ended with the establishment of the Han dynasty in 207 BCE, a mere 14 years after it had been established. The Qin dynasty's lasting success was in setting up many of the institutions that were used for the next two thousand years in imperial China.

9

The Han Dynasty, 206 BCE–220 CE[1]

History and Development

There were a number of rebellions against the Qin dynasty after the death of the First Emperor. Liu Bang, who began as a farmer, was one of the rebels, and he led forces that captured the Qin capital, Xianyang, in 206 BCE.

During the civil war, when Liu Bang was fighting against Xiang Yu for control of China, Liu Bang's armies encircled the capital of the old state of Lu. In the city, Confucians, many of whom had supported Xiang Yu, carried on discussions, chanted poetry, and performed music. In a show of courage and defiance, they ignored the imminent attack from the leader they had not supported and "the sounds of their playing and singing did not cease."[2] Liu Bang went on to establish the Han dynasty as its first emperor, Gaozu.

The Han dynasty lasted for four hundred years and was roughly contemporary with the Roman Empire in the West. It was, in general, a very successful dynasty, expanding its territory both north and south to include much of what we think of as China today. Iron tools and weapons were mass-produced in factories. Han military successes were aided by the use of the crossbow, not seen in Europe till the 900s. The government encouraged settlement in the newly opened north and northwest by tax breaks and grants. Improvements in food production,[3] which had begun during the Warring States era, meant that there was a surplus of food produced by farmers who often owned their own land. The government sponsored irrigation projects and the building of roads, bridges, and dams. The result was a strong internal economy. Foreign trade boomed too: by the first century BCE, silk and other goods were being sold along the "Silk Road" to the west, to India, to what is now the Middle East, and beyond, as far as Rome.

There were other technological advances. Horse harnesses were changed to put the pressure on the horse's chest, not its windpipe, to make it easier for a horse to pull greater loads. The wheelbarrow was invented. Astronomers calculated the orbits of the sun, moon, and planets, the path of meteors, and the occurrence of eclipses. The Han dynasty had accurate water clocks, used paper, and calculated the value of *pi*.[4]

Liu Bang, the Gaozu Emperor, had no reason to admire Confucians, but he did have a government to run. He imitated the Qin bureaucracy and set up a system like the Qin dynasty's, with senior and junior ministers each having his own ministry and clear responsibilities. An edict in 196 BCE to bring "men of merit" into the government is often marked as the beginning of Confucian influence in government. Fifty years later, the government prohibited men who had studied Legalist texts from taking office. In 136 BCE, the government established five seats of learning for experts in five texts: the books of *Poetry*, *History*, *Ritual*, and *Changes*, and the *Spring and Autumn Annals*. By 124, Emperor Wu had established an academy where students could study the classics and were examined on them; if the student passed the examination, he would be eligible for government employment. The numbers of students at this academy grew dramatically: it began with 50 and by 144 CE had, it is said, 30,000 students.[5] This did not immediately end hereditary posts held by nobles, but it began the process.

Traditionally, it has been thought that the establishment of seats of learning for each classic in the government-sponsored academy was the "triumph of Confucianism." Those trained in the Confucian classics became, by virtue of this training, the political elite, bringing philosophy and morality to the institutions of government. Instead of being merely one voice among many in the Warring States era, from the Han dynasty on Confucianism becomes the single dominant voice, and this continues throughout Chinese history up to the 1900s.

Things are, unfortunately, never this clear-cut. Throughout the Han, thinkers educated in the classics were mostly ignored and occasionally threatened with execution. Among the Confucians, there was little agreement about what constituted a Confucian orthodoxy or the correct way to interpret the classics, as we shall see shortly. Finally, scholars were not, by any means, all Confucians. Despite their one year's study at the imperial academy, many thinkers were advocating everything from Legalism to immortality techniques. Confucianism does not seem to have had much impact on either government or society until very late in the Han dynasty.

While the Han dynasty cannot be seen as an obvious triumph for Confucianism, still, the establishment of the academy and the elevation of the Five Classics did allow for the Confucian appropriation of the classics and for vigorous activity among scholars that laid the foundations for developments in the Confucian tradition throughout the imperial period.[6]

The Classics in the Han

Whatever the truth about the First Emperor's orders to destroy books, by the time of the Han scholars believed that the textual tradition had been broken. They thought that the texts they had were incomplete and so their focus was on restoring, preserving, and interpreting these texts. Sima Tan (d.110 BCE) and his son, Sima Qian (145–c.86 BCE), wrote the *Shi Ji*, the *Records of the Historian*, a history meant to restore what had been lost in the Qin. Liu Xiang (79–78 BCE) and his son, Liu Xin (46 BCE–23 CE), imperial librarians, rewrote the texts in the imperial library into the standard characters of the time. They took the material they had and divided it into books, further subdividing these books into chapters. They also deleted some material. The result was the form of the texts that we use today.[7]

Confucians of the Han dynasty should be seen less as a school than as scholars of the classics. They saw themselves as interpreters of the Five Classics, and these five classics were problematic. The *Spring and Autumn Annals* is a prime example of their problems. Confucius had said that his reputation stood on the text. But, as we have seen, the text consists of terse notes of events in the state of Lu. During the Warring States period the *Zuo Zhuan* was written as a commentary on it. By the time of the Han, Confucian scholars were left with a cryptic classic, the *Annals*, and its commentary, the *Zuo Zhuan*, neither of which seemed to reflect Confucius' teachings very much. How could this be?

The New Text School

In the Han dynasty, Confucians disagreed about what versions of the classics to use and how to understand them. The dominant group is called the "New Text" School. Their name is based on their use of the new style of writing begun in the Qin and used by the Han. Their versions of the classics were written in that style, they used the yin-yang and five phases theories to interpret the classics, and they understood Confucius to be a very special kind of person. The New Text School's was the dominant interpretation of the five classics in the Han dynasty.

The most well known of the New Text scholars is Dong Zhongshu (c.179–104 BCE). His thought is systematized in the marvelously named text *The Luxuriant Dew of the Spring and Autumn Annals*.[8] Dong Zhongshu's interpretation was based on two theories that we find throughout the New Text School: the yin-yang theory and the five phases theory. These theories were used by the New Text School to find the hidden meanings in the classics, especially in the more obscure texts like the *Spring and Autumn Annals*.

Figure 9.1 Yin-yang symbol

The Yin-Yang Theory

References to yin and yang can be found in the Warring States era.[9] "Yin" originally meant "shade" as in the shady side of a hill; "yang" originally meant "sunshine," as in the sunny side of a hill. These meanings were extended to include ideas like cold and dark, hot and light. The yin-yang theory began as an observation about the seasons and yin or yang was assigned to them. So in the spring, yang begins to grow, while yin declines; yang grows until it reaches its height in the longest, hottest days of summer. Then yang begins to decline in the autumn, while yin grows and the days become shorter, the weather cooler. Yin continues to increase until the coldest, shortest, darkest days of winter. Yin reaches its height and then begins its decline as yang begins to grow, moving us again to spring. Yin and yang work in a continuing cycle.

The yin-yang system can also be applied to the cycle of day and night: yang reaches its height at midday with the highest point of the sun and begins its decline as yin increases. Yin reaches its high point with the darkest time of the night, then begins its decline, and so on. Westerners are usually familiar with the yin-yang symbol (figure 9.1).[10]

As neither yin nor yang dominates the other, but ebbs and flows in concert with it, the yin-yang system has been seen as "complementary." This means that, unlike a dualist system of opposites, where good fights evil, for example, yin and yang may be opposites, but they complement each other rather than conflict with one another.

Han dynasty scholars were very much taken by the yin-yang theory. With it, and the five phases theory, which we will look at next, they believed they had found the secret to the ways in which everything in the universe worked. As a result we have a number of texts describing the yin-yang theory and categorizing everything as yin or as yang. The rule of categorization was "likeness." This means that yang is hot, so is the sun, so the sun is also yang. Similarly, yin is cool, so is snow, so snow is yin. Elaborate lists were developed dividing all sorts of things into the categories of yin or yang.

Yang	Yin
heaven	earth
round	square
day	night
big states	small states
ruler	minister
superiors/above	inferiors/below
man	woman
father	son
older brother	younger brother
noble	base
broad-minded	narrow-minded
giving	receiving
active	passive
hot	cold
straight	curved
birth	death
full	empty

By understanding which item is yin and which is yang, it should be possible to figure out how things work and how they work together. Human beings can either follow the proper order and measure of yin and yang or run counter to them. If we act against the cycle of yin and yang and disrupt its balance, we can, for example, become ill. Illness is the imbalance of yin and yang in the body. The idea that we must all move with the universal actions of yin and yang is the reason that many of the yin-yang texts are concerned about the actions of the ruler, the representative of all human beings, whose actions, emotions, rituals, dress, and food must follow the proper measure appropriate to the movements of yin and yang. For example, rulers who go to war and bring death during the season of yang, life and growth, are running contrary to the natural balance of things and will pay the price. Should the ruler not follow yin and yang properly, the seasons could be disrupted, the harvests fail, or the state be lost. The yin-yang theorists often argued that it was extravagance and imbalance that ruined states and that the ruler should restrain himself and act according to the universal yin and yang.

Yin-yang theorists believed they had discovered a universal system that explained how all things worked and provided a blueprint for the best actions of the individual and the state. Following this blueprint would lead to balance, harmony, and success; working against it would lead to illness, famine, social chaos, and the loss of civilization.

The yin-yang theory has some serious problems, of course. First it assumes that "like moves like" and so the reason we feel sleepy on a rainy day is that the yin in the rain evokes the yin in us. It is true that we often feel sleepy on a rainy day, but it is not because of the yin in the weather evoking yin feelings of sleepiness in us; going to war in the summer takes farmers away from their work and tramples crops and so it may be unsuccessful, quite aside from anything to do with the workings of yin and yang. Second, many of the pairs of opposites in the yin-yang system do not work in the same way that yin as winter and yang as summer work. So, for example, a government minister does not increase to his height and then decline in relation to a ruler who also increases and declines. Many of the pairs of opposites are not opposites in the same cyclical way that summer and winter are. Third, as you can see from the list there is a preference for yang, something the yin-yang texts openly admit. Things that are more affirmative or appreciated have ended up in the yang column: broad-minded, noble, active, and birth for example. Finally, assigning gender in the way that the yin-yang texts do is problematic. Male is yang: "Spring [plays the role of] father and gives birth to things; summer [plays the role of] son and nurtures them."[11] In the yin-yang system, if nowhere else, the statement "yang is male and gives birth" makes sense. Yang is heaven, heaven gives birth to things in the yang seasons; yang grows in spring and reaches its height in summer, crops grow in spring and reach their height in summer.[12]

Qi

The yin-yang texts talk a great deal about "*qi*," saying things like, it is the yang *qi* that grows in the spring. There is no good English equivalent for the Chinese word *qi*. It has been translated in many ways, as "air," "vital spirit," "energy," "ether," and so on. You will find today many Westerners using the word, often incorrectly, with no clear idea of what it means.[13] Early in Chinese texts, *qi* was used to describe a person's character, to describe emotions, or to describe the atmosphere of a place, and it is still used that way in words in modern Chinese. Later theories about *qi* became more elaborate. It was argued that *qi* makes up all things and comes in various forms. Scholars called it "heavy" or "light" *qi*. In its lighter forms, *qi* can be air, light, electricity, or energy; *qi* in its heavier forms makes up things like the earth, a desk, or objects perceivable by the senses. An object, like a desk, may look inert, but it is *qi*, just *qi* moving very slowly. Human beings are made up of *qi* in many forms: heavy *qi* forms the bones, slightly less heavy *qi* is the flesh, *qi* in its liquid state is the blood and fluids of the body, *qi* is the character and emotions of a person, and *qi* as sheer energy animates us as a living person.

The New Text scholars argued that, given that *qi* is found in the universe and in human beings, it is what connects everything. Human government, human life, and human health are all based on the same processes that everything else in the universe is based on. So when the yin of a rainy day evokes the yin in a person to cause sleepiness, it is the yin *qi* of the universe reacting with the yin *qi* of the human being that makes this happen.

Taking this further, Dong Zhongshu argues that the *qi*, the energy and emotions found in human beings, are also found in Heaven, the workings of the universe itself. Human emotions are influenced by the actions of Heaven, and Heaven, in turn, is influenced by human actions and emotions. All things share the same *qi* and this is the way the microcosm – human beings – and the macrocosm – Heaven – interact.

The New Text scholars see Heaven as both anthropomorphic, acting like a human being, and as a natural process, but do not discuss how this works.[14] They do, however, talk about Heaven and Earth (nature, the universe) and human beings as forming a triad. In this triad, the actions of one part affect the actions of another. They say,

> Heaven, earth, and human beings are the origin of all things. Heaven gives birth to everything; earth nourishes everything and human beings perfect them. Heaven gives birth by providing filial piety and respect for elders; earth nourishes by providing clothing and food; human beings perfect everything through ritual and music. These three are like hands and feet that come together to form a body – no one part can be dispensed with.[15]

In this cosmic triangle, human beings, Heaven, and earth all work together. Matched with Heaven and Earth, human beings hold an exalted place in creation. The *Luxuriant Dew of the Spring and Autumn Annals* says,

> The essence of Heaven and Earth gives birth to all things and none is more noble than human beings. Human beings receive the choice of Heaven and this is what elevates human beings above all creatures. Other creatures are incapable of practicing humanity and rightness, only human beings can. Other creatures are incapable of matching themselves with Heaven and Earth, only human beings can.

The passage continues with some fantastical comparisons of the human body to the sun and moon and other natural phenomena and concludes by saying that human beings have a "mind/heart that expresses sadness, happiness, joy, and anger – the same class of feelings as the spirit-like feelings of Heaven."[16]

It is the responsibility of human beings, in particular of the ruler, to make sure that actions and emotions match the cycles of Heaven and earth. The ruler has the choice of Heaven and is the Son of Heaven. As the representative of human beings, the ruler's moods and actions are reflected in the moods and actions of Heaven. So, for example, the ruler must not be angry or carry out executions in the spring as this works against the growing yang of Heaven. If the ruler runs counter to the cycles of Heaven, Heaven will send signs and omens like floods, famines, or three-headed calves to show its displeasure.

The Five Phases[17]

The New Text school used a second theory in concert with the yin-yang theory to map the movements of human beings and the universe. This is the five phases theory, which is based on five basic elements that move from one phase to another. These are wood, fire, metal, water, and earth. Each presides over a season, changing, as yin and yang do, from growth to decay in the cycle of a year. They fit with the movements of yin and yang. Wood overcomes earth, metal overcomes wood, fire overcomes metal, water overcomes fire. Like the yin and the yang, the five phases move through a cycle:

wood	east	green	growing yang
fire	south	red	full yang
metal	west	white	growing yin
water	north	black	full yin
earth	center	yellow[18]	

The five phases correspond to five colors, the five notes of the pentatonic scale, five organs of the human body (liver, heart, spleen, kidneys, and lungs), five tastes (sweet, salty, bitter, spicy, and sour), and so on. Looking back in history, each dynasty was assigned one of the phases, along with a color, direction, and so on. As one dynasty fell to another, this was explained by the movement from one phase to another.

Just as the ruler had to reflect the movements of yin and yang, so too was he required to align himself with the movements of the five phases. The colors of the clothes he wore, the food that he ate, the direction of the palace rooms he lived in were all set out according to yin, yang, and the five phases. If the ruler did not follow these minute directions, the forces of nature would be confounded; famine, floods, and the loss of the state would follow. The yin-yang and five phases theories could be applied to many things: government, history, or medicine. They also provided the key to unlocking the real meaning of texts like the *Spring and Autumn Annals*.

The Status of Confucius

During the Han dynasty, Confucius came to be seen as something more than just an ordinary person who tried to work out solutions to the problems of his time. Confucius began to be called the "uncrowned king."[19] The thinking behind this title was that Confucius did indeed possess the choice of Heaven, even though he did not unify China and become its sole ruler. The jealous machinations of those who envied and feared him, along with the simple stupidity of those who did not understand him, kept Confucius from achieving his political goals.

Confucius' biography was expanded. In the *Records of the Historian* Confucius is no longer just a minor bureaucrat and little-known teacher. According to Sima Qian, Confucius held positions in the state of Lu, beginning as the police commissioner and moving up to the senior minister levels, first as the Minister of Public Works and then as the Minister of Justice, finally becoming the Chief Minister of the state of Lu.[20]

During the Han dynasty many of the pious stories about Confucius appeared, which included his miraculous birth and his supernatural powers. Even descriptions of his appearance were magnified to make him look more like the typical sage-king.[21]

Confucius did not exactly become a god, but certainly he was understood as someone with more power and a higher status than ordinary people.

The Old Text School

Countering the scholars of the New Text School were those of the, predictably named, Old Text School. The first difference between them was the texts that they used. The Old Text scholars used texts that were supposedly concealed during Qin and had been rediscovered; these texts were written in the older form of writing. The more general grounds of disagreement were the use of the yin-yang and five phases theories, the growing dependence on divination texts, and the view that Confucius was a semi-divine person. While there are still disputes about whether the New or Old Text versions are the "real" texts, gradually the Old Text versions won out. By the 900s they were in general use, and they are the ones we read today. However,

the issue was never as much about the texts themselves as about the commentaries, the interpretations of the texts. Scholars knew what Confucius
had taught, the debates were over what that meant.

The leading scholar of the Old Text school is Wang Chong (27–97).[22] He
rejected what he saw as the "superstition" of the New Text School, arguing
against most of the popular scholarship and beliefs of his time.

Wang Chong says that *qi* is natural and spontaneous; it has no purpose
and no emotions. *Qi*, like the Dao of the philosophical Daoists, does
not intend anything towards us. While it is certainly true that human
beings are made from the same *qi* as the universe, all that this means
is that we are alike; it does not mean we are connected. Dong Zhongshu
had written that

> Spring has the *qi* of happiness and thus gives birth; fall has the *qi* of anger,
> and thus things die off; summer has the *qi* of joy, and thus nourishes things;
> winter has the *qi* of sadness, and thus things are hidden. The four seasons
> are in the same unity as are heaven and human beings.[23]

This connection between the workings of Heaven and human beings is
rejected by Wang Chong. He replies,

> The way of heaven is to not have any intention. Therefore, spring does not
> give birth to things; summer does not grow them; autumn does not ripen
> them; winter does not hide them away. The yang *qi* comes out spontaneously
> and things are born and mature; the yin *qi* rises spontaneously and things are
> ripened and hidden away.[24]

The world works as it works. It does not act for our benefit. We can take
advantage of spring planting and autumn harvest, but they are not pur-
posefully provided for us. Heaven, the universe, and *qi* act naturally and
spontaneously, and have no aim. There is no special unity among Heaven,
earth, and human beings. The world is here for us to use. It is not here
because it wants to help us:

> Heaven gives birth to all creatures everywhere. Some creatures are hungry
> for grain and, feeling the cold, need clothing; therefore, people eat grain and
> wear clothes. Heaven did not produce the five grains and silk and hemp just
> so people could eat them or wear them, nor are calamities sent down to
> punish people. Things are spontaneously produced and people wear them
> or eat them.[25]

The reason that human beings cannot affect what Heaven does by our
moods or behavior is that Heaven, the universe, is simply the natural workings of *qi*. Criticizing the New Text scholars, Wang Chong says,

When discussing heat and cold, people say that when the ruler is happy, there is warmth, and when he is angry, there is cold. How is this supposed to work? Happiness and anger, they say, develop inside the ruler and are expressed on the outside in the form of rewards and punishments. With these widespread expressions of happiness, anger, reward and punishments, they can, in the extreme, cause things to wither and do harm to people. ...

The Way of Heaven is spontaneity and spontaneity means it does not act with any ego or intention. It may be that, when people perform divination, this matches with human events, but this is only by chance. To see these things as heaven responding to the actions of human beings is to deny the spontaneity of heaven.[26]

As Heaven just flows on its course, no behavior, good or bad, from rulers or any human being has any effect on what it does. Heaven does not send us omens to warn us about our behavior; it does not care. If there are floods and famines, they are natural events; they are not meant to warn us of faults in individual or government behavior. The New Text School is wrong in its application of yin-yang and five phases theories. It does not matter what color clothing the emperor wears, what palace rooms he lives in, what he eats, and when he orders executions. What matters is that he govern properly.

Human beings have no special place in the universe. Like other animals or like plants, we are made of *qi*, we live in a world of *qi*, but we have no special status in a triad of Heaven, earth, and human beings. Human beings have no way to influence Heaven. Wang Chong argues that a flea may live under a jacket. However, that flea cannot influence the thoughts and activities of the person wearing the jacket. So, too, human beings cannot influence the workings of the universe. To think that human beings hold such an exalted status is to not understand how the world works.[27] The New Text scholars are wrong in thinking that Heaven and earth give birth to human beings on purpose: human beings are born just as all other creatures are born. There is nothing special about us.

Another fad of the time, the search for immortality, also came under Wang Chong's fire. He attacked the whole idea of immortality, saying that it is natural for human beings to die. Animals all die; what would make human beings so special that they could somehow avoid death? When we are born, our *qi* comes together; when we die, our *qi* comes apart. This is a natural process that cannot be avoided. Similarly, the idea of ghosts makes no sense. Many, many people have died, Wang Chong said, so why do we not see millions of ghosts? Why do we not see ghost birds, ghost ants, and ghost fish? What makes human beings so special that there are human ghosts and not mouse ghosts? Finally, ghosts are always reported to be clothed. Where do their clothes come from? Can they buy them in ghost stores?

For Wang Chong we live in a world of nature that is like us; we are part of it, but nature does not concern itself with human beings. Human beings have no elevated status in the universe; we are just like all the other animals. Wang Chong did not argue against the yin-yang and five phases theories in themselves; they had become part of the fabric of the culture. He did reject the New Text School's use of these theories to elevate the status of human beings, to think that we live in a universe that cares about us, and to create a system that they thought explained everything.

Other Confucian Texts in the Han Dynasty

In addition to the commentaries and texts generated by the New and Old Text Schools, other scholars were writing other kinds of texts. One, the *Biographies of Women*, was a tribute to extraordinary women, like Mencius' mother, written by Liu Xiang (*c*.80–7 BCE).[28] The women Liu Xiang chose were almost always women who respected their parents and their husbands while caring for the children and the family as a whole. One theme that began in these biographies that we will see more of is the idea that, once widowed, a virtuous woman will not remarry. She should remain loyal to her husband's memory and to her husband's family that she has married into. In the biographies, virtuous women who were forced into remarriage committed suicide rather than compromising their loyalty. The same sorts of themes can be found in *Admonitions for Women* by Ban Zhao (*c*.45–51—*c*.114–20 CE). Sister to a famous historian, Ban Zhao was a well-educated woman who completed her brother's history. She argued that in order to be virtuous, women must be chaste in all ways and obedient to their parents and husbands. However, women should be encouraged to develop as moral beings and be educated in order to cultivate this morality. This would allow women to nurture their children and provide a good model for them.

The second kind of book that became very popular and influential by the end of the Han dynasty and far beyond was collections of stories about sons and daughters who were fine examples of filial piety.

For much of the Han dynasty, families were small, usually consisting of four or five people related in the sort of nuclear family we are used to now. As the Han dynasty began to decline, families that could afford to do so banded together for protection and economic strength. The families of the elite became extended families, including brothers and their wives and children. The tensions in these large families were usually between brothers who wanted to go their own way outside of the control of their father, and who wanted their share of the family fortune to do so. The senior males in these large families needed some way to maintain their control of the family. To do this, they found the ideas of filial piety very useful. Just as a minister is loyal to a ruler, so, too, a child must be loyal to parents; just as a servant must be obedient to a master, so, too, a child must be obedient to parents. The ideas of filial piety coming out of the Confucian tradition and the yin-yang theory's paired opposites fit into this very well. Loyalty and obedience on the part of children were as natural as the movement from spring to summer and just as ordained by Heaven.[29] A common motif in these stories was the filial child, who, when his parent was very ill, would slice off a part of his flesh in order to make a medicine to cure them. It was considered a sovereign remedy.

An example of these filial piety stories is one about Han Boyu, who would grow up to become one of Confucius' students.

> Han Boyu made a mistake. His mother beat him. When he began weeping, she said, "On other days I have beaten you, you have never wept. Why do you weep today?" He answered, "On other days when I have committed an error, your beating always hurt, but today, because of your failing strength, you are no longer able to cause me pain. This is the reason I weep."
>
> Therefore it is said, "The highest form of conduct is that, when your parents become angry, resentment does not even register in your thoughts, nor does it show in your appearance. Also you deeply accept your guilt to the extent that it causes your parents to feel sorry for you. The medium form of conduct is that, when your parents become angry, resentment does not even register in your thoughts, nor does it show in your appearance. The lowest form of conduct is that, when your parents become angry, resentment registers in your thoughts and shows in your appearance."[30]

As Keith Knapp points out, Confucian notions of filial piety allowed the primary male to have authority over the children, no matter what age, and Confucian rituals made for a formalized relationship between parent and child in which the parent held the authority. The result was a family hierarchy based on generation, age, and gender. The Confucian tradition did not invent large patriarchal families; instead, large patriarchal families needed certain Confucian ideas to be able to function.[31]

Summary

The political and economic success of the Han dynasty meant that China was a stable and unified country. The status of Confucian texts and ideas began to rise with the establishment of five seats of learning in the five Confucian classics and an academy for the study of these classics.

Dong Zhongshu of the New Text School believed he had found the key to understanding Confucius' thought and texts in the yin-yang and five phases theories. Both of these theories reflect a dependable cycle that works with everything from the universe to human beings. Basic to New Text School thought is the idea that *qi* is shared by the universe and human beings. Heaven's moods and actions are reflected in human beings; human actions and moods are reflected in Heaven because we all share the same *qi*. The ruler represents all human beings and so is subject to minute regulations in order to ensure that he will at all times follow the yin-yang and five phases cycles. In the view of the New Text School, Confucius has a special status beyond that of all other people. Confucius was the "uncrowned king" of his time. It is during the Han that we find more supernatural stories about Confucius' life.

The opponents of the New Text School, the Old Text School, held that the overuse of yin-yang and five phases theories had led to "superstition." Wang Chong argued that, while all things in the universe do indeed share the same *qi*, this *qi* is natural and spontaneous and does not pay any attention to the wishes and actions of human beings. We live in a natural world and we cannot influence it through our actions or our emotions.

During the Han we see the beginnings of biographies of virtuous women – something we will see more of as we go on. By the end of the Han we also see the beginning of the popularity of stories about filial piety. It is these tales of filial piety, not scholarly debates, that will bring Confucianism through to the Middle Ages.

10

From the Han to the Tang Dynasties, 220–907 CE

After the fall of the Han dynasty in 220 CE China was torn apart by rival kingdoms and invasions by peoples from the north and northwest. For almost four hundred years, there was no unifying Chinese dynasty that lasted for very long and fitful peace was all that anyone could hope for. Finally, in 589, the Sui dynasty unified China under Han Chinese rule and was replaced in 618 by the great Tang dynasty (618–907) that stabilized the country and is famous for its art, governance, and international relations.[1]

Buddhism and Its Development

It was during this period that Buddhism, which had come from India, grew and prospered, adapting to Chinese culture and becoming both a spiritual and a political force. Buddhism attracted people from every social rank and built great temples, monasteries, and convents; some Buddhist monks became tutors of the ruler's children and trusted officials in various governments.

Buddhism, unlike the Confucian tradition, offered a system where one could expect reward for good deeds – a good rebirth. There was justice for those who did evil because they would have a bad rebirth or go through lifetimes of hells. For those who aimed higher, Buddhism offered enlightenment through study and meditation, freeing them from the chains of rebirth. All of this was open to everyone, or at least all men, no matter their class, and was presented in beautiful temples, carvings, art, and many texts.

Formed in India, Buddhism brought with it Indian habits of thought and practice. Monks and nuns left their families and were celibate, not carrying on the family line; they shaved their heads and wore odd clothes. While they claimed to be holy people, they shocked Chinese people at first by begging on the streets for their food. Over the centuries, as Chinese people practiced Buddhism, Buddhism, not surprisingly, adapted to Chinese culture. Monks and nuns stopped begging for food and accepted donations instead. They argued that becoming a monk was a filial act of the highest kind as a holy monk prayed first for his parents and, should he become an enlightened *bodhisattva*, would save his parents first. Buddhist temples began to hold services for the dead and for ancestors, as they do today.

Objections to Buddhism continued throughout imperial China, especially criticism of institutional Buddhism for having too much political and economic influence. Even today, some people still criticize Buddhism for being "superstitious" and, even worse, "foreign" – this even though Buddhism has been practiced in China for almost two thousand years.

The form of Buddhism that became most popular in China was Mahayana and its schools. The most popular school is the Pure Land school. Through faith in Amitabha Buddha, one can be reborn in the Pure Land and there have the time, intelligence, and teachers to study Buddhism and become enlightened. Another popular, and essentially Chinese, form of Buddhism is Chan, more commonly known in the West by its Japanese name, Zen. This is the meditation school.

However, during the Tang and early Song dynasties, the schools that aroused the most interest were philosophical schools. Bizarrely enough, even today, you can still find texts, written by Westerners and even some Chinese authors, that say that the Chinese are not interested in philosophy or not philosophically inclined. If you have gotten this far in this book, you already know that is not true. Further proof, if needed, can be seen in the great discussions that took place over issues in the philosophical schools of Buddhism that formed in China.

Many of these schools based themselves on thinking from Indian philosophical schools like the Yogacharin school.[2] In the early Tang dynasty, a Chinese monk, Fazang (643–712), began a philosophical school of Buddhism called Hua Yan. Fazang used terms and ideas from earlier Chinese philosophy and began to argue that there are two things going on in all things. The first is "principle." This is what makes the thing that thing: a tree is a tree, not a book, because the principle of "tree-ness" is "within" it. The second is "phenomenon": this is the physical reality of that tree, its roots, trunk, branches, and leaves as they exist in this world, right now. Principle and phenomenon exist together in order for there to be a tree we can look at. Fazang and his Hua Yan school, along with other Buddhist schools like Tiantai, developed these ideas to deal with issues in Buddhism that do not concern us here, but the ideas of the Hua Yan school had a great impact on the Confucianism that would develop later.[3]

Confucianism from the Han to the Tang Dynasties

With the fall of the Han dynasty, scholars of the classics busied themselves with writing commentaries, commentaries on commentaries, studying the development and meaning of ancient Chinese characters, and other dusty pursuits. As historians of philosophy describe it, Confucianism fell into a long sleep. There were no new Confucian interpretations and no new insights. This does not mean, though, that the Confucian tradition disappeared. Instead it went in another direction.

We have seen the popularity of filial piety stories in the later Han dynasty. This popularity increased at an even greater pace during the period of disunity after the Han. Not only were there more and more texts describing the great feats of filial children, but imperial histories began to include examples of those who served their parents in extraordinary ways, and tombs were decorated with scenes from famous stories of filial behavior.[4] The reasons behind this were the same ones we saw in the later Han: elite families found that maintaining a large extended family gave them protection, economic power, and political influence. To keep this extended family in order, hierarchy was needed and, to keep the hierarchy functioning, children had to be raised with tales of filial behavior. Even as adults, sons and daughters were taught to see their parents' interests as primary; they too would be rewarded with a "proper" family and, in the future, children who would respect them in the same way.[5]

The second major influence on the Confucian tradition began during the early 600s, in the Sui dynasty. The Sui instituted the beginnings of the civil service examination system organized by the Board of Civil Office. Examinations were held every three years: candidates were required to show their knowledge of a classic, and awarded three levels of degrees. Successful candidates were offered a job in government. This developed into an even more elaborate system in later dynasties.

Civil Service Examinations and the Imperial Civil Service

Chen Shimei left for the capital to sit in the civil service examinations. His family heard nothing from him for three years, during which time his parents died and his wife and children began to starve. His wife, Qin Xianglian, took her children and went to the capital to search for her husband. She discovered that he had attained first place in the examinations and had married the emperor's daughter. She went to their mansion, but her husband pretended not to know her and had her thrown out. He refused all further attempts from her for a reconciliation and finally hired one of his followers to kill her and the children. The follower could not go through with it and Qin sued her husband at court for desertion and attempted murder.

The judge was Bao Zhang (999–1062) who was well known for his disgust at corruption and for upholding the highest standards of justice. As an investigating officer, he had scores of officials demoted or fired for their corruption. Despite interventions from the palace, Bao Zhang tried Chen Shimei, found him guilty, and executed him.

Over time, Bao Zhang became celebrated as Bao Gong, the god of justice, and is prayed to, especially in his main temple in Kaifeng, even today. He is also represented as the black-faced official in Chinese opera.

The reason for establishing an examination system was to provide a method of recruiting people to the civil service based on something other than noble birth. While the Chinese examination system changed and adapted over its 1300-year history, its general form remained much the same. The examination system lasted up to 1904, when the last examinations of this kind were held. The Chinese system influenced Western governments: civil service examination began in the 1870s in the UK and in 1883 in the US. Even today, in many countries around the world, tests are required for anyone wanting a civil service job.

Study for these exams began at anywhere from five to eight years of age. Both boys and girls were taught easy texts like the *Three Thousand Character Classic*. Boys went on, under the guidance of a tutor, to memorize all the Confucian classics and then their commentaries. What constituted a classic and whose commentaries a student read changed over time.

Once a young man had memorized the classics and the commentaries on them, he would attempt his first level of exams. The examinations were open to all men except those in prohibited occupations, like actors, who were considered too low-class. The examinations were held at district, provincial, and national levels. At each examination, the candidate would be given a phrase from one of the classics and would have to write out the entire passage the phrase came from. There were also questions on philosophy, history, government theory, and the theory of poetry. Questions became more difficult with each level.

The first level, the district examination, was generally taken at about the age of fifteen. If the candidate passed, he was then allowed to take the prefectural examination in the biggest city of the area (a province usually had ten to twelve prefectures). If he passed that one, he was given the qualifying examination by an authority from the provincial government. Success at this level gave the candidate a title, "licentiate," and the successful candidates were taken to the temple of Confucius where they swore to become followers of Confucius.[6]

With their distinctive clothing and caps, students who reached this level had no official government post, but were respected as if they did. With further study, often by their late twenties or early thirties, candidates went on to the provincial, metropolitan, and palace examinations. All of these examinations were held in special enclosed examination areas. Inside a walled area were lanes containing rows of small cells, about six feet or two meters wide. In each cell there was nothing but three boards that, when placed across the cell, became a shelf, a desk, and a seat. Candidates at the provincial level spent three days and two nights in these cells, bringing with them inkstones, ink, brushes, pots, food, and bedding. The exam papers were brought to the candidates, who spent their days and nights answering them.[7]

Great efforts were made to eliminate cheating: candidates were strip-searched before the exams and their clothing searched for crib notes; before they took their places, a guarantor had to authenticate their identity; candidates were assigned a number so that their names would remain secret throughout the testing and marking; their answer sheets were recopied so that their handwriting could not be recognized by the examiners. Public interest in the outcome of these examinations was intense, and if the examiners were thought to have fiddled with the outcome there was a great outcry, often leading to imperial investigations. It was said that to pass the exams, the candidate needed "the spiritual strength of a dragon, the physique of a donkey, the insensitivity of a wood louse, and the endurance of a camel."[8]

As the examination system took hold, Confucianism's central place in Chinese culture was solidified. The examinations were based on knowledge of Confucian classics and their commentaries and the result was a civil service well versed in Confucianism and governments that talked like Confucians – even if they often did not act like Confucians. As the Confucian tradition became central to the government and to the rich and powerful, it trickled down into the general culture. As well, it was these educated Confucian civil servants and scholars who wrote books on proper rituals for family occasions, like funerals and weddings, and, by their explanations of these rituals, helped spread Confucian ideas throughout the culture.

These examinations were, in theory, open to all men of any class. However, the rich were the only families who could afford the books and tutors, and to have their young men spend their early lives in study. There were occasional students from poorer backgrounds who were sponsored by a town or guild, but, by and large, the examination system was a way in which the rich and powerful maintained their riches and power. Because inheritance was divided among the sons, a family's wealth could disappear within two or three generations. Having sons who did well in the examination system meant that the extended family rose with them as these sons reached the higher levels of the civil service. It was the responsibility of each generation to further the family's influence and wealth by entering the civil service.

The Civil Service

The government was divided into national, provincial, and local levels. The civil service consisted of a relatively small number of bureaucrats for a country as large and populous as imperial China. Estimates are that in the Tang dynasty there were 13,500 officials for 50 million people; by the Qing dynasty, with a population of about 425 million people, there was one magistrate for every 300,000 people.[9]

The foundation of the civil service was the local magistrate. Most successful candidates in the examination system began at this bottom rung. The "law of avoidance" meant that magistrates were not allowed to serve in their native areas. The new magistrate arrived as a stranger and often could not speak the local dialect, so he would usually speak to the local gentry who would be fluent in "Mandarin" or "official" dialect. To help him with his duties he had a staff of about a dozen subordinates. A magistrate, as pretty much the sole representative of the imperial government, had enormous duties to perform. He had to investigate and prosecute crimes, judge civil disputes, collect taxes, impose corvée, and raise a local militia if needed. He acted as the judge, police, and prosecutor at trials. He was required to know all the laws and the punishments that went with them: punishments varied from ten blows to execution, mitigated in some circumstances if the person was old or mentally ill. His court proceedings were public and his sentences and decisions were subject to the people's approval. His legal duties also included acting as a mediator, especially in civil cases.[10]

If a magistrate was competent, he would be promoted to the provincial and then national levels. Given the small world of the civil service and its enormous powers, this was the route to power and wealth. Although paid small salaries, civil servants made up for this by accepting "gifts" for the consideration of assistance or to hear civil cases.[11] This was only considered to be a problem if, for example, a magistrate let himself be so influenced by the bribes he had received that it caused unrest in his district.

The Status of Confucius in Imperial China

With the dominance of Confucianism in the civil service and its examination system and Confucian ideas filtering down through society, what did people think about Confucius himself?

In 57 CE, the imperial college began sacrifices to Confucius; in 492, the emperor bestowed the title "Accomplished Sage" on Confucius. Titles continued to be bestowed until, in 1530, the emperor stripped Confucius of previous titles such as duke (1 CE), king (739 CE), and emperor (1106) and gave Confucius the title "Greatest Sage and Ancient Teacher" so that Confucius was unique.[12] This title was expanded in 1645 to "Classic Teacher, Accomplished, Illustrious, and Perfect Sage." Titles were not just awarded to Confucius: the Kong family was ennobled, and financially supported, by the Chinese government up until the 1940s.

Confucian Temples

You can apply for a ticket to the government office of the Council of Cultural Affairs in Taipei for admission to the celebration of Confucius' birthday, also called "Teachers' Day," on September 28th. And, if you are willing to get up before four in the morning, you can attend the celebration of Confucius' birthday that begins just before daybreak in the Confucian temple in Taipei. Delegations of municipal and governmental dignitaries, foreign visitors, and a sizeable crowd follow an ancient liturgy. Young boys dressed in Zhou dynasty costume perform ancient dances and play ancient musical instruments – pipes, zithers, bells, and drums.[13] Offerings are made. Similar ceremonies are held at the older Confucian temple in Tainan.

These ceremonies are sponsored by the government and by a local committee that oversees the Confucian temple. From Taiwan to Indonesia, China, Korea, Vietnam, and Japan you will find Confucian temples. Some are still used; others are museums or tourist sites.[14] The Confucian temple in Beijing, built in 1302, was renovated in 1981. When I last visited it in the mid-1990s, it was still run down and looking for donations to its building fund. It is called the "Capital Museum" and is open to the public for a small fee. The general sprucing-up of Beijing for the 2008 Olympics completed the renovations. The Shanghai Confucius temple is also a tourist draw along with its Sunday second-hand book fair.

Many of the Confucian temples in China decayed through long neglect from the 1920s to the 1940s. With the establishment of the Communist government in 1949, some were used for other purposes and some were demolished. Signs of destruction caused by the Cultural Revolution (1966–76) can still be seen today in patched-together pieces of inscriptions. In contrast, one can also see renovation in, for example, the brand new statue of Confucius in the main temple in Qufu built in 1984.

Veneration of Confucius officially began in 195 CE, when the Han dynasty emperor venerated Confucius in Qufu at Confucius' tomb. Later

Figure 10.1 Main building in the Temple of Confucius in Qufu

in the Han, scholars at the imperial academy offered sacrifices to Confucius and his favorite student Yan Hui. In the 450s, the imperial government built the first Confucian temple, and during imperial China any city of respectable size had a temple to Confucius.

Imperial governments throughout Chinese history built and managed Confucian temples and celebrated the spring equinox, the birthday of Confucius, and the successful candidates of the civil service examinations with public rituals in these temples. The ceremonies were complex and followed an officially mandated liturgy.

In 1530, after much government debate, it was decided that there should be no statues in a Confucian temple. It was thought that having statues and portraits of Confucius and his followers smacked too much of Buddhist and Religious Daoist temples. Instead, Confucius and his followers were represented by memorial tablets inscribed with their names and titles. The only exception was, as it is today, in the temple of the Kong family in Qufu.[15]

Throughout imperial China there was also considerable argument as to which scholars deserved to be enshrined in a Confucian temple. In theory the scholars should have played a significant part in the transmission of the Confucian Way, but the list of the men to whom that applied changed, reflecting the orthodoxy of the time.[16]

Imperial governments also supported the Hanlin Academy. Founded in the Tang dynasty, it was staffed by the elite of scholars who performed library duties for the court, including interpreting the Confucian classics.

Confucius as a God

We will look at the question of Confucianism's status as a religion below (chapter 13), but this is a good time to stop and ask if Confucius is a god. There are those who say that Confucius is indeed a god, particularly when one looks at imperial China. Confucius has been, at many times, prayed to, and the worshippers expected to receive happiness or help from him. Others say that Confucius was respected and venerated as a guide for behavior.[17] How can there be such different views?

As with many things in the study of Chinese religions and traditions, much depends on who you talk to and what expectations you have when you look at things. So, for example, you can today go to the Confucian temple in Taipei, and you will see a temple dedicated to Confucius. You see people burning incense and bowing to the memorial tablet of Confucius. When you ask them what they are doing, they tell you they are asking for Confucius' favor in something like the upcoming national university entrance examinations. You can also see students studying quietly in the study halls or in the garden courtyards. Ask them why they are studying there and they will tell you that it is a quiet place, and some will say that the influence of Confucius will help them in their studies.

Are these people in modern day Taipei, just like people in imperial China, seeing Confucius as a god? Possibly. From conversations I have had, it is clear that some people see Confucius as possessing supernatural powers, able to help those who pray to him, especially in petitions concerning school and examinations. However, when I talk to other people, they say that burning incense and studying at the Confucian temple is a way to show respect to the first teacher, to concentrate the mind, and to build motivation. Confucius is someone to whom one should show respect and that is why people go to the Confucian temple and bow to his memorial tablet.

So, is Confucius a god? Sometimes.

What we can say with more confidence is that, throughout most of imperial China, Confucianism was the state cult. Do not panic at the word "cult." While the media uses the word "cult" to describe some scary group that brainwashes its followers, the word itself simply means "following." A state cult, or a state ideology, is the religion that the state uses or the way the government talks. Most governments have something like this. Remembrance

Day or Memorial Day ceremonies are often set up, and paid for, by governments. Fallen soldiers are prayed for using the liturgy and terms of whatever the dominant religion is, or has been, in that country. In imperial China, the emperor followed Confucian rituals in matters of marriage and funerals, and in the sacrifices he alone carried out to Heaven and to Earth. The government built and maintained Confucian temples; the government decided on titles for Confucius and his followers. Imperial governments talked like Confucians – no surprise, given the bureaucrats had all been trained in the classics. For example, they referred to neighboring Korea as a "younger brother." Throughout their laws and decrees, imperial Chinese governments acknowledged their responsibility to care for the people.

Confucianism outside of China

Korea

As early as the fourth century CE, Koreans began to study Confucian classics and establish academies for their study, but Confucianism did not have a huge impact on government and culture until the Choson dynasty (1396–1910). Early in the Choson dynasty, Confucianism became the state cult.[18] This was specifically the Confucianism of Zhu Xi (see chapter 11). Korean scholars worked on, refined, and developed the School of Principle. During the 1500s, Korean scholars took part in famous debates over how one might interpret the ancient Confucian texts in light of Zhu Xi's thought. Throughout all of these debates and the development of schools of Zhu Xi's thought, there was a common call for reform: reform of society and the economy so that Korea might become more like a Confucian ideal state.[19] Throughout the 1400s and 1500s Korean scholars refined and developed Neo-Confucian thought (see chapter 11) in more sophisticated ways than could be found elsewhere. The Koreans used a civil service examination system, but as Korean society differed from China's only the sons of certain lineages from elite families could sit for these examinations. When the Ming dynasty in China fell to the Manchus in 1644, the Koreans proclaimed themselves, with some justification, the only state in East Asia that followed orthodox Confucianism.

Imperial patronage of the Confucian tradition ended with the fall of the Choson dynasty in 1910 as Korea was swallowed by Japan. In modern times, there are still venerable institutions, such as the College of Confucian Studies, part of Songgyun-gwan University, where the Confucian tradition is still studied. When members of the Korean National Classical Music Institute visited Taiwan in 1967, their renditions and understanding of classical music were of such antiquity and of such a high standard that the Confucian temples in Taiwan changed the music they had used in the celebration of Confucius' birth.[20]

While Confucianism no longer has a place in modern Korean government, the Confucian influence on Korean society is deep and the attitudes of Koreans, whether towards their family, teachers, or international affairs, are still couched in Confucian terms.[21]

Japan

Starting in the 600s, the Japanese upper class went through a great fad for "chinoiserie." They imported Chinese clothing, architecture, the writing system, and everything Chinese. All of these things, including Confucianism and Buddhism, were brought to Japan by Koreans. Confucianism became part of the education of the upper class.[22] Confucianism was taught in Buddhist schools and monasteries, which may sound odd, but Buddhist teachers saw Confucianism as a moral teaching for this life, and Buddhism as a teaching for the next life and for enlightenment. This was a Confucianism for the upper class; for much of Japanese history it did not percolate down to ordinary people.

It was also a Confucianism adapted to the needs of Japanese society and culture. The emperor of Japan was understood to be a *kami*, a being with a supernatural status based on his divine descent. This status was passed down to the emperor's heir in an unbroken line. Confucian ideas around the "choice of Heaven" would not work in Japan where the emperor was chosen on grounds other than the choice of Heaven. So Confucianism had to adapt. There were no meaningful civil service examinations in Japan either, as clan loyalty and family relationships were the way to government positions.

There was an imperial academy, and over time rich and powerful families set up their own academies. Competition among these families was reflected in competition and factionalism among the Confucian scholars at their academies during the ninth and tenth centuries. The Confucian virtues promoted were loyalty and filial piety – a filial piety that extended respect to elders and leaders so that one's own aims and ambitions were subordinated to one's parents or lord.

Loyalty to one's lord was of interest in teaching samurai warriors and, along with self-control and faithfulness, Confucian loyalty and filial piety became part of *bushido*, the code of the samurai. The status of women, which had begun its long slide downward since the 600s, was further debased by *bushido* and its contempt for emotions, love, and women, and its admiration for manly values and the military.

It was during the Tokugawa shogunate (1603–1868) that Confucianism came into its own in Japan. A shogun was a military ruler, and, while there was still an emperor, it was the shogun who had real power. The Tokugawa family, headed by the shogun, the military ruler, was interested in keeping order – and power – and so set up a virtual caste system: society was rigidly controlled. The Tokugawa used Confucianism, focusing on the idea of loyalty, as part of their way of enforcing order. The Tokugawa proclaimed an orthodox Confucianism, and in 1790 they banned all schools of Confucianism considered to be not following that orthodoxy.[23] Not all Confucian scholars followed the Tokugawa: they were divided between those who supported the continued feudal rule of a shogun and those who advocated nationalism and a return to the real rule of the emperor.

As a result, Japanese scholarship took up issues and ideas from China and Korea; this scholarship was stimulated by the business elite families who set up Confucian academies for their sons. The production of children's books on Confucian lines and their dissemination among the population at large finally brought Confucian ideas to ordinary people.

Confucian scholarship continues today in Japan. Confucianism, understood as teaching moral virtues, focused on loyalty and filial piety, continued throughout the 20th century and can still be found today being taught in Japanese schools.

Vietnam

Vietnam was influenced by Confucianism, but that influence was less than in Japan. While an examination system existed by the eleventh century, candidates were not tested just on Confucian topics, but on Buddhism and Religious Daoism as well. The Ming dynasty Chinese occupation of Vietnam in the early 1400s led to a significant use of Confucianism in the following Nguyen dynasty (1428–1883). Confucianism may have been accepted by the ruling elites, but does not seem to have percolated through society. This Confucianism was confined to the court and to some of the upper classes as the court began a more bureaucratic style of governing, but there was no system of academies or widespread publication of texts. As in Japan, the Confucian ideas that found most favor with government and society were the ideas of loyalty and filial piety. However, the impact of Confucianism on everyday life, on government, and on scholarship was not deep. By the nineteenth century, rulers used Confucianism and established a bureaucracy based on it. It was then that most Vietnamese became familiar with Confucian ideas and terms, but by the mid-twentieth century Confucianism as a system faded. What remains are the ideas of loyalty and filial piety, commonly recognized and practiced. More modern Vietnamese scholars have often interpreted their past as a Confucian past, but this may be only either to decry the fall of standards or to criticize a stifling and closed history. The Confucian tradition made much less of an impact on Vietnamese history and culture than the impact we find in Korea and Japan.[24]

Summary

While vigorous intellectual debate in Confucianism disappeared from the Han to the Tang dynasties, Confucianism did not. Filial piety, so closely associated with Confucian teachings, became an even more popular idea, celebrated in texts, art, and histories. The development of the civil service examination system, in which candidates were tested on their knowledge of Confucian texts, led to Confucianism's continuing close relationship with government. Confucianism became the state cult or state ideology of imperial governments, naturally reflecting the training of the members of the civil service. The status of Confucius continued to rise as he was awarded title after title and Confucian temples could be found in cities and towns across the country.

Confucianism spread to Korea where it had a deep impact on both government and people; this impact on Korean culture can still be seen today. The Japanese adapted Confucianism to their own culture, emphasizing loyalty, filial piety, and hierarchy; the impression of Confucian thought can also still be seen in Japan. Vietnam was also, but to a lesser extent, influenced by the Confucian tradition.

The popularity of Buddhism in China posed real problems to Confucians in imperial China. Not only was Buddhism politically powerful and edging into what Confucians saw as their proper sphere of influence, but Buddhist ideas circulated through the culture. Confucian scholars were both influenced by Buddhist ideas and keen to reject them, as we shall see in the next chapter.

11

Neo-Confucianism

Neo-Confucianism fully developed during the Southern Song (1127–1279), after the humiliating defeat and loss of northern China at the hands of non-Han Chinese invaders. The name "Neo-Confucianism," a new Confucianism, was invented by those same Jesuit missionaries who gave us the names "Confucius" and "Mencius." In Chinese, Neo-Confucianism is called *Daoxue Jia*, the school, or study, of the Dao, and this is further divided into *Lixue*, the school, or study, of principle, and *Xinxue*, the school, or study, of the mind/heart. Neo-Confucianism was a reaction to the rote learning of the examination system, the intellectual and political power of Buddhism, and the loss of Chinese territories to non-Chinese invaders. Neo-Confucian thinkers saw themselves as returning to the original Confucianism, sweeping away all the inaccurate interpretations that had gone before, and developing a new interpretation that really explained the Confucian tradition.

In this section we will look briefly at the changing times of the Song dynasty, the ideas of early Neo-Confucian thinkers, the great system maker Zhu Xi, who brought their ideas together, opposition to Zhu Xi, particularly the thought of Wang Yangming, and the impact all of this had on Chinese culture and the Confucian tradition.

The Northern and Southern Song Dynasties

The Song dynasty is divided into two parts. In the Northern Song, from 960–1125, Chinese emperors held much of the north of China and the capital was in Kaifeng, near the Yellow River. In the Southern Song, 1127–1279, Han Chinese rule was pushed south, back to just north of the Yangzi River, and the capital moved to Hangzhou.

Even with the loss of the north to non-Han Chinese invaders, the Song capital in Hangzhou was the biggest city in the world at that time, with a population of two million by 1200.[1] International trade boomed. Muslims moved to port cities like Guangzhou (Canton), helping to spread trade from the East Indies to India and to East Africa. This sea trade made use of the world's first compartmented ships, rudders for steering, charts, and compasses. The economy also grew with the widespread use of paper currency, something that had begun in the Tang dynasty.

The technological invention that had the greatest impact on the literati was the invention of the printing of books. Paper had been used in the Han dynasty, but the widespread availability of books, printed first in woodblock and then, by 1000 CE, with moveable type in both China and Korea, meant that the Northern Song was the first society in the world with printed books.

Western mythology holds that the first printed book was the Bible, printed by Gutenberg in 1455. Certainly this was the first book printed in Europe, but the Diamond Sutra, a Buddhist text in Chinese, is the oldest printed book in the world, printed in 868 CE in the Tang dynasty.[2] The availability of printed books spread ideas throughout China and beyond. It had an enormous effect on the establishment of schools and, as we shall see, the development of ideas in the Song dynasty.

The civil service examination system continued for most of the Song. By the Southern Song, the number of successful candidates in the examination system began to outnumber the government posts available, so elite families used their literati status as a sign of prestige and became more involved in negotiating their power on the local scene. From the Southern Song to the end of the Qing dynasty in 1911, China's social structure centered around the "gentry." In imperial China, this gentry class had economic, social, and governmental roles. They were often landlords of sizeable portions of land that they rented or leased to farmers. The aim of this gentry was to maintain, and further, the economic and political power of their family. A gentry family would include men who had passed the civil service examinations. Gentry families lived in towns and often lived grandly. As landlords, they had the biggest impact on the life of local farmers. As civil servants, or as men who had passed the examinations, they were equal, if not superior, to the local magistrate, and thus had political power.

Neo-Confucianism

Among these gentry families, sons studied hard to pass the civil service examinations, but how "Confucian" were those who passed? These men are generally called "literati" rather than "Confucian," and many were attracted to Buddhist ideas;[3] some literati learned and discussed Buddhist ideas, especially those of the Hua Yan school (see below), while others studied under Chan (Zen) masters. The literati also spent time reading Daoist philosophy in the *Laozi* and the *Zhuangzi*, reading and writing poetry, painting, collecting antiques, and gourmandizing. They cannot really be called "Confucians" just because they had been trained in Confucian texts and commentaries.

Issues in Neo-Confucianism

It was clear that the examination system did not produce people who lived a serious "Confucian" life. Men who passed the exams were often just looking for wealth and power and had no intention of actually practicing anything they had just spent half their life memorizing. One of the first concerns for Neo-Confucian thinkers was how to reform the examination system so that the result would be men who took Confucianism seriously. All the Neo-Confucian thinkers rejected Confucian studies in earlier times, seeing them as merely textual studies, not really felt or practiced.

Given the collapsing political situation in the Song, there was also a call for political reform: the emperor should employ "real" Confucians who would reform government and the examination system, and who would guide the people. This was how to save the nation from invasion, venal officials, wealth-obsessed merchants, and a discontented population. Neo-Confucianism was never just a philosophy, but concerned itself with economic and political reform.

Finally, Neo-Confucian thinkers faced a major challenge from Buddhism. Buddhism had set the terms and issues being discussed by anyone interested in ideas since the Tang dynasty. Neo-Confucians saw Buddhism as dangerously "other-worldly," that is, focused on enlightenment and not involved in the problems of this world. The compelling issues of the time were of no interest to Buddhists who spent time building up good karma for a good rebirth or on meditating so as to free themselves from the chains of this world. Buddhist monks were trying to escape from this world, said Neo-Confucians, while a good man should face up to life's responsibilities.

Early Neo-Confucian Thinkers

In the later half of the Tang dynasty, many of these problems were already being discussed by thinkers like Han Yu (768–824). His anti-Buddhist attitudes can be seen in his memorial, or position paper, the "Bone of the Buddha," addressed to the emperor in 819. He complained that the government was spending far too much money to acquire and house relics of the Buddha, "these decayed and rotten bones, an ill-omened and filthy relic" of a barbarian.[4] Han Yu came close to execution for this and was banished to a minor post in the boondocks. In addition to his opposition to Buddhist influence, Han Yu argued for social action, not withdrawal, and a return to the sources of the Confucian tradition. In his essay "On the Origin of the Dao," he defines the Way as the one transmitted from sage-king to sage-king, then to the early rulers of the Zhou dynasty, then to Confucius, and then to Mencius where it stopped. It was misunderstood by Xunzi, he says, and by later Confucians. There is an orthodox or proper understanding of the Way, the Dao, a *Dao tong*, and it is this that must be studied.

Han Yu's contemporary, Li Ao (*c.*844), was the first thinker in imperial China to advocate paying special attention to one of the chapters in the *Book of Rites*, the "Great Learning." As we have seen, this chapter contains the idea of the investigation of things and extending knowledge – something that we will see a great deal of later.

During the Northern Song dynasty, Zhou Dunyi (1017–73) produced what he called the "Diagram of the Supreme Ultimate" along with a text to explain how it all worked (see figure 11.1). At the top is the Supreme Ultimate, Tai Ji, which is also the Supreme Ultimate-less, Wu Ji.

The Supreme Ultimate is an entity beyond time and space and an entity that is abstract (or "transcendent" and "metaphysical" in philosophy-speak) as opposed to concrete.[5]

Why is it both the Supreme Ultimate and, at the same time, the Supreme Ultimate-less? Some of these "it is" and, at the same time, "it is not" statements that one runs across in Chinese philosophy can be frustrating. What Zhou Dunyi is trying to point to is that this is an entity that can be thought of as existing (Supreme Ultimate) and should also be thought of as something beyond our very notions of what "existing" means, the Supreme Ultimate-less. This entity, as Zhou Dunyi goes on to explain, is an abstract principle that is the foundation of the movements of yin and yang and that underlies the universe.

Once a thinker has established an entity that is abstract and beyond time and space, the difficulty he now faces is how to connect that to our world of time, space, and concrete things we can know with our senses. The Supreme Ultimate is the abstract principle underlying the universe. This means that our senses cannot perceive it and it is something apart from our physical world. The Supreme Ultimate, through movement, produces yang (from the Han dynasty yin-yang theory), and when yang reaches its height, it slows and stills; this is yin. Yin and yang alternate. The alternations of yin and yang produce the five phases: water, metal, fire, wood, and earth – just as we saw in the Han dynasty theories. As the yin-yang and five phases interact ceaselessly, we come to the physical level, the level of *qi*.

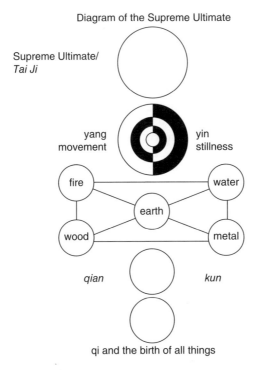

Diagram of the Supreme Ultimate

Figure 11.1 Diagram of the Supreme Ultimate

The next two terms, *qian* and *kun*, are taken from the Confucian classic, the *Book of Changes*. They are the names for the two basic hexagrams in the divination system and are here, as is often the case, assigned gender: *qian* is male, *kun* is female. As they too join the mix of yin and yang and the five phases, all things in the universe are born.

Zhou Dunyi says that just as there are yin and yang in the universe, so there is humanity and rightness in human beings; similarly, the five phases evoke five moral qualities in human beings (humanity, rightness, proper behavior, wisdom, and sincerity). It is the virtue of sincerity, as described in the *Doctrine of the Mean*, that is the basis of all moral behavior and the way in which we can decide good and evil. Human beings are imbued with the Supreme Ultimate itself, as human beings and cosmos are united by human beings' sense of order. The sage matches the movement and stillness of the ultimate.

Another of the early thinkers in Neo-Confucianism was Zhang Zai (1020–77), who lived during the Northern Song dynasty. He argued against the Buddhist doctrine of *sunyata*, emptiness, which says that this world is not real. Buddhists say that all things are compound things and all things will change. This means that there is no eternal thing in the universe. Yogacharin Buddhism went further and argued that all the world we perceive is an illusion – much like the situation presented to Neo in the movie *The Matrix*.[6]

The Buddhists are wrong, Zhang Zai said. There is an eternal, primal, substance that is real and that substance is *qi*. *Qi* condenses and disperses. He argued that *qi* has always existed and that all things are made of various kinds of *qi* and, when they dissolve, they dissolve back into other forms of *qi*. So, the world is not an illusion, it is real and there is something eternal in it.

He saw *qi* as identified with the Supreme Ultimate, and it is through *qi* that human beings are part of the Supreme Ultimate. He carried this further in his "Western Inscription." He applied his theory of *qi* to argue that all people are made from the same *qi* and, by extending the Confucian virtue of humanity, one could embrace all people. We must extend affection, humanity, from our family out to all people until we form one body with everyone.

> Heaven is my father, Earth is my mother, and even such a small creature as I finds an intimate place in their midst. Therefore, that which fills the universe, I regard as my body and that which directs the universe, I consider as my nature. All people are my brothers and sisters and all things are my companions. ...
>
> Respect the aged – this is the way to treat them as the elderly should be treated. Show deep love toward the orphaned and the weak – this is the way to treat them as the young should be treated. ... Even those who are tired, infirm, crippled or sick, those who have no brothers or children, wives or husbands – all are my brothers who are in distress and have no one to turn to. ...
>
> Wealth, honor, blessing, and benefits are meant for the enrichment of my life, while poverty, humble station, and sorrow are meant to help me to fulfillment. In life I follow and serve Heaven and Earth. In death I will be at peace.[7]

This "Western Inscription" became the manifesto of Neo-Confucianism.

Zhang Zai's nephews built upon his work. The two brothers, Cheng Hao (1032–85) and Cheng Yi (1033–1107), also studied under Zhou Dunyi. They used their uncle's ideas about *qi* and added to them the concept of principle.

We have seen the idea of principle earlier, in Hua Yan Buddhism. Fazang's understanding of principle was taken over by the Cheng brothers. Principle is a metaphysical, abstract idea. It is what makes a thing what it is. It is the principle of "tree-ness" that makes a tree a tree. If you cut the tree down and saw it up, you still have all the material that made up the tree, but what has been lost is the principle of "tree," so that the wood you are looking at is not a tree. A rose is a rose because it has the principle of "rose" and not the principle of "fork." The practice of filial piety has a basic principle that does not depend on the particulars of this son and this father. Everything, no matter whether it is an object, an action, or a situation, has a principle. All events, affairs, and things, like a rose, the relationship of parents and children, the invasion of China during the Northern Song, and so on, have a principle. There are principles that make things the things that they are and there are principles that make historical events, family relationships, and the actions of government what they are.

Principle is found in all things. Although we say principle is "within" all things, this does not mean that you can take apart a rose and find the "piece" of principle. Principle is abstract and does not exist physically "inside" the rose. Principle is "in" all things and all things can be understood once one understands their principle. For example, the principle in human beings is human nature, what it is that makes us human beings.

Working with principle is *qi*, the material by which things are produced. Principle may give the tree its "tree-ness" or a human being a human nature, but there has to be material as well. The material is *qi*. Wherever there is *qi*, principle is present; without *qi*, principle would have no way to manifest, or show, itself.

Through thought and study, one can begin to understand the principle of one thing and then another, finally moving to the realization of principle itself. This realization is sagehood. It is the understanding that all things in the universe are, as Mencius said, "complete within me." The way to do this is to rid the mind of desires and to control the emotions. The mind must become serious, sincere, controlled, and balanced. The mind, and how to change its habits, then became central to the discourse and Neo-Confucians began to focus on the inward side of the self.

All of these ideas – the Supreme Ultimate, the roles of principle and of *qi*, the idea of investigating things and extending knowledge, showing that Buddhists are incorrect in saying the world is an illusion, controlling and balancing the mind – are brought together by the most famous of the Neo-Confucians, the great systematizer, Zhu Xi.

Zhu Xi (1130–1200) and Li Xue, the School of Principle

Zhu Xi taught at an academy until his death at the age of 70. He attracted many students and established what would be called the "School of Principle" because principle is central to his thinking. Zhu Xi brings together earlier ideas about *qi*, principle, the Supreme Ultimate, and an orthodox transmission of Confucianism.

Zhu Xi's understanding of principle is the same one we have just seen in the discussions from the Cheng brothers. Principle is abstract and beyond a particular time or space. It is much like the essence of a thing. There is a principle for all things, and things can only exist with a principle. Principle is eternal. It is shown in the physical world in a particular thing or event, like a rose or the practice of filial piety, but even though the rose fades and dies, principle continues to exist. Principle always exists: this means that, when we invent something new, like a computer, we are discovering the principle of computer – a principle that already existed.

On the *qi* level, we live in a physical world of particular things or events. *Qi* is found in the concrete, physical world where things are created and destroyed. *Qi* condenses and disperses as things, people, and events move through time and space.

As we saw with Zhou Dunyi, the Supreme Ultimate contains the principles of movement and stillness, operating actively as yang or congealing as yin, and, with the five phases, produces all things in the physical or *qi* world.

The Supreme Ultimate, the *Tai Ji*, and/or the *Wu Ji*, the Ultimate-less, is the most perfect principle, the totality of principle. It both changes and does not change; it both exists and does not exist. It is abstract, beyond time and space, and the "entity" that is the source of all things in the universe.

We have come to another instance of what we saw in Zhou Dunyi and his diagram. The Supreme Ultimate moves but does not move, exists but does not exist, changes but does not change. The questions are: what does this mean and why does Zhu Xi argue for it? By using two names, the Supreme Ultimate and the "Supreme Ultimate-less," Zhu Xi wants to argue that it is beyond us and requires a special insight in order to understand it. Saying that it moves allows for the next movements of yin-yang and the five phases, but, as an abstract principle – actually, as *the* abstract principle – the Supreme Ultimate cannot be said to move. If Zhu Xi had argued that the Supreme Ultimate exists, the next question is going to be, "where is it?" He wanted to say that it cannot exist in a place because it is an abstract principle. It has no form. If the Supreme Ultimate changes, then Buddhists will argue that it is like all other things that are compound and change. So, like Zhou Dunyi, Zhu Xi used both the Supreme Ultimate and the Supreme Ultimate-less as names for the highest.

The Supreme Ultimate is One; it is the totality of all principle. All things share in it because all things have principle. This means that every thing and event has the Supreme Ultimate "within" it. Zhu Xi says,

> one Supreme Ultimate exists, which is received by all individual things. The Supreme Ultimate is received by all individual things as an entire and undivided Supreme Ultimate. It is like the moon shining in the sky reflected in the lakes and rivers.[8]

Just as there is one moon with many reflections, so, too, the Supreme Ultimate is "in" all things, creatures, and events.

If, after reading this, you object that none of this sounds very much like the Confucianism you read about in chapters 2 and 3, Zhu Xi is coming to that. In human beings, principle is human nature, while the body is made up of *qi* in its different forms (bones, flesh, blood, animating energy, emotions). Principle is good, human nature is good. This, if you remember, is part of what Mencius argued, that human nature is good. Zhu Xi, however, says that, while what Mencius said is true, *qi* can cloud our human nature. Some people are simply born with a purer *qi*, while other people have a muddier *qi*. Mencius, says Zhu Xi, was talking about principle when he said that human nature is good.

For Zhu Xi, the principle in people is human nature. The mind/heart is where principle (human nature) and *qi* meet. The mind/heart is pulled in two directions: first toward the morality of the principle/human nature within us; second, toward error and desires because of the mind/heart's involvement with *qi*.[9]

Emotions are produced by *qi* and have to do with the physical world. Emotions move the mind/heart, leading to desires and excess. When mind/heart is still, like still water, emotions and desires cannot move it.[10]

As Mencius said, the sprouts of sympathy, shame/dislike, modesty, and a sense of right and wrong are found in one's principle, human nature. And, as Mencius said, when expressed concretely in this world they lead to humanity, rightness, ritual, and wisdom. While drawing heavily on Mencius, Zhu Xi's interpretation of Mencius is different from any we have seen before. Zhu Xi's position is that the state of one's *qi* leads us to develop, or not develop, the seeds within us.

Knowing that we have this marvelous principle within us, we need to find it. We do that, Zhu Xi says, by "extending knowledge and investigating things." This phrase, as we have seen, comes from the *Great Learning*. In the *Great Learning*, extending knowledge and investigating things form the basic step that will lead us to complete knowledge, then to sincerity, then to a proper mind/heart, then to the cultivation of the person, the regulation of the family, the proper government of the country, and peace for all.

When we read that we should extend our knowledge and investigate things, we might think that this would lead to the study of both humanities and sciences. However, Zhu Xi interprets the phrase to mean we must learn the principles of things.

If we contemplate things, through what Zhu Xi calls "quiet sitting" and by studying all things – history, human relations, political issues, moral behavior, the teachings of Confucius, and so on – we will come to understand the principles of each of these areas fully. We need to come to this project with sincerity and seriousness. Learning each principle is a cumulative process. While principle is different in different things, all principle is one and differs only in the way that it is manifested in *qi*. So, when we have an exhaustive knowledge of the principles of all things, we can come to an inner enlightenment, a knowledge of the principle that contains all these things, the Supreme Ultimate.

All things can be understood by reasoning, thinking, and reading. Self-cultivation is important for Zhu Xi, just as it was for early Confucians. Study is the way to self-cultivation; knowledge comes before action. We must cultivate a calm mind/heart, like still water, unstirred by emotions that can overwhelm it like waves on the water.

We can all become sages, as Confucius and Confucians have always maintained. The sage gets rid of the obstructions of *qi* and finds the principle within. Clearly this is an intellectual way to sagehood: the human problem is an intellectual problem that can be solved intellectually through study and thought. If we think, focusing on principle, in "quiet sitting," we can come to the conclusion that the Supreme Ultimate itself is reflected in us. This is an inward way where we focus, in the end, on our own natures, our own principle, our own inward processes.

Zhu Xi has given Confucianism a formally set out cosmology that links the structure of the universe with the moral and political concerns of human beings. Our moral behavior is behavior in harmony with the Supreme Ultimate. This allows Confucianism to now compete with systems like Buddhism.

Zhu Xi, like the Neo-Confucians before him, called for learning for learning's sake, not just to pass the examinations. Real learning would make a man a responsible adult, taking on family and social responsibilities. Zhu Xi firmly believed that by understanding and practicing the search for principle, a student can come to understand the true teachings of Confucianism and internalize them – not just learn them by rote.

Politically there is a principle for the organization of a state and that is the moral Dao of early Confucianism. The ancient sage-kings, Confucian heroes like the Duke of Zhou, and Confucius himself, all knew, and lived by, this principle. When the ruler and government follow it, there will be good government. Political reform is based on the reform of the individual and that, in turn, is based on a deep philosophical understanding. As with early Confucianism, the best ruler is a sage, but, according to Zhu Xi, a sage who has gotten rid of the blockages of *qi* and reaches the principle within, the Supreme Ultimate.

Zhu Xi argued adamantly against Buddhism. He said that it is because Buddhists do not understand principle that they think that this world is not real, but an illusion. Buddhists think that human nature is not really real: it is an illusion that changes at every moment and is brought together only by particular circumstances. They are wrong, says Zhu Xi, because they do not understand principle. Principle is eternal, and the belief that nothing is eternal is wrong.

Zhu Xi was a prolific writer and wrote commentaries on the classics, with a focus on the classics he used as the basis for his interpretation. These were the *Analects*, seen as the authentic words of Confucius, and the *Mencius*, a text Zhu Xi appreciated for Mencius' theory that human nature is good and for statements in the text like, "all things are complete within me," which Zhu Xi saw as the foundation of his teachings. The other two are shorter texts, the *Great Learning* and the *Doctrine of the Mean*, chapters taken from the *Book of Rites*. The *Great Learning*, as we have seen, begins with the investigation of things and extension of knowledge, leading to the moral cultivation of the individual and the peace of the world. Moral behavior and politics are firmly linked. The *Doctrine of the Mean* describes living in a state of harmony and balance. It also talks about developing the virtue of sincerity that connects us to the universe. These four books, as understood and commented on by Zhu Xi, reflect Zhu Xi's theories most closely. Zhu Xi saw them as the real foundation of Confucian thought.

While all the Confucian classics we have seen earlier[11] remained part of the official Confucian canon, these "Four Books" – the *Analects*, the *Mencius*, the *Great Learning*, and the *Doctrine of the Mean* – were singled out as the most important texts of the Confucian canon and, to a large extent, are still seen that way today. Zhu Xi's commentaries and choice of classics became the orthodox interpretation of Confucianism, maintained by the examination system and imperial patronage. This orthodoxy remained in force for the next seven hundred years and is often the foundation used by modern Confucian scholars.

Zhu Xi not only established the Four Books and his interpretations of them as the foremost texts, he also established an orthodoxy called the *dao tong*, the orthodox transmission of proper Confucianism. Zhu Xi set up a list of Confucians from Confucius to Mencius, and on throughout history. These Confucians were, according to Zhu Xi, proper Confucians. They and their texts were celebrated in the tradition. Thinkers and texts seen as dissenting from the tradition were not allowed in the imperial library and, in some cases, their books were prohibited.[12]

As intellectual interest turned to Neo-Confucianism and it became influential in the state and society at large, there was a tendency to inwardness, as people focused on inner principle, and a tendency to conservatism, as Zhu Xi's interpretations were understood to have explained everything.

Zhu Xi's *Family Rituals* set out the principle for families: the father and husband are the leaders, the wife and daughter are explicitly secondary and inferior. Just as Heaven is superior to earth, and yang is superior to yin, women are subject to the three obediences: to their father when young, to their husband when married, and to their son on the death of their husband. Neo-Confucians were adamant that widows should not remarry, but should stay loyal to their husband's memory. Histories, from local gazettes to imperial histories, began to record the fidelity of widows and they were rewarded with commemorative arches in their city or town, recording their virtue.

Zhu Xi and his successors wrote a number of pieces describing the ideal woman, who was focused solely on the family and who would subordinate herself to her male relatives and, humbly, help them in the path to achieve the Way. Women themselves were not eligible to study the Way.[13]

The highest virtues for women were loyalty and chastity. Chastity meant being a virgin before marriage; being faithful to one's husband during marriage; and remaining loyal to his memory and not remarrying after his death. Men, as you might have guessed, were not subject to these rules of chastity: male sexual behavior was only a problem when it threatened the stability of the family, and widowers were encouraged to remarry in order to carry on the family line.

The Neo-Confucian demand that widows should not remarry was based in part on the ideal of loyalty and in part because widows might well have to hold a household together, managing its finances. By tracing laws and customs governing ownership of property and of inheritance, Bettine Birge shows that up to the end of the Song dynasty women had far more property and inheritance rights than previously thought. This changed, to the detriment of women, in the following dynasties, for many reasons, including a far more rigorous application of Neo-Confucian ideals.[14]

Throughout the Song, women, particularly upper-class women, became more confined to the home. A number of factors contributed to that; one of them was the practice of footbinding. Footbinding was first mentioned in the Song dynasty, in the 1300s, but might be an even older practice. Scholars suspect that it originated with dancers in the palace, spread among palace women, and then filtered down through the population who followed it in imitation of the leisured upper classes. By the Ming dynasty (1368–1644) footbinding was widespread. Having one's feet bound was a sign of good breeding; girls with unbound feet would find it hard to marry. It was thought too that it decreased the likelihood of female unfaithfulness. The proverb was, "If you love your son, don't go easy on his study; if you love your daughter, don't go easy on her feet" – a proverb that applied of course to the gentry, but that lower classes imitated.

At about the age of four or five, two yards of bandages were wrapped around the feet to keep the feet from growing. The toes were bent under and into the sole, bones broken, and the toe and heel brought close together. The result was a three- to five-inch long foot, repulsively called "golden lilies." The practice could lead to paralysis or gangrene and death and many women could not walk without help, or needed to lean on something while standing. It was outlawed in 1911, but continued in some places into the 1920s and 30s.[15]

In the twentieth century, when Confucians were blamed for just about everything, they were blamed for footbinding as well. Given the explicitly inferior status of women in many Neo-Confucian texts, one can understand how this connection was made. However, the practice began, and spread, outside of the Confucian tradition. It is true that most Confucians did not condemn it, but the few scholars who publicly opposed footbinding did so on the Confucian grounds that it ran contrary to filial piety. Binding feet deformed the body, and, according to filial piety, we must keep our body whole, just as our parents gave it to us.[16] Many factors contributed to the status of women in imperial China, and Neo-Confucianism was only one.

Neo-Confucianism has also been criticized for being so influenced by Buddhism. Despite the rejection of, and attacks on, Buddhism, by the Song dynasty, it would have been impossible for anyone not to have been influenced by Buddhist ideas and habits of thought. Zhu Xi's contention that principle, an eternal unified ultimate, is found in all things echoes the Hua Yan Buddhist idea of principle and phenomena. The Neo-Confucian ideal of the sage who has mastered his mind, controls his emotions, understands all principle, and then understands his interconnection to all is something like the Buddhist path of meditation. However, most of these similarities are natural enough given the culture of the time. Neo-Confucianism is quite clearly "Confucian" in its loyalties, its texts, and the self-cultivation of the individual that is meant to lead to an individual taking on responsibilities in his family, society, and government.[17] It is no surprise that Neo-Confucians talked about "quiet sitting," finding the ultimate in the universe, and a number of other issues that come from the Buddhist tradition. We are all influenced by our times, and when we talk about Confucianism now we talk about it in light of science, democracy, and human rights – just as modern Confucians do.

Neo-Confucianism is Confucian in its values and terms; it is clearly not Buddhist as it affirms the world and continues the Confucian notion that human beings reflect the universe in our sense of order and value. Neo-Confucianism, especially Zhu Xi's School of Principle, was successful in turning the attention of the educated back to Confucianism and in establishing an orthodox interpretation of Confucianism that would last for centuries. With the widespread availability of books, Zhu Xi's ideas spread across China and beyond to Korea and Japan.

This does not mean, of course, that all Neo-Confucians agreed.

The School of Mind/Heart

Lu Jiuyuan (1139–93) was a younger contemporary of Zhu Xi and disagreed with him. They met to discuss their differences and carried on an extensive correspondence, but never resolved the issues that divided them. In brief, Zhu Xi argued that only human nature is principle. The mind/heart becomes involved in the *qi* world of emotions and things. As we have seen, the point is to find the principle within, and that can be done by stilling the mind/heart.

Lu, on the other hand, argued that our mind/heart is fundamentally one with the universe. Principle, he said, is nothing other than mind/heart; the mind/heart is nothing other than principle. This oneness becomes obscured by desires and the ego as we separate ourselves from the universe. In addition, Zhu Xi's ideas were too complicated and involved; understanding something innate to us should not be so difficult.

Wang Yangming

Lu's somewhat sketchy approach was taken up later in the Ming dynasty (1368–1644) by Wang Yangming (1472–1528). While still a teenager, Wang had tried to follow Zhu Xi's instructions. He spent days contemplating a stand of bamboo, trying to understand its principle, but he was unsuccessful. Giving up, he went on to pass the civil service examinations and reached high office. When he was 35, he used his office to defend other officials who had complained about corruption at court. He was arrested and beaten with 40 strokes in a public ceremony. It very nearly killed him. He was then demoted and exiled to a remote area. On his way there, his enemies at court attempted to assassinate him, but Wang escaped. It was in exile in Guizhou that Wang Yangming came to his great insight about Zhu Xi's thought. He taught, wrote, and, restored to favor, became a successful general who put down a number of rebellions against the Ming dynasty.

Wang Yangming argued first that the almost total dependence on Zhu Xi's thought had become nothing more than textual studies and that it restricted new thinking. Second, that finding principle in things was a hopeless task: he himself had spent days studying the principle of bamboo, but still there was a separation between principle and his mind. And, finally, as he realized in Guizhou, one's own nature is sufficient – it is wrong to look for principle outside of one's self in external things and events. If principle is understood as something separate from one's self, then the mind/heart is divided from principle. Principle must be seen as the same as the mind/heart. We can only understand principle by doing it.

Knowing about something and doing it are the same. If we study to find the principle of filial piety, looking for it in books, we will not really find it. But, when we love and respect our parents, we know and act out the principle of filial piety. This shows us that principle cannot be known or found outside of the mind/heart. Zhu Xi's attempt to find principle outside of the mind/heart is based on the incorrect understanding that knowledge and action are separate.

In another example, Wang says that as soon as we see flowers, we appreciate them. The knowledge of beauty and the action of appreciation are woven together; the knowledge of how to do calligraphy cannot be separated from the practice of calligraphy. So, Wang says, "Knowledge is the beginning of action and action is the completion of knowledge";[18] they are mutually interdependent.

All human beings possess an original mind/heart. As Mencius said, the four sprouts or beginnings are the external manifestations of this original mind/heart. This original mind/heart is what Wang calls "intuitive knowledge."

Our innate faculty of knowing, our moral consciousness or intuitive knowledge is the same for sages and for ordinary people. Because of our intuitive knowledge, we can see whether we are on the right or wrong course; intuitive knowledge acts like a compass. It is intuitive knowledge that promotes the good in us and it contains an emotional dimension. A truly good heart feels the emotion of sympathy for the child at the well. Intuitive knowledge is innate, as can be seen in the natural love children have for their parents. If we know about filial piety only in theory, but do not practice it, it is because knowledge and action have been separated by selfishness and we have looked for principle outside ourselves, not following our intuitive knowledge.

Like Lu Jiuyuan, Wang Yangming argued that the universe has never separated itself from people; it is people who have separated themselves from the universe through selfishness, ignorance, or incorrect thinking. We are already one with the universe because our mind/heart is the universe's mind/heart. If we have this sense of the universe, then everyone in the world is one family, as Zhang Zai said; however, if we are imprisoned by seeing principle as outside of the self, then we can see only difference and separation.

Zhu Xi and earlier Neo-Confucians were right to talk about principle and the Supreme Ultimate; they were right to say, as the "Western Inscription" does, that we are intimately connected to all people and all the things of the universe. Where they went wrong was to use an intellectual method to find principle. This will always lead to our understanding principle as something separate from us.

Wang Yangming was criticized for being a Chan (Zen) Buddhist and not a Confucian. The Chan idea that the mind naturally and intuitively knows without any dependence on anything outside of the mind certainly influenced Wang's thinking. Wang's followers debated the nature of intuitive knowledge: some argued it needed training to be found, others said it was simply natural. Some followers said they could do anything at all, as long as their intuitive knowledge justified it. The crux of the problem in Wang's thought is that it is subjective, so there is no outside standard by which behavior can be judged. If your intuitive knowledge says there is nothing wrong in killing me, I can hardly argue that your intuitive knowledge is not saying that. I can only argue that your intuitive knowledge is wrong, and, according to Wang Yangming, how can I say that?

Wang Yangming was a great example of someone who was both a Confucian scholar and active in government. His challenge to the Zhu Xi School of Principle was a serious one, and by responding to it the School of Principle had to bring its emphasis back to action.

Summary

Zhu Xi's School of Principle and Wang Yangming's school of mind/heart agree about the existence of the Supreme Ultimate, principle, *qi*, moral cultivation's relation to political action, and so on. They both agree that all human beings are related to the Supreme Ultimate. They disagree on how we should go about finding and expressing the principle within us.

Zhu Xi's School of Principle remained the dominant approach. As one might expect, by setting up an orthodox interpretation, one used in the examination system, Neo-Confucianism began to fossilize. It resulted, once again, in men who simply memorized Zhu Xi's commentaries and ignored their real meaning. However, while most literati were not very interested in practicing the Confucianism they had read, there were always those, like Han Yu and Wang Yangming, who tried to act on Confucian values. They were courageous enough to "speak truth to power," and many were demoted, or even executed, for doing so.

For example, Wei Zheng (580–643) was a famous minister to the even more famous Taizong emperor of the Tang dynasty. Wei Zheng did not hesitate to criticize his emperor and, in a letter in 637, warned the emperor that when he began his reign he had used rightness as his guide, but as time had gone on, the emperor had become careless and arrogant, and lived in luxury. Unlike most of the dynastic rulers of China, the Taizong emperor accepted the criticism. When Wei Zheng died, the emperor said that he used three mirrors: one was to straighten his cap, a second mirror was the history of the past that showed him his errors, and his third mirror was Wei Zheng. Now that Wei Zheng was dead, he said, "I have lost the most important mirror of all." Su Shi (1037–1101) was a well-known writer, poet, and statesman. He was appointed to the government of the city of Hangzhou. When he arrived, he found that drought and famine had devastated the city, and set up soup kitchens to feed the hungry. He sold rice though the government granary at a reduced rate and had the local government provide rice, soup, and medicine to those in need. He used his own money to establish hospitals. Liu Zongzhu (d.1645) was a great scholar and supporter of the Ming dynasty in its last days. Despite the Ming clearly having lost Heaven's choice in their defeat by the Manchus, Liu remained loyal to them and starved himself to death rather than serve the new dynasty. These are just a few examples of the many men who, through the centuries, tried to live according to Confucius' teachings.

Neo-Confucianism may not have been the source for the dramatic decline in the status of women during the imperial period, but it did contribute to it with its insistence that women are secondary. Women were to express Confucian values by being loyal, serving their families, and maintaining their chastity.

Neo-Confucians completed Chinese society's assimilation of Confucian ideas by producing ritual handbooks. Thinkers like Zhu Xi wrote texts setting out the proper way to conduct funerals, ancestral veneration, or weddings. Along with the rules, he explained the reason behind them and those reasons, of course, were couched in Confucian terms. They also promoted the commemoration arches for loyal widows and filial children along with government and gentry support for the building and upkeep of Confucian temples.

Neo-Confucians challenged the Buddhist idea that this world is not real, that it is a dream. The world is not an illusion, they said, nor is it a prison we must escape from. The universe holds a secret – the relationship between human beings and the Supreme Ultimate – but the universe is not a dream.

Neo-Confucianism was successful in turning intellectual interest toward Confucianism. Neo-Confucianism remained the orthodoxy for the rest of imperial China, and most modern scholars of Confucianism continue to base their interpretation of Confucianism on it.

12

Confucianism and Modernity

The Qing Dynasty, 1644–1911

The Ming dynasty was defeated by the invading Manchus in 1644. The Manchus set up their own dynasty, the Qing dynasty, and governed China in much the same way it had been governed in the Tang, Song, Yuan, and Ming dynasties.[1] The Manchus of the Qing dynasty had a problem: while they were the rulers of China, they were outnumbered one to ten. Their major concern, therefore, was to hold on to power.

While there were internal rebellions against the Manchu rulers, the real threat was to come from foreigners. Since the 1500s European powers had been traveling the globe, taking over countries and making them into colonies that they added to their empires. By the 1700s European traders had arrived in China and had accepted limited trade on Chinese terms. For the British, the one thing they wanted to buy from China was tea, and China was the only place they could get it. The British were paying gold and silver for this tea and it began to disrupt the British economy.[2]

British traders came upon another product they could sell to China to make up the gold and silver they were losing on the tea trade, and that was opium. By the 1820s opium was being smuggled into China for about one million addicts. For this kind of trade, the British needed to have a steady supply and so the British East India Company forced Indian farmers to grow opium in India, moving it to the smugglers in China. The Chinese government, facing a growing number of addicts and the drain of money flowing out of the country, continually tried to suppress the trade, finally arresting and executing some British smugglers.

So, from 1840 to 1842, the nation of Great Britain went to war with China for the right to trade in opium. The fighting was unequal: Chinese soldiers armed with muskets and lances faced British artillery and rifles. The result was defeat for China and a series of unequal treaties. These treaties guaranteed foreigners "treaty ports," that is, part of the city set aside for foreigners to live and trade in. Foreigners also had the right of extraterritoriality: the right to be tried by one's native country's courts and law system, rather than the Chinese system, even though the crime occurred in China. Foreigners ran their own courts, police, legal, and tax systems. China gave up Hong Kong and the right to set tariffs to protect Chinese industry; it lost the right to collect customs duties on trade goods and the right to control its own waterways: foreign navies could sail on any lake or river in China.

Once these concessions were made to the British, other imperial powers flooded in. China gave concessions to the French, the Germans, the Russians, and later, the Japanese. As the German Kaiser said, "We shall carve up China like a melon." Because so many imperial powers were involved, no one of them ever dominated China as the British did India. However, many foreign countries would continue to control much of China until 1949.

This foreign takeover of China had enormous effects on everything from the economy to politics to philosophy. China had always been technologically ahead of the West and had always considered itself superior to "lesser" nations abroad, but obviously the West had developed technology more quickly and much further than China. It was clear that something had to be done; what Chinese thinkers disagreed about was what to do.

Kang Youwei (1858–1927) and the Reform of Confucianism

Confucian scholars understood the problems facing China as a problem of how to apply Confucianism to a radically changing modern world. One solution they proposed was to view Confucianism as the "substance" of Chinese culture, providing moral direction, while accepting Western technology as the "application," a practical expression of modernity. This "substance/application" approach continued to be promoted by Chinese thinkers throughout the twentieth century and can be found in Japan and Korea as well.

Many reform-minded Confucian scholars established study societies to discuss how to wed the old and the new, Confucianism and modernity. They called for an end to the civil service examinations and argued that China should take ideas from the West. One of the most famous of these scholars was Kang Youwei, whose book *Confucius as a Reformer* brought a radical new interpretation to Confucianism. Confucius, Kang argued, had always been in favor of democracy, science, and women's rights. These positions had been understood by the New Text scholars of the Han dynasty, but were lost when the Neo-Confucians returned to the Old Text versions of the classics and added their own stultifying system. Returning to an "original" Confucianism, Kang argued, makes clear that Confucianism and modernity are not in conflict.

Kang Youwei continued to write, and in his *Book of the Great Unity* he argued that an elected government could evoke true humanity, allowing for the autonomy of women and a universal harmonious state. This was what Confucius had really taught, but over the centuries it had been lost. The "national essence" of Confucianism could be maintained and would fit well with modern ideas and practices. In 1898, Kang proposed that Confucianism be recognized as the official religion of China and that a Confucian "church" be set up. He proposed this again in the 1915 debates on a new constitution for China, but he was not successful. Kang's followers did set up what were called "Kongjiaohui" meeting centers, which they compared to churches.[3]

However odd Kang Youwei's ideas may sound to us now, he found support with the emperor who, in 1898, decreed a series of reforms, including a new system of national education, a new government structure, and a modern military. These reforms, and they were reforms, not a radical restructuring, are called the "100 Days of Reform" because they lasted only a few months.

The Dowager Empress, Cixi, the person really in charge of the government, put the emperor under house arrest, revoked the reforms, and executed the reformers. Kang Youwei's brother was killed and Kang himself fled to Hong Kong. This horrific response did not end the agitation for change: Chinese thinkers, Chinese living overseas, and Chinese students returning from study abroad all continued to call for the end of the Qing dynasty and for a new China. The examination system was abolished in 1905 as the Qing attempted some reform.[4] The abolition of the examination system carried the message that Confucianism was no longer the state cult, but left open the question of where China would go from there.

The Qing dynasty was overthrown in 1911 and the Republic of China established. The Republic was weak and faced a host of problems: two thousand years of tradition had evaporated; the foreigners were still in China with the same powers; there was a growing provincialism as much of China was ruled by warlords; and no one had a very clear idea of what to do.[5]

The May 4th Movement

The May 4th movement got its name because of student demonstrations against Japan's increased appetite for taking over parts of China. Students demonstrating against Japan in Beijing were shot by British troops on May 4, 1915. The May 4th movement was a movement, not a political party and not an organization. It had no membership cards and no single leader. It was more of a cultural movement articulated by novelists, poets, newspaper and journal writers, and academics, all of whom flourished in the 1920s and 1930s. They shared a strong sense of patriotism and a desire for radical change in Chinese society, government, and culture. They also shared a common enemy: Confucianism.

Confucianism was seen as the cause of all the failures of Chinese society and government. Confucianism maintained superstitious ceremonies. Confucianism's blind loyalty had led to a monolithic and fossilized society. Confucian emphasis was on the family, not the individual, as the basic unit of society. Filial piety, understood as the main teaching of Confucianism, made people subservient and dependent. It led to oppression of women and the oppression of the young by the old. Confucianism was opposed to freedom of thought, to democracy, and to science. Confucianism was the root of China's failure to fend off Western powers. Confucianism was to blame for almost everything. The slogan of the May 4th movement was, "Down with Confucius and sons," as if Confucianism was a shop where false ideas were sold.[6]

Lin Yutang wrote a play, "Confucius Meets Duchess Nanzi," drawing on the story in the *Analects* about the only woman Confucius is said to have spoken to: the traditionally wise Confucius is portrayed as a fool, while the traditionally salacious Nanzi is portrayed as wise.

Countering Confucianism, people in the May 4th movement extolled science and democracy. Science was better than the superstitious past; democracy would bring an end to filial piety and family values. Ibsen's play *A Doll's House* became wildly popular, as it was in Europe and North America. Nora's decision to leave her husband and go out of the house to find her own destiny resonated with these young people, especially women.

The May 4th writers wrote in modern Chinese, not the classical form that Confucian scholars had used for centuries, and they produced magazines, literary journals, novels, and newspapers[7] where they debated the future direction of Chinese politics, society, and culture.

One of the best-known writers of the May 4th movement was the short story writer Lu Xun. He did not spare the new Republic, arguing that the 1911 revolution was controlled by crooks and had led to death for the gullible and innocent. He criticized those who found it convenient to blame China's backwardness on the superstition of the common people: this was just an example of the educated elite deflecting blame. In one of his short stories, a madman claims that, after reading the Confucian classics for years, he has found a secret command between the lines. This secret command is "eat people." Confucian classics have taught this for so long that the entire society has become a cannibal society. Confucianism, in the end, teaches people to devour others, especially their children.[8]

The May 4th view of Confucianism is problematic in a number of ways. First, it assumes a single and unchanging Confucian tradition; second, this tradition is seen as responsible for everything evil in "old China," from footbinding to child marriages to a lack of scientific development. Obviously there were many reasons for these things. As well, they demanded the complete removal of Confucianism from Chinese culture, something that, as we shall see, is easier said than done.

However, in many ways the May 4th thinkers were accurate: Confucianism, in its orthodoxy, had become fossilized; the elevation of filial piety as the primary teaching of Confucianism allowed for all sorts of excesses in both government and the family; the Confucian tradition had contributed to a contempt for women. But is that all Confucianism is?

The May 4th movement was successful in challenging, and often overthrowing, cultural norms like footbinding, but its members never took political leadership roles.

The Guomindang and the New Life Movement

While the May 4th movement attacked Confucianism, the leadership of the Republic of China had been taken over by Chiang Kai-shek as the new leader of the Guomindang (Kuomintang, KMT), the National People's Party.[9] Thinkers in the Guomindang had understood the May 4th movement's criticisms, but argued that these criticisms applied only to decaying Manchu rule in the Qing dynasty. Confucianism was not responsible for the mess that the Qing had created. Chiang Kai-shek proposed a "New Life Movement" that used Confucian ideas of loyalty and filial piety as one of the ways to develop a responsible, patriotic, and obedient new citizen.[10] The New Life Movement wanted to use Confucian terms to reform people and, it was hoped, to make people proud supporters of the Guomindang. This was not the first time Confucian ideas had been used for other purposes. It would become a popular strategy in modern times.

The Guomindang government had the "Four Books" taught in schools, restarted the performance of rituals in Confucian temples, and officially recognized Confucius and his followers as national heroes. While this had no impact on the civil wars going on in China during the 1920s and 1930s, it did lay the groundwork for the status of Confucianism on the island of Taiwan after 1949.

The Communist Party and the Communist Government

From the 1920s on, the Chinese Communist Party accepted most of the criticisms of Confucius that had been made by the May 4th movement.

Communist theoreticians added a Marxist level to these criticisms. They argued that the Zhou dynasty had been what they described as a slave-holding society.[11] Confucius' desire to return to the Zhou made him a reactionary, fighting against the historical movement to feudalism. Coupled with this was Confucianism's association with intellectuals, a group especially despised by Mao Zedong. After the attack on intellectuals in the "Anti-Rightist Campaign" in 1957, Mao is reported to have said that, while the First Emperor buried 460 scholars alive, "we have buried 460,000 scholars, surpassing him a hundredfold."[12] By the 1950s, when the Communists had taken over China, Confucianism seemed to be pretty much a dead issue.[13]

However, when Mao Zedong, as Chairman of the Chinese Communist Party, initiated the Cultural Revolution (1966–76), Confucius once again became a player.

Mao's Cultural Revolution was meant to bring him back to power, but publicly it was painted as a revolution against those, especially in the Communist Party, who were gradually leading the country away from communism. Young people were formed into groups of Red Guards and told to destroy the "four olds," old culture, old thinking, old habits, old customs. They arrested, tortured, and killed people. They destroyed Buddhist, Religious Daoist, and Confucian temples, statues, inscriptions, art, and books.

As Confucian ideas had not been taught in China for decades, the first job was to explain who Confucius was, what he thought, and why he was an evil reactionary. Enemies of Mao, and thus of the revolution, were equated with Confucius because, it was said, they wanted to return to the bad old days of capitalism and misery, just as Confucius wanted to return to the bad old days of the slave-holding Zhou dynasty.

Once Mao Zedong died and the Cultural Revolution ended in 1976, Confucius and Confucianism in China seemed completely dead: its temples were destroyed, its books were nowhere to be found, and Confucius was a great villain of the past. But some funny things happened in the last quarter of the twentieth century.

New Confucians

While communism was attacking Confucianism inside China, scholars outside of China, especially in Hong Kong and Taiwan, were reconsidering Confucianism. What had happened to the Confucian tradition that made it so vilified by the May 4th movement and others? What had happened to China that it had fallen so far behind the West? Why was it that communism, not Confucianism, had succeeded in unifying China and making it finally independent of foreign powers?

One of the things that many Westerners often do not appreciate about China in particular, but many other East Asian countries as well, is the shock that Western imperialism brought and the corresponding pride in the defeat of that imperialism. As China's GNP grows, as China sends a manned rocket into space, as China hosts the Olympics, pride and patriotism grow. The defeat of Western imperialism, whether military or economic, is celebrated as East Asian countries not only catch up to the West but also surpass it. New Confucianism shares in this same pride and patriotism.[14]

New Confucian scholars poured their patriotic feelings into Confucianism, and in 1958 several important scholars[15] joined together to call for a return to the Confucian orthodoxy of Zhu Xi and its religious and philosophical truths. They were to begin a movement called "New Confucianism."[16] Do not confuse this with the Neo-Confucianism of imperial China. New Confucians described themselves as the "third wave" of Confucianism following the first wave, Confucius, and the second wave, Neo-Confucianism. China, they argued, had a long and unique culture that the West has not understood and this culture is based in the Confucian tradition. The original New Confucian scholars were not noticed outside of academic circles, but events outside of academia would soon change that.

Up until World War II, many Western, and some Chinese, thinkers had said that Confucianism was opposed to capitalism. With its emphasis on hierarchy and ritual, and its dismissal of merchants as just money grubbers, a Confucian society, it was said, was unable to develop a modern capitalist system.[17] This was why China and other East Asian countries had not developed economically until they dismantled their old Confucian system.

This view was proven wrong when, from the 1950s to the 1970s, Japan, Hong Kong, Taiwan, South Korea, and Singapore experienced tremendous economic growth. How had these economic miracles happened? The answer, simplistic in the extreme, was that all of these states were based on Confucianism. Confucianism had taught a strong work ethic, deference to family, obedience to authority, emphasis on education, and the virtues of thrift and self-sacrifice. These were the virtues that allowed East Asian countries to modernize so well and so quickly. The undemanding connection was made: Confucianism was common to all these cultures; therefore, Confucianism had been responsible for their success.[18]

This economic success was most gratifying, given the economic decline of the West and the slow disintegration of Western culture. Western journalists, most not well versed in Asian history and culture, bought into this notion and began to tell Western corporations that they would have to follow the Asian, and particularly the Japanese, business model. Less discussed was the backbreaking work of ordinary people, the poor pay, poverty, social inequity, and pollution that had made the East Asian economic miracle.

With the economic miracles of East Asian countries, New Confucians developed a new confidence in the Confucian tradition. Governments throughout East Asia began to bring Confucian ideas into their thinking and to have them taught in their schools. Confucianism began its comeback, even weathering the Asian stock market crashes of 1997 that might have made one doubt the "Confucianism = economic success" theory.

Confucianism as the Foundation of Chinese Culture

New Confucians like Tu Wei-ming (Du Weiming),[19] a Chinese American scholar, describe the Confucian revival as a search for roots: for him, finding one's cultural roots is finding Confucianism. New Confucians argue that only by returning to a Confucian foundation can Chinese societies maintain a solid culture. "Confucian values" are basic to the culture, attitudes, and behavior of these societies. Confucianism is not a thing of the past. It permeates Chinese culture. This is true even for the China of the time, where there was no sign of Confucianism.[20]

This is because all Chinese people share a common culture: this includes the importance of family, "family values," ancestral veneration, rituals, and the celebration of festivals. This core of Confucianism is not the Confucianism that was the state cult of imperial China; it is a "real" Confucianism, practiced by Chinese people. Real Chinese culture is based in Confucianism, New Confucians say. This has led to a debate about the role Confucian thought and values play in modern East Asia. It has also led to an examination of the problem of differentiating "Confucian" and "Chinese" values. For many New Confucians, Confucianism is understood as having a special status in China's identity both in the past and in the present. We can find people talking about a thread running through Chinese culture and history: this thread is Confucianism.[21]

Substance/Application

Back in the late 1800s, Chinese scholars had attempted to keep Confucianism as the "substance" of Chinese culture and Western technology as the practical application or function of modernity. A superior Confucianism was to act as the base of a modern society, while Western technology was only for practical use.

Many New Confucians do a version of this "substance/application" approach, saying that "Chinese culture is spiritual; Western culture is materialistic." There are criticisms of the West's obsession with consumerism and its neglect of spiritual and moral values. Implied again is the

184 Confucianism and Modernity

superiority of Chinese culture and a more religious or mystical version of Confucianism, as we shall see. Confucianism is the antidote to the faults of Western culture.[22] It is not only Chinese scholars who have developed this kind of thinking; leading scholars in the West like Roger Ames and David Hall, in their book *Thinking Through Confucius*, argue that rationality in Western thinking has failed and that the "aesthetic" approach of Confucianism works much better.

The Confucian Core

If Confucianism is the substance, the base, of all Chinese culture, and Confucianism is a good thing, how are you going to explain all the terrible things that happened in imperial China when Confucianism was in charge? The New Confucian response is that the tyrannical governments and backward societies of the past do not represent "real" Confucianism and, in fact, they stopped "real" Confucianism from developing, as it naturally would have, ideas of democracy.

What was practiced as "Confucian" from the Han dynasty to the Qing dynasty was not "Confucian" at all, just as the so-called "Christian" states of Europe did not practice real Christianity.[23] The May 4th movement's criticism of Confucianism was a criticism of social and political Confucianism, not "real" Confucianism. There is a radical difference between the "real" Confucianism, with its universal message, and the institutionalized Confucianism that was practiced in imperial China by people who did not understand Confucianism.

Do not be too surprised by this. Around the world, many traditions have been re-evaluated in this way. For example, burning women at the stake may have been done by both Catholic and Protestant Christians, but modern Christian thinkers say that was not "real" Christianity. What you may be surprised by is the description of Confucianism as religious and even mystical.

Confucianism as Religion

Most New Confucians focus on a religious dimension in Confucianism, arguing that Confucianism is a religion and always has been, when properly understood. This approach is based on passages in the *Mencius* ("all the things of the universe are complete within me") and later works like Zhang Zai's "Western Inscription." The connection between human beings and the universe has been described throughout Confucianism and it defines Confucianism. These things have been labeled as "mysticism"[24] in Confucianism, and the existence of mysticism in the tradition proves that Confucianism is a religion, according to many New Confucians. There are

Figure 12.1 Students studying at the Confucian Temple in Taichong, Taiwan

also Western scholars of Confucianism who agree that Confucianism is a religion, or at least a spiritual experience. The reason for seeing Confucianism as a religion is a desire to experience the Confucian Way. In imperial China, people simply memorized the classics to pass the examinations. The real Confucian Way must be experienced, felt, and self-transforming.

The religious, mystical understanding of the Way began with the great sage-kings of antiquity, was articulated best by Confucius and then Mencius, was lost and then picked up again by the Neo-Confucians, lost again, and rediscovered by the New Confucians. This is what the *daotong*, the orthodox teaching of the Way, is.

New Confucians often emphasize the *Book of Changes* as the one Confucian text that describes the universe as a great flow of change in which human beings find their proper place. Much of the debate about the religious status of Confucianism among Chinese scholars has also focused on issues like whether or not Confucius believed in the spirits, to what extent Heaven is a deity, and whether Confucius had the status of a god. It is interesting to note as well that many New Confucians are affiliated in one way or another with Buddhism.[25]

If Confucianism is more like a religion, New Confucians say that in order to truly understand Confucianism, one must practice it. Confucianism, New Confucians argue, is not to be understood intellectually, but should be felt and should be practiced. In order to truly understand the Confucian classics, one must approach them with respect and reverence. The core of Confucianism is reached by self-cultivation and it is only those who practice this who truly understand Confucian teaching.[26] The difficulty with this argument is that it can be used to deflect criticism from outsiders: after all, only those inside the tradition really understand it.[27]

Asian Values

The world is changing in East Asia as it is in the West. These changes make some people worry that modernization will kill traditional values. For example, industrialization splits up families; social status is decided solely by wealth; women are becoming more independent as they are able to earn a salary, and so on.

New Confucianism is often used to critique the West: Westerners do not care about their family or their elderly; Westerners are individualistic to such a degree that they are rootless; Westerners are self-indulgent; Western culture is only materialistic and this accounts for its high degree of sleaze.[28]

"Asian values" or "Asianness," on the other hand, contains the values of hard work, thrift, emphasis on education, respect for the family, humanity towards others, a connection to the past, sense of community where the community is the priority, and self-discipline.[29] These are all Confucian values, New Confucians argue, and these values have led to Asian economic dominance. Cultural or societal changes are a problem when they begin to change Asian values.

Governments

Government leaders were happy to sign on to this sort of Confucianism. After all, it leads to tremendous economic growth, an emphasis on education, harmonious relationships among citizens, and a strong state.

Taiwan

The New Life Movement, which we looked at above, was set up by Chiang Kai-shek's Guomindang party and emphasized the Confucian ideas of filial piety and loyalty. In the late 1940s, when the Guomindang lost the civil war in China to the Communists, they retreated to the island of Taiwan and continued to support Confucianism.[30] The Guomindang government saw itself as the preserver of Chinese culture and tradition, in contrast to the godless communism of mainland China. Confucianism was taught in the schools and the government financially supported Confucian temples, Confucian societies, and academic research. While this has all had a major impact on society, it is not clear that it has resulted in people identifying Confucianism as a religion, let alone their religion. When interviewed in the 1970s and asked "What is your religion?" only 1 percent of people in Taiwan replied "Confucian."[31] Despite Confucian ideas and practices being so common in Taiwan, people there have not identified themselves as practicing Confucianism as a religion. With democratic elections in the last twenty years, and the election of Democratic People's Party (DPP) candidates, government support of Confucianism declined, but the rhetoric of Confucianism has not disappeared and Confucianism continues to be taught in schools. In Taiwan, it is generally accepted that public education should include moral education and Taiwanese texts emphasize the usual filial piety, loyalty, and patriotism. People in Taiwan have, however, begun to debate Confucianism's place in a modern society.

Singapore

The city-state of Singapore, under the dictatorship of Lee Kuan Yew, had worked very hard at producing a first-class education system, and successfully graduated top-ranking computer programmers, engineers, physicists, and medical researchers. To Lee's dismay, while these young people were highly educated in their field, they had no clear sense of morality and many of them told researchers that they saw nothing wrong with cheating and dishonesty. A society that so emphasized technology had turned into a moral nightmare. In the 1970s the government responded to this situation by building up the study of Confucianism at all levels in the schools. The Confucianism that was chosen was that of the New Confucians. The level of Confucian study in Singapore had been so low that scholars from abroad had to be brought in to set up the textbooks and courses.[32] The textbooks contain many of the messages of New Confucians: there is a real Confucianism that is not the Confucianism of imperial China; learning and practicing Confucian ethics will lead the student to the self-cultivation of a strong character; when everyone practices Confucianism, society will be harmonious and Singapore will be economically prosperous.

China

In the 1970s, Deng Xiaoping, the successor to Mao Zedong, had brought in major economic reforms. People in China had realized that the Cultural

Revolution had been a hoax and now the very foundations of communism were changing too. Communism, which had given people a set of values, was bankrupt. Confucianism could be used to replace those values in ways that would be "natural" to Chinese culture. Confucianism promised, as well, to help with economic growth.

As time went on and capitalism took hold in China, the government began to worry about what they saw as the bad effects of that capitalism: dishonesty, corruption,[33] selfishness, drug use, and pornography. By the 1980s it was decided to have Confucianism taught in schools to counter the evils of capitalism and Western "spiritual pollution." As in Singapore, the level of Confucian scholarship in China was so low, given the Cultural Revolution, that foreigners had to be brought in to set up courses and textbooks at public, high school, and college levels.[34] The Confucian classics, with annotations, have been reprinted and are for sale everywhere, along with comic book versions of the *Analects* and other stories about Confucius. The government established the Academy of Chinese Culture (*Zhongguo Shuyuan*), sponsored conferences on Confucianism, and has now set up the China Confucius Foundation that has established Centers for Classical Studies all over China and abroad. In 1994, the Chinese Communist government sponsored a major conference in Beijing to celebrate the 2,425th anniversary of the birth of Confucius – a conference attended by many scholars and dignitaries, including Lee Kuan Yew of Singapore. At this celebration, the International Confucian Association (*Guoji Ruxue Lianhehui*) was formed. It continues to hold conferences and publishes a journal, *International Confucian Research (Guoji Ruxue Yanjiu).*[35]

The textbooks in schools in Singapore, China, and Taiwan all draw a line between "core" Confucianism and the Confucianism practiced in the past. In some cases "core" Confucianism is described as different from the "folk culture" of the past that developed things like the concubine system or footbinding. Texts teach students to have filial piety, to extend that respect to teachers and authorities, to be loyal to their family and country, to study hard so as to make their family proud and contribute to the economic and social well-being of society. In general, Confucianism is taught as supportive of capitalism, but also as the antidote to some of the consequences of capitalism like individualism, selfishness, and materialism.

It is not just textbooks but government policy and the laws it enacts that reflect their support for Confucianism. For example, in China, Taiwan, and Singapore there are laws requiring adult children to provide support for their parents. Critics point out that it is laws of this kind that allow the government to avoid providing old-age pensions.

Why are dictatorial governments so happy to promote Confucianism? When some scholars and government officials define Confucianism as focused on filial piety, loyalty, and hierarchy, then it is a Confucianism that fits well with authoritarianism. This kind of Confucianism is what Joseph Tamney calls "the stripped-down version of Confucianism."[36] If Confucianism is nothing more than filial piety, loyalty, and hierarchy, then Confucianism can be used to teach the acceptance of a paternal form of government that citizens, as good Confucians, should happily accept. If the family is paramount, then governments are not required to set up unemployment insurance or old-age pensions: families will take care of their own. If Confucianism contributes to a good economy and a rise in the standard of living, then the hard work and self-sacrifice of one generation benefits the next. If Confucianism is the core of Chinese culture, then it promotes patriotism.[37]

This close relationship with dictatorial governments does not reflect the views of all New Confucians. Many New Confucian scholars protested the massacre at Tiananmen Square in 1989. Xu Fuguan in Taiwan has always been a staunch supporter of democracy and has criticized Confucian scholars who aid and abet authoritarian rule, as does Martin Lee in Hong Kong. Other New Confucians, however, have not found a way to situate themselves independently in regard to authoritarian governments. However, it is not just totalitarian governments that promote Confucianism. Taiwan is a good example of a democratic form of government that also uses the "stripped-down version" of Confucianism.

Critics of New Confucianism

It is not just on the political level that New Confucianism has come in for criticism. Inside academic circles there is considerable debate. Some scholars see New Confucianism as too Western influenced; others criticize the idea of Confucianism as a "moral religion." The emphasis on an "orthodox" Confucian transmission has, in some cases, led to an idolization of the early New Confucians. Others criticize the "orthodox" transmission idea as sealing off Confucianism from new directions. Many criticize their fellow scholars for being far too anxious to support repressive and dictatorial governments. Others argue that Confucianism, understood as based on relationships and respect, chains individuals to their roles and makes them dependent on their superiors. The three basic bonds, father–son, husband–wife, ruler–minister, are criticized as domination by virtue of age, gender, and power. Others say that Confucianism developed in a world that accepted a monarch, and its political and social thought is therefore completely antithetical to democracy.[38] Still others say that Confucianism did not lead to Asian economic success and, in addition, the whole notion of "Asian values" is an artificial one dreamed up by authoritarian states to make citizens obedient to their rule. Modern Chinese scholars do not all agree: some, like Tu Wei-ming, argue that Chinese cultural traditions must be preserved; others respond that those very cultural traditions have kept China backward in the past and can lead to authoritarianism.

Outside of academia, New Confucianism has been criticized as being too interested in theory and not able to deal with the real problems of ordinary life. The use of New Confucian ideas by authoritarian governments is also, clearly, a problem. Far harsher criticisms come from people who do not accept that there is a "real" or "core" Confucianism that is different from the Confucianism that was practiced in the past. Confucianism is Confucianism and it is responsible for the disgraceful dismemberment of China at the hands of Western powers. Confucianism demands that people live, and think, in a straightjacket. Confucianism is a foe of modernization and democracy. The 1988 six-part television series *He Shang, Yellow River Elegy* argued that the backwardness of Chinese civilization, represented by the Yellow River, could only be thrown off by the rejection of tradition, especially its Confucian tradition. Some argue, too, that Confucianism can never work with modern capitalism: Confucianism emphasizes ritual and hierarchy – contrary to the cash relationships of capitalism – and Confucianism dismisses the mere accumulation of wealth.

In the New Confucian movement there are probably thousands of people, each with an individual approach to New Confucianism. People often do not agree with each other and debate is vigorous. There are, however, some commonalities among them. First, they are almost entirely male. Second, most of the New Confucians see Confucianism as central to Chinese culture. Third, they describe an "orthodox" transmission of Confucianism. Fourth, New Confucians mostly see Confucianism as religious, or at least with an emphasis on the spiritual.

New Confucianism's Impact and Importance

Chinese societies in Taiwan, Hong Kong, Singapore, and China are not all the same. Societies in other countries like South Korea and Japan are different again. Surveys find support for "Asian values" in all of these societies, but less, for example, in Hong Kong than in China. So things like divorce are becoming more socially acceptable.

However, ideas like paternal authority, that women are responsible for the housework, and that children should obey their parents are still common throughout East Asia. Rising rates of domestic violence and divorce are often blamed on Western influence. Given that government propaganda identifies Asian values with traditional family practice, changes in attitudes proceed slowly, but do proceed. It begins to look like the attempt by both governments and New Confucians to stem the tide of change may not be working.

Why should we care about New Confucianism and the way in which it plays out in governments and society? First, the government of China in particular has promoted Confucianism for a number of reasons, one of which is to establish common ground with, especially, Taiwan, Korea, and Japan.[39] Second, China is a major player on the world stage, and it will shortly be *the* major player on the world stage. How Confucianism is defined and developed in light of Chinese cultural and governmental attitudes will be crucial. How Confucius is evaluated and how Confucianism is taught is not just important in East Asia; it will affect the West in ways we cannot imagine.

Summary

There is a new movement among Asian and Western scholars called "New Confucianism." This is a re-evaluation that finds tendencies to democracy, scientific thought, and economic growth in classical Confucian thought. New Confucians argue that Confucianism as it was practiced throughout Chinese history was not authentic Confucianism, but was a misunderstood and manipulated Confucianism. These scholars say that, by understanding Confucius' teachings properly, we have a guide for modern life that is superior to the morally bankrupt Western world.

Confucianism is now taught in schools in Taiwan, Korea, Japan, and Singapore, and has been for the last 20 years in China; governments in these countries sponsor conferences, seminars, university chairs, and programs in Confucianism. The relationship between New Confucian scholars and government policy and support is not always a direct one. The Confucianism taught in schools focuses on filial piety, loyalty, forbearance (the way in which "humanity" is understood), hierarchy, hard work, education, and "Asian-ness." Critics of the New Confucians argue that theirs is simply one more interpretation and an interpretation that is not reliably based in the classical texts. Critics of Confucianism taught in schools say that this version of Confucianism is crafted merely to keep authoritarian governments in power and to teach obedience and passivity to future citizens.

By the 1970s, Confucianism looked like a dead tradition, practiced only in Taiwan and overseas Chinese communities and discussed only in abstract terms in academic circles. Within the space of a few decades, Confucianism had staged a major comeback. The tradition has revived in the twenty-first century, especially in China.

13

Issues

What is Confucianism?

By now you should have enough information to answer the question "What is Confucianism?" with another question, "Which Confucianism?" The Confucianism of the Warring States? of the Han dynasty? of the Neo-Confucians? of the May 4th movement? of the New Confucians? or of the present-day Chinese government? So, when we come to try to answer some broader questions about Confucianism, the first thing we need to do is to be clear that there is more than one Confucianism. Confucianism, as Lee Seung-hwan says, is a "discourse with a thousand faces."[1]

You also know by now that there is really no such thing as "Confucianism." The *Ru* Confucians follow *Ruxue*, the Confucian school that is not understood as based on a founder, Confucius (Kongzi), but is a tradition that began before Confucius. Confucius is the revered sage who articulated the tradition best. Confucian ideas began to gel around Confucius' teachings and around a set of texts. These ideas have been interpreted in all sorts of ways by all sorts of people in all sorts of times.

These interpretations depend a great deal on the time: the things people were talking about, the ideas floating around, the problems people in the Confucian tradition found themselves facing.

To take one example, Zhu Xi, the great systematizer of the Confucian tradition, set up a system under the impetus of Chinese Buddhism, drawing on Confucian texts and ideas, and using the Han dynasty yin-yang and five elements systems. He was educated for, and passed, the government-sponsored civil service examinations. He expressed his Neo-Confucian ideas by writing commentaries on the Confucian classics, selecting some classics as more important than others, writing ritual textbooks for people, and assigning a lower status to women. His interpretation went on to become the orthodox understanding of Confucian ideas, was mandatory study for the civil service exams, and was backed and enforced by imperial power. How can one ever disentangle "Confucianism" from imperial Chinese culture and society? What parts of the life and thought of Zhu Xi are "Confucian" and which influenced by the culture at large and the political system of the time?

We can see this all playing out again in our times with the New Confucians as they try to answer the criticisms of the May 4th movement and deal with issues like democracy and human rights – problems Zhu Xi never faced.

Another question has to do more generally with modern Confucianism's identity. Confucianism lost its official status with the end of the examination system in 1905. There were no more civil service examinations and no more Confucian-trained civil servants. Confucianism was no longer the state cult. An important New Confucian scholar, Yu Ying-shih (Yu Yingshi), has argued that without the institutional expression of Confucianism found in imperial China, Confucianism now has no specific identity.[2]

A further question arises from this: who is a Confucian and what does it mean to be one? Scholar-officials have traditionally been seen as the "Confucians," but as there is no more examination system and no more Confucian civil service, who can be a Confucian: intellectuals? all intellectuals? women? ordinary people practicing filial piety? only Asians?[3]

The "Boston Confucians" are a group of New Confucians centered around the city of Boston. They include Tu Wei-ming of Harvard, and Robert Neville and John Berthrong of Boston University.[4] They examine ways in which Confucianism can be adapted to Western culture. For example, the virtues of sincerity and honesty can be applied to any culture. They argue that Confucianism does not have to be confined to China and the Chinese, but can be practiced by anyone from any background who follows any belief.

There is no Pope in Confucianism, no head, no central council. Since the end of the Hanlin Academy in 1911, there is no one person and no body to speak with authority about what Confucianism is or is not.

Democracy

Bearing this in mind, when we want to ask the question "Can Confucianism co-exist with democracy?" we have to think carefully about what aspects of Confucianism we are talking about.

The New Confucians' answer is that had Confucianism never become tangled up with imperial politics and government, it would have developed the idea of democracy on its own. They argue this by drawing on certain strands of Confucianism. The first strand is that anyone can become a gentleman, or even a sage. It is through education and self-cultivation that we can become gentlemen or sages; it is not based on birth or social status. If we have within us the possibility of self-cultivation, then, as in a democratic ideal, we are all equal.

This presumes, of course, that education and self-cultivation are open to women, as well as men, and open to all classes of people. So it is argued that as education has been extended to include everyone as much as possible, democracy is completely compatible with the Confucian tradition.

The second strand of Confucian thought that would have developed into democracy, they say, is the idea that government exists for the benefit of the people. While Confucius and later Confucians lived in times of kings and emperors, the idea that government should benefit the ordinary person is one that, over time, could have easily developed into ideas of democracy. Surely democracy is defined as government for the benefit of the people and by the people. This is the inevitable conclusion of the Confucian ideal of government for the benefit of the people.

The third strand is the idea of the "choice of Heaven." From *The Book of History* to Mencius we find the idea that the right to rule, the "choice of Heaven," is bestowed on those who rule with the welfare of the people as foremost. The supporters of democracy use this to argue that it is obvious that ordinary people are the best judges of what benefits them and that the natural extension of the "choice of Heaven" is democracy. The "choice of Heaven" need not be a supernatural idea. If, for example, a government knows that one of its cities is in danger of flooding and, despite recommendations, does nothing about it and then does nothing much to help after the flood, it has surely lost its moral authority to rule.

Some have argued that the idea of the "choice of Heaven" includes in it the right to rebel. If a government has lost the "choice of Heaven," its moral authority to rule, then rebellion is not only justified, but proper.

Finally, "putting words right" tells us that, if rulers are good rulers, then they deserve the title of "ruler" and should continue to be the ruler. Confucians who support rulers who are bad rulers are running counter to the Confucianism they claim to follow.

"Putting words right" is an excellent tool for dealing with government issues. Not only does it get at social problems ("your call is important to us") but using it could check governments that tell us that another war is "patriotic" or a way to fight terrorism. The word "terrorism" is a good example of when we need "putting words right" to define carefully what is really meant by "terrorism."

These ideas – inclusively (that Confucianism is open to all equally) along with developing the ideas of government for the benefit of the people, the "choice of Heaven," and "putting words right" – can all be a good fit with modern ideas of democracy.[5]

Others argue that Confucianism is irredeemably elitist and anti-democratic. It is no coincidence, they say, that Confucianism has flourished under authoritarian and dictatorial governments, whether those of imperial China or modern dictatorships. This argument is based on what is seen as an "elitist" view in Confucian thought and practice.

It is not hard to find this elitist point of view. Thirty or forty years ago, one could easily find the argument that, of all the people in the world, the Chinese were a singular people whose culture could not support democracy. During the 1970s and 1980s, I began to feel that I was eternally condemned to having to argue against this. My arguments were with a number of educated Chinese people and some Westerners. Both groups cited the particularity of Confucian culture as the reason for their anti-democratic views. Lee Kuan Yew, the leader of Singapore, wrote in 1994 that "The Confucianist [*sic*] view of order between subject and ruler helps in the rapid transformation of society. I believe that what a country needs to develop is discipline more than democracy. Democracy leads to undisciplined and disorderly conditions."[6] One would have thought that the development of democratic elections in Taiwan would have ended this view, but fist fights in the legislature and instances of corruption are used as further "proof" that democracy cannot exist in Chinese culture.[7] Of course, all modern democracies began this way. Still, it is not hard to find an elitist view throughout East Asia. The educated and competent, it is believed, should rule on behalf of the uneducated and dim-witted masses – benevolently of course.

Critics argue that the ground of this elitist view is the Confucian notion of government. While government is for the benefit of the people, Confucianism argues that this is a moral obligation of the gentleman in government who must guide the people because they are incapable of making decisions for themselves. The idea that an educated gentleman is responsible for caring for the people is, in itself, anti-democratic. This argument is backed up with quotations like the one from the *Analects*: "The virtue of the gentleman is like the wind and the virtue of the common people is like the grass: when the wind moves, the grass is sure to bend."[8] Critics say that elitism is part of the fabric of Confucianism and so Confucianism is not compatible with democracy.

The Emphasis on the Economy

Whether in the West or in East Asia, it is the modern conceit to judge all things by money. We are dominated by Mozi's thinking, not Confucius': if something is a good thing, it is because it makes money. Everything is quantified in terms of dollars and cents. Movies are judged not by whether they are any good, but by how much they make at the box office. The aim of education is to give us a job that pays well. Heaven help poor students who are "just" getting an Arts degree: whatever will they do with their lives? They will not be able to make money and so the degree is useless.

Many New Confucians credit Confucianism with an important role in the economic success of East Asian countries, as we have just seen. Confucianism is a good thing because it leads to greater wealth. This, however, runs against classical and imperial Confucian ideas about money. Confucius says, "Eating ordinary food, drinking water, and having one's elbow as a pillow – there is joy in this! Wealth and high position – when gotten improperly – are no more to me than passing clouds."[9] In the *Thousand Character Classic*, the first book studied by children in much of imperial China, merchants are given last place in the social structure. Throughout the Confucian tradition, making money was seen as somewhat undignified. It certainly took second place to becoming educated.

So what are we to make of this? Following Confucianism does not exclude becoming wealthy, say some. Others argue that we cannot follow Confucius by buying into the values of the modern world, particularly its obsession with money.

Ritual

While we are unlikely to want to return to a world of bows, curtseys, and "at home days," any more than we would want to start wearing powdered wigs, Confucian ideas of ritual may be something we would want to consider. Ritual, defined as an exchange of mutual respect, is not a bad thing. Ritual is a moral action that ensures a proper, civilized society. Ritual is civilized behavior and it can also function as a way to restrain our selfishness and channel our emotions. Would the practice of ritual help us cure the modern-day blight of rudeness? Would teaching rituals to children make for a better society? Would relationships based on ritual, rather than the exchange of money, lead to a better society or a worse one?

We still practice rituals like weddings and funerals. One ritual that Western cultures no longer have is coming-of-age rituals. Maybe we should. One of the things that coming-of-age rituals do is to define what it is to be an adult. In Western culture, we see a continual infantilization of adults, who are not expected to act like adults, and, indeed, are encouraged to be childish.[10] Conversely, in places like Taiwan and China there is a lot of conversation about the notion of responsibility and what it means to be an adult.

Filial Piety

Can filial piety work in a modern society? When I survey my students, I find that most of them like the idea of filial piety, but understand it more as affection for parents than as obedience to parents. When it comes down to it, the doctrine of individualism, taught to us in movies and TV, dictates that children should follow their own hearts, no matter how much they love their parents. Should we pay more attention to parents' wishes? After all, our parents cared for us for all the years that we were helpless. Parents are older and may have more experience of the world. Most parents want the best for their children.

Should parents expect more filial piety? In much of Chinese culture, it is not the parents who enforce respect and filial piety from the children; the onus is on the children to provide it. If there is conflict between children and parents, it is not a failure in parenting, but the children's fault for not understanding what they are supposed to do.

Can filial piety be taken too far? How far is a child expected to go in practicing filial piety? In the *Analects* Confucius says that a good son should protect his father, even when his father is a criminal. Most of us would feel uncomfortable with this. Again, the tool of "putting words right" is useful. If a parent is abusive, then that parent is not behaving as a parent should and does not deserve the title "father" or "mother" and thus does not deserve filial piety. This is not what Confucius and the Confucian tradition construed filial piety as meaning: for most of them filial piety was to be unquestioning obedience.

Education

Much has been made recently of Confucianism's emphasis on education. From Confucius himself encouraging his students to learn, through the classical and imperial eras, and today, education is a constant in Confucianism.

But what kind of education are we talking about? Is it education, as much education is today, that aims at teaching job skills and turning out technocrats? Both West and East spend the bulk of their education dollars on education that is "useful." A "useful" education is thought to be one where the student learns useful, often quantifiable, things that will get them a good job and, in return, the student will be useful to the economy when he or she graduates. The spirit of Mozi is alive and well.

In classical Confucianism, education was not seen that way. Education aimed at producing knowledgeable people who learned moral lessons from what they were taught. They were then expected to go out into the world and change it, making society more civilized and government more caring and responsible. Apparently, students who are "just" getting an Arts degree are doing exactly the right thing. Given the corrupt governments and morally bankrupt societies most of us live with and in, perhaps we might give the classical Confucian ideas about education a second thought.

Self-cultivation

The Confucian idea of "self-cultivation" is also a notion worth looking at. We can tend to the moral virtues within us, practicing them daily, watching ourselves carefully. We are building up the virtues of honesty, sincerity, sympathy for others, and so on. The point is to come to humanity, an ethical attitude. Confucius did not demand that we become perfect human beings immediately; this is a task that takes some time and considerable care. If we do this, and do it properly, then in a crisis or a situation where we have to make a quick decision, we can trust a moral compass within us. Self-cultivation is not something we practice for our private satisfaction or because it leads us to some sort of enlightenment. It is meant to allow us to act, and act properly, in our family, our neighborhood, and our country. Perhaps our society would be better off if we talked about self-cultivation.

Does Confucianism Include Women? Can Confucianism Include Women?

> Mao Zedong said, "Women hold up half the sky" and Chinese women say, "But why is it always the heavier half?"

In the last 50 years, scholars around the world have looked again at the great traditions and re-evaluated them in light of feminist theory and gender discourse. In general, modern scholars have used four main approaches to question the tradition about the history of women and to establish a place for women in the modern tradition.

First, they look at women in the history of the tradition, their accomplishments, and their status. Second, they look at the texts of the tradition, if applicable, to see what attitudes there have been about women, how these may have changed over time, and what reasons there were for these changes. Third, they look for a basic message in the tradition to see if that can indeed include women. Finally, they re-evaluate the past in light of this basic message.

Taking Buddhism as an example, in step one scholars find that women played an important role in early Buddhism, had more social freedom in the Buddhist community, were students, teachers, and missionaries, and became enlightened. In step two, they find that the later the Buddhist sutras, the more anti-women the sutras tend to be, until finally women are told they cannot become enlightened as long as they are women. In step three, in Mahayana Buddhism, the basic message, they say, is that all sentient beings contain the Buddha nature and therefore men and women can become enlightened equally. Finally, they reject a past that discriminated against women as incorrect and not in keeping with the basic message of Buddhism. One should note that this does not mean that Buddhist attitudes around the world have changed and that women are admitted equally with men – scholarly influence is slow in moving thousands of years of culture.

Scholars re-evaluating the Confucian tradition do many of the same things. First they look at women in the history of Confucianism. Unlike the enlightened female followers of the Buddha or the female disciples of Jesus, there are no women recorded as Confucius' students. One can begin with a text we looked at in the Han dynasty (chapter 9), the *Biographies of Women* by Liu Xiang, containing over one hundred biographies of famous women, like Mencius' mother. We see portraits of women in traditional roles, but being active and virtuous, that is, Confucian. More famous is Ban Zhao. Ban Zhao's *Admonitions for Women* advocates education for women because of their important role in the inner world of the home, which is a foundation for the outer. She believed the rules of proper behavior had been set out in the Confucian classics and that they applied to both men and women. Ban Zhao is the first example of a long list of female authors who, throughout imperial China, wrote texts for women, poetry, and biographies.

Second, scholars look at the Confucian canon to see what attitudes there have been about women, how these may have changed over time, and what reasons there were for these changes. As we saw in chapter 3, *The Book of Poetry* contains love poems by women, but we find negative sayings about women as well. In *The Book of History* we see active women, involved in the politics of their day, but more often women are portrayed as leading rulers astray. In both *The Book of History* and the *Zuo Zhuan* the bad decisions of rulers are often said to have been caused by the beautiful women around them. In the texts devoted to rituals, we see both men and women venerating ancestors, for example, and the growth of the idea that men should be active outside the family, while women are active inside the household. The separation of the sexes and the division of their responsibilities is found in all the ritual texts. Other Confucian classical texts continue these themes. None of the Confucian classics label women as evil, but there is debate as to whether this division between men and women means equality or inequality.

When we move to the Han dynasty yin-yang texts, the debate continues: some argue that the yin-yang texts cement the inferiority of women in a cosmic scheme; others claim that the yin-yang theory is complementary and works for the equality of men and women.[11]

Most agree, however, that the status of women declined throughout imperial China. At birth, a girl was called a "small happiness" or "goods on which one loses" because of the custom of daughters marrying out of the natal family and living with their husband's family. By the Song dynasty, daughters had their feet bound. Daughters in well-to-do families received some education, though not as much as their brothers.[12] Most women had little power in their husband's household and were subject to attitudes – and laws – about maintaining their chastity and prohibitions against remarriage if they were widowed.[13]

Two very famous stories with Confucian themes about quite different women come from the imperial age. The first is the story of Yang Guifei, the beautiful concubine of emperor Xuanzong (712–55), who was deeply in love with her. In the face of a rebellion, the emperor was forced to flee the palace and his military escort demanded the head of Yang Guifei. They said that she was the cause of the emperor's misrule and this rebellion; apparently the emperor himself had nothing to do with it. Broken-hearted, the emperor agreed, and, after her death, returned to his throne, saddened, but poetic about it. The second is the story of Hua Mulan (*c*.500). When China was divided between the Northern Wei dynasty and the Liang, she was a great example of filial piety: her ill father was conscripted and her brother too young, so she disguised herself as a man and went in his place. Her chastity was preserved because no one suspected she was a woman. She served brilliantly in the army for twelve years, becoming a general. She returned home and took up her womanly duties.[14] The story of Yang Guifei is like the stories in the Confucian classics in which a beautiful woman leads her emperor to destruction. The story of Hua Mulan is like the stories of filial piety in which the filial daughter offered her life in place of her father's.

So, if there are no female models among Confucius' students, can one look to women like Ban Zhao and Hua Mulan as examples of a Confucian woman? Is there a basic message in Confucianism by which to judge the history of Confucianism and which would include women? Yes, say some. This is "education without distinction." Some argue that Confucius meant to include women in his view that education should be open to all; others say that, even if that was not what Confucius meant, it can now be understood that way. Confucians never argued that women were irrational or incapable of morality. So, given the same education, women can become just as moral as men.[15] The point is that if education is open to both men and women, then both men and women can study the classics, use self-cultivation, and become gentlemen. In English, the sentence "a woman can become a gentleman" sounds a little odd given that "gentleman" is a word with obvious gender expectations, but in Chinese, saying a woman can become a *junzi* works better (even though, as a class of knights originally, it too has some gender expectations).

The basic message of Confucianism is that everyone, man or woman, can become an ethical person through education, and everyone can work in society for the betterment of society.

If that is so, then how do we understand the past? Like New Confucians, some scholars of Confucianism argue that much of the past was not real Confucianism.[16] Excluding women from a real education was not following the message of Confucianism. The Confucians of the past were too much influenced by the culture around them and did not really understand the message of Confucianism. Confucian ideas of gender were formed by the culture around them; as well, they did not think through the moral implications of "real" Confucianism. It is perfectly possible to reject Confucianism's view of women while remaining faithful to Confucianism.

Critics

As you can imagine, all of this is extremely controversial. Critics of Confucianism argue that Confucianism is a male-dominated philosophy that has always spoken to men's concerns. Confucianism has in the past, as it does now, excluded women from public life. Confucianism supports rigid gender roles that make women secondary to men. It supports a patriarchal family and a patriarchal state.

The Confucian classics set out this secondary status for women quite clearly and it was then cemented in place by the ideas of yin and yang which made women's lowly status a matter of cosmic order.

The basic message of Confucianism is that what men do and what men think is important, while what women do is not. This, critics argue, is the only way to understand the Confucian tradition and its history. When Confucianism excluded women from the public arena and believed that women could only be active in the home, this meant that women did not need an education and so could not practice self-cultivation or become gentlemen. Confucianism not only theoretically and practically excluded women from government roles, but also limited women's ability to be independent moral actors by demanding women's obedience to father, husband, and son.

This plays out even today, critics say, in the New Confucian movement, where almost all the participants are male and where discussions of modern ideas of gender equality are very rarely heard. New Confucianism teaches filial piety and loyalty, but this is filial piety and loyalty in the context of a patriarchal family and society. All that many New Confucians say to women is that they must preserve Asian values and not become Westernized – that is, independent.

The differences between those who would redeem the Confucian tradition and make it more open to women, and those who think that Confucianism cannot be redeemed and cannot include women, are wide indeed.

How this will play out is still very much up in the air. There are reports that women in both Taiwan and China are beginning to perform ancestral veneration for their own, natal, ancestors in the female line. As well, women in East Asia are becoming better educated and, gradually, have more job opportunities. What will that mean for their acceptance or rejection of Confucian ideas?

Is Confucianism a Religion? A Philosophy? Something Else?

As you have gone through this text, it may have seemed to you that Confucianism is more like a philosophy than a religion in one section and then more like a religion than a philosophy in the next. So, which is it?

Westerners have a long history of discussing this problem. When the Catholic missionary order, the Jesuits, first went to China in the 1500s they saw people bowing to Confucius' tablet in Confucian temples. When they asked if this was a religion they were told it was not. It was simply an offering of respect and reverence to the great teacher. Of course, the people they asked about this ritual were the upper class, educated, elite. Similarly, when they saw people performing rites of ancestral veneration, they under-stood these rites as reverence for one's ancestors and rituals of thanks and praise. They conflated ancestral veneration and Confucianism, and the Jesuits decided that Confucianism was not a religion. Once the Jesuits began to translate "Confucian" texts, these translations had an enormous impact on European and North American thinkers of the Enlightenment[17] who were delighted with an example of a non-religious state that could still be civilized and successful.

When another Catholic order, the Franciscans, went to China, they worked with the poor and found Chinese people "worshipping" their ancestors as if they were gods. This, the Franciscans said, was idolatry and not the memorial service the Jesuits, who had been talking to the educated elite, had said it was. This began the "Rites Controversy" about whether or not ancestral veneration was a memorial service or an idolatrous worship of gods. This controversy spread all over Europe and was a major subject of debate – despite it being based on the smallest possible amount of knowledge. In the late 1700s the Pope decided in favor of the Franciscans. Ancestral veneration was religious and any Chinese person who wanted to convert to Christianity must cease practicing it. Confucianism, so closely identified in the Western mind with ancestral rites, was then thought to be a religion.

While both Protestant and Catholic authorities eased the restrictions on performing ancestral rites by the 1920s, the Western assumption that

Confucianism is a religion has continued. Confucianism is generally – though not entirely – taught in university departments of Religious Studies and appears, labeled as a religion, in most textbooks that cover world religions. Confucianism is rarely taught in Philosophy departments – reserved for the study of white European males – though courses may be offered in East Asian Studies departments.

Confucianism is defined as a religion not just in the Western mind, but, as we have seen, the New Confucians often stress a religious dimension to Confucianism, arguing that Confucianism is not just rote learning, but something to be practiced and experienced.

If Confucianism is a religion, what are the kinds of things we would expect to see? We think of religions as having moral teachings, a history of maintaining an orthodoxy, temples, ritual, a following (though not a congregation in, for example, the Christian sense), a set of texts considered to be very important, and some sense of the metaphysical in, for example, the concept of Heaven. Confucianism has all of that.

What would we expect to find in a religion that we do not find in Confucianism? There is no priesthood, no central leader, no congregation (that might, for example, support the building and upkeep of a temple), no sacred texts, no God or gods.

So it may be that the expectations we have around the word "religion" make for the difficulty in defining Confucianism.[18] Are we the ones who assume that religion is separate from secular activities? Are we making assumptions that religion must be defined as something centered around temples, texts, and a sense of the sacred? Is this why the Confucian school (*jia*) or teachings (*jiao*) do not fit our expectations? Perhaps it is our definition of religion that is the problem here. So when we look at Confucianism and see things like an emphasis on practice, temples, and lack of a central deity, we find ourselves at a loss.

The same sorts of problem develop when you try to define Confucianism as a philosophy. What sort of things do you expect to find in a philosophy? How is philosophy distinguished from religion?

Another consideration for this discussion is one thing Confucianism does not do, and has never done: there are no sanctions in Confucianism. Many Christians believe that bad people will go to hell when they die. In Buddhism, bad people build up karma and will have a very unpleasant rebirth in the next life. In the Confucian tradition, if someone behaves badly, the worst you can do is say to them, "Well, you are no gentleman!"

This lack of sanctions has, historically, allowed the corrupt, the cruel, and the bullies to do whatever they like, safe in the knowledge that not much can be done about them. I have witnessed instances of ill-treatment of children, students, and subordinates by parents, professors, and bosses that I would describe as abuse. The children and subordinates have, almost uniformly, tried to practice humanity and moral virtues in the face of this abuse, but no such reflection ever seems to have been required from the parents, teachers, or employers. Expectations about behavior and attitude often seem to apply only to some. This lack of sanctions has, in practice, associated Confucianism with all the things the May 4th movement complained about.

On the other hand, this lack of sanctions is a grand thing. The Confucian tradition does not threaten one with hellfire, but calls us to look at ourselves first and monitor our own behavior. If we know that we should act with humanity, we are then supposed to do that. We act from humanity not because we will be rewarded in the next life, but simply because it is the right thing to do. We are, in the end, adults who are responsible for what we do, and we are responsible for doing it well, none of which, unfortunately, can answer the question of whether or not Confucianism is a religion, a philosophy, or something else.

Summary

Over 2,500 years ago, Confucius lived in a world where standards were declining, sleaze and corruption were everywhere, and most people were behaving badly. Confucius' solution to the problems of his time was twofold: reform of the individual and reform of society. He taught filial piety, dutifulness, honesty, sincerity, rightness, wisdom, moral courage, and sympathy for others. These are things we can cultivate within us. If we study and cultivate the virtues within us, we can come to the general moral attitude of humanity. Humanity, expressed through ritual, allows us to act properly in the world. Doing this makes us gentlemen or, if we do it very well, sages.

Not only are we to act as moral people in the world, we can transform our society by putting words right, by ensuring that government acts for the benefit of the people, and by being models for others.

After his death, Confucius' followers faced attacks from Mohists, Daoists, and the many thinkers of the Warring States era. In defense of Confucius, Mencius was the first to come up with an interpretation of Confucius' thought that would deal with the new problems Mencius faced. He argued that our human nature is good and reflects the goodness of Heaven. Confucius' ideas of morality were not just a matter of taste, but natural to human beings and linked to the cosmos itself.

Xunzi rejected Mencius' interpretation and defended Confucius, using another approach. Human nature is evil. The sage-kings set up an artificial morality and that is what Confucius taught. Confucius understood that morality was imposed on us; that was the true basis of his teachings.

In the Han dynasty, the New Text scholars believed that they had found the universal basis of Confucius' teachings in the yin-yang and five phases theories. This too connected Confucius' ideas to the workings of the universe. During the Han dynasty four important developments began for the Confucian tradition: the use of the yin-yang and five phases theories; the association of Confucianism and certain texts; the beginnings of a civil service examination system; and the growth of interest in the Confucian idea of filial piety.

For the next seven hundred years, Confucian studies slept, while intellectual interest turned to Buddhism. Confucianism did not disappear because of its relation to the important idea of filial piety and the revival of the civil service examination system. Imperial governments built and funded Confucian temples, loaded Confucius with titles, and used Confucianism as the state cult. Confucianism also spread to Korea, Japan, and Vietnam.

Confucianism went through a great revival in the Southern Song dynasty as Neo-Confucian thinkers reshaped Confucius' ideas. This all came together in the thought of Zhu Xi, who connected Confucius' ideas with the Supreme Ultimate and with principle. Through study and introspection, we can come to know all principle, the Supreme Ultimate itself. Zhu Xi's system became the standard and orthodox interpretation throughout imperial China and, for the most part, remains so today.

The twentieth century saw the uncoupling of Confucianism from the Chinese state with the end of the civil service examination system. The May 4th movement attacked Confucianism, blaming it for the backwardness and weakness of Chinese society and government. Attacks continued under the Communist government, and by the early 1970s Confucianism in China seemed well and truly dead.

However, two things restored Confucianism: the New Confucian scholarly movement and the economic success of "Confucian" societies like Japan, South Korea, Taiwan, Singapore, and Hong Kong. Bringing in its own economic reforms, China followed suit. Confucianism is now taught in schools all over East Asia and governments support Confucian temples, institutes, and scholarship.

Confucianism in our times still faces a number of problems: how compatible is it with democracy, human rights, feminism, and consumerism? Who can tell in what ways Confucianism will develop? Despite the pounding it has taken in its trip through the rapids of history, Confucianism has arrived, somewhat the worse for wear, in the twenty-first century. Throughout history, Confucianism has seemed to be heading toward extinction only to revive in a new incarnation.

As for Confucius himself, surely it is the breadth and depth of his ideas that have allowed so many, and so many different, interpretations throughout history. We might want to look very carefully at what Confucius says, because, like him, we live in a society that is simultaneously childish and sleazy, where ignorance and the military are celebrated, and where socio-paths are applauded as men with business sense.

It is not just Confucius' thought but also his life that can be a model. We can get rid of our cartoon picture of Confucius. He was no boring old fogy churning out dull maxims, but a person who fought with passion and wisdom against the enveloping darkness.

Notes

Notes to Chapter 1

1   Confucius say, "Man who run in front of car get tired." Confucius say, "Man who keep feet firmly on ground have trouble putting on pants." And so on and so on.
2   Lonely Planet, "Shanghai Confucian Temple" entry; see www.lonelyplanet. com/china/shanghai/sights/369485.
3   There are two systems of transliteration for Chinese: the older Wade–Giles system and the newer Pinyin system. I will use the Pinyin system in the text, but both systems in the notes and glossary. The Pinyin comes first, then the Wade–Giles, divided by a slash, for example Kongzi/K'ung Tzu. As Pinyin is still sometimes daunting for English speakers, I have included an approximate pronunciation in the Glossary.
4   For a description of Western attitudes toward Confucianism, see Seung-hwan Lee, *A Topography of Confucian Discourse: Politico-philosophical Reflections on Confucian Discourse Since Modernity*, trans. Jaeyoon Song and Seung-hwan Lee (Paramus: Homa and Sekley Books, 2006), Ch. 2.
5   Lewis argues that the emerging elite of the Warring States sought sanction and precedent and so re-imagined Chinese history where gods become sage-kings. The point the elite was making was that institutions were neither natural nor supernaturally created, but created by human beings. It was rulers, through their powers, who created civilization and society, perhaps the most radical claim to political authority ever. See Mark Edward Lewis, *Sanctioned Violence in Early China* (Albany: State University of New York Press, 1990), 210–12.
6   *The Book of History*, "Zhou, Jin Teng"; compare James Legge, *The Chinese Classics. Volume 3: The Shoo King, or The Book of Historical Documents* [*Shu Jing, Book of History*] (1865; reprinted Hong Kong: University of Hong Kong Press, 1960), 351f. For more on *The Book of History*, see chapter 8.
7   Ghost-spirits, *guishen/ kui-shen*, is a phrase commonly used in classical texts to refer to supernatural powers of gods, ancestors, and the spirits of the dead.

8   *The Book of History*, "*Da Yu Mo, Gao Yao*"; compare James Legge, *The Shoo King [Shu Jing, Book of History]*, 74.

9   The period of the Eastern Zhou, where the capital city is in the east, is further divided into the Spring and Autumn period (named after the Spring and Autumn annals), 722–481 BCE, and the Warring States Era, 403–221 BCE. Officially, Zhou rule lasted until 256 BCE when the last Zhou ruler was killed, but effectively the Zhou had no power by 403 BCE.

10   *Zuo Zhuan*, Duke Huan, 16th year. For more on the *Zuo Zhuan*, see chapter 8.

11   The *Zuo Zhuan* is full of such stories. In 548 BCE, Duke Zhuang of Qi carried on an affair with the wife of one of his advisors. His advisor, allying himself with another state, surprised the duke who was visiting his lady friend and had him killed (Duke Xiang, 25th year). King Ling of the state of Chu had become ruler by murdering his nephew. He accused his grand marshal of treason and took all of his property, seized the lands of another noble, and took over various regions that had been fiefs of other noble families. His rule was so corrupt and violent that three of his younger brothers revolted against him and killed him in 529 BCE (Duke Zhao, 12th year). Compare Burton Watson, trans., *The Tso Chuan [Zuo Zhuan]: Selections from China's Oldest Narrative History* (New York: Columbia University Press, 1989), 168f.

12   *Zuo Zhuan*, Duke Ding, 3rd year; compare Watson, trans., *The Tso Chuan [Zuo Zhuan]*, 178.

13   *Zuo Zhuan*, Duke Xuan, 2nd year. Duke Ling also is described as imposing heavy taxes to decorate his buildings; compare Watson, trans., *The Tso Chuan [Zuo Zhuan]*, 77f.

14   *Zuo Zhuan*, Duke Ai, 1st year.

15   *Zuo Zhuan*, Duke Ai, 16th year. Compare Watson, trans., *The Tso Chuan [Zuo Zhuan]*, 206.

16   *Zuo Zhuan*, Duke Xiang, 25th year. Compare Watson, trans., *The Tso Chuan [Zuo Zhuan]*, 47.

17   For an excellent description of the changes in the Warring States period, see Mark Edward Lewis, *Sanctioned Violence in Early China*. To see the kind of clothing people wore, the weapons they used, and the palaces royalty lived in, see the movie *Hero* (Zhang Yimou, 2002). The plot, however, is fantastical.

18   *Analects* 14.38. The standard translation of the *Analects* is D. C. Lau's *Confucius: The Analects* (New York: Penguin, 1979 and reprinted frequently). In the citations from the *Analects* I am using Lau's standard numbering system; readers can compare that to other translations. Since Lau's work there have been more scholarly translations including Roger Ames and Henry Rosemont, Jr., *The Analects of Confucius: A Philosophical Translation* (New York: Ballantine Books, 1998), which includes useful information about the formation of the text, including the partial text discovered in 1973 in Dingzhou, Hebei. See also Edward Slingerland, *Confucius: Analects with Selections from Traditional Commentaries* (Indianapolis/Cambridge: Hackett Publishing, 2003), which includes helpful commentaries to explain the terms and sometimes cryptic sayings of the *Analects*. Two good, non-scholarly translations are David Hinton's *The Analects* (Washington: Counterpoint, 1998) and Simon

Leys (Pierre Ryckmans), *The Analects of Confucius* (New York: W.W. Norton and Co., 1997); the translations are readable and the books include good introductions to the text.

19 I will give a brief description of these texts as we go along, but for a more complete description, see chapter 8.

20 For discussions about the composition of the *Analects*, see Bryan Van Norden, "Introduction" in *Confucius and the Analects: New Essays*, ed. Bryan Van Norden (New York: Oxford University Press, 2002), 3–36. See also E. Bruce and Taeko Brooks, *The Original Analects: Sayings of Confucius and His Successors* (New York: Columbia University Press, 1998), for a good description of the theories around the formation of the text and their own proposal that the *Analects* is layered in four levels. For a description of a number of the versions of the *Analects* and related texts from the Han, see Mark Csikszentmihalyi, "Confucius and the *Analects* in the Han" in Van Norden (ed.), *Confucius and the Analects: New Essays*, 144f.

21 *Analects* 5.10.

22 *Analects* 10.17.

23 For a painstaking examination of the issues involved in the accounts of Confucius' life, see Shigeki Kaizuka, *Confucius: His Life and Thought*, trans. Geoffrey Bownas (New York: Macmillan, 1956).

24 His dates are tentatively given as 624–529 BCE. For a reference to He of Zou, traditionally identified as Confucius' father, see the *Zuo Zhuan*, Duke Xiang, 10th year (563 BCE); compare Watson, *The Tso Chuan [Zuo Zhuan]*, 139.

25 In some stories, we are told that her first son was deformed and so unable to perform sacrificial rituals. Confucius was a second son.

26 Later, as was customary, taking another name or "style," Zhongni.

27 Some scholars are suspicious of the reports of Confucius' rise in rank in the government of Lu that we find in the traditional stories. They think that, as time went on, there was a gradual addition to Confucius' rank. See, for example, David L. Hall and Roger Ames, *Anticipating China: Thinking through the Narratives of Chinese and Western Culture* (Albany: State University of New York Press, 1995), 201.

28 *Analects* 9.6.

29 For a discussion of the use of the word "knight" as noble or true manhood, based on noble birth, see Lewis, *Sanctioned Violence*, 32.

30 Enumerated in *The Book of History*, "Shun Dian," and in the *Zhou Li*. "Accomplishments" is often translated as "arts," but they were skills, not fine art, crafts, or techniques.

31 *Analects* 2.2. The Book of Poetry is a collection of 305 poems and songs, taught by Confucius and, it was believed in the past, edited by him. The poems include everything from praise of the early Zhou rulers to romantic love poems. See chapter 8.

32 *Analects* 16.13.

33 *Analects* 17.9.

34 *Analects* 7.32.

35 *Analects* 11.26.

36   *Analects* 7.14. The *Shi Ji* adds to this story by saying that when Confucius was in Qi, he discussed music with its Music Master and, when he heard the *Shao*, studied it. *Shi Ji* "Kongzi Shi Jia."
37   *Analects* 17.21.
38   *Analects* 7.8.
39   *Analects* 9.23.
40   *Analects* 9.4.
41   *Analects* 2.4.
42   *Analects* 7.3.
43   *Analects* 7.16.
44   *Analects* 5.26, following Slingerland, *Confucius: Analects* 50.
45   *Analects* 7.19.
46   *Analects* 9.12.

Notes to Chapter 2

1   The term filial piety is not found on the oracle bones from the Shang dynasty. It develops an independent existence quite late. It is found on the bronze vessels and in *The Book of Poetry* and *The Book of History*. From the early Zhou on, filial piety is closely tied to blood relationship, particularly in the performance of family and clan sacrifices. Many commentators argue that, although the character itself is not found on the oracle bones, the Shang and earlier societies give clear evidence of clan and family solidarity and a continuation of the clan's relationship with the dead. This is the basis of the ideal of filial piety. Rosemont and Ames suggest alternative translations for *xiao* such as family responsibility, family deference, family feeling, or family reverence; see Henry Rosemont Jr. and Roger Ames, *The Chinese Classic of Family Reverence* (Honolulu: University of Hawai'i Press, 2009), 1.
2   *Analects* 2.5.
3   *Classic of Filial Piety*, SPPY ed., 2.8; compare Rosemont and Ames, 111.
4   *Classic of Filial Piety*, SPPY ed., 2.7b; compare Rosemont and Ames, 110.
5   *Analects* 17.21.
6   *Analects* 13.18. See also the *Mencius* 7A:35 for a similar point of view. Mencius used the example of the sage-king Shun, and the stories of his filial piety toward parents who did not love him, as the highest examples of moral behavior.
7   Quoting the *Analects* 2.5, Liu JeeLoo says filial piety is not blind: respect is not due an elder who is not virtuous. See her *An Introduction to Chinese Philosophy* (Malden, MA, and Oxford: Blackwell, 2006), 52. See also John H. Berthrong and Evelyn Nagai Berthrong, *Confucianism: A Short Introduction* (Oxford: Oneworld, 2000), 27 for a similar evaluation.
8   *Analects* 4.18.
9   The *Book of Rites*, "Nei Zei" (Domestic Regulations); compare Legge, *The Li Ki* [*Li Ji*] *Sacred Books of China*, trans. James Legge (Oxford: Clarendon Press, 1879), vol. 1, 456–57. See also the "Qu Li Xia" chapter that says, "The proper ritual for a minister is that he should not remonstrate in public. If the minister

remonstrates with his lord three times and the minister is not listened to, the minister should resign. As for a son and his parents, if the son remonstrates three times and is not heard, crying and in tears, the son must also go along with them." Compare Legge, vol. 1, 114.

10 *Analects* 4.20.
11 Compare Rosemont and Ames, *The Chinese Classic of Family Reverence*, 113.
12 *Analects* 2.8.
13 The *Book of Rites*, "*Nei Ze*" (Domestic Regulations); compare Legge, vol. 1, 449–54.
14 *Analects* 14.43.
15 *Analects* 1.2.
16 See the *Doctrine of the Mean* (*Zhong Yong*), discussed in chapter 8.
17 *Analects* 1.2.
18 *Kongzi Jia Yu*, SPPY ed., 1.7a.
19 *Classic of Filial Piety*, SPPY ed., 2.9; compare Rosemont and Ames, 114.
20 See Keith N. Knapp, *Selfless Offspring: Filial Children and Social Order in Medieval China* (Honolulu: University of Hawai'i Press), 2005, 3f. This text gives a thorough description of filial piety's role in Chinese thought and society.
21 *Analects* 5.19.
22 "*Zhong* is often translated as 'loyalty,' but 'dutifulness' is preferable because the ultimate focus is upon one's ritually-prescribed duties rather than loyalty to one particular person and, indeed, *zhong* would involve opposing a ruler who was acting improperly (13.15, 13.23, 14.7)" Slingerland, *Confucius*, 34–5. Liu understands *zhong* as loyalty, though she agrees it is loyalty to a task, not a person: *An Introduction to Chinese Philosophy*, 48f.
23 *Analects* 14.7. See also *Analects* 13.15.
24 The *Book of Rites* "*Nei Ze*" (Domestic Regulations) noted in Slingerland, *Confucius* 35. See above, note 12 for the quotation.
25 "Integrity" as a translation is suggested by David L. Hall and Roger T. Ames; see their discussion in *Thinking from the Han: Self, Truth, and Transcendence in Chinese and Western Culture* (Albany, NY: SUNY, 1998), 161.
26 *Analects* 4.16; 19.1.
27 *Analects* 16.9, following Slingerland's translation.
28 *Analects* 7.20; 7.28.
29 "'Knowing' then, in classical China is not a knowing *what* provides some understanding of the environing conditions of the natural world, but is rather a knowing *how* to be adept in relationships and *how*, in optimizing the possibilities that these relationships provide, to develop trust in their viability." Hall and Ames, *Thinking from the Han*, 150. See also *Analects* 15.8.
30 *Analects* 12.22.
31 *Analects* 2.17.
32 *Analects* 2.24.
33 *Analects* 17.23.
34 *Analects* 4.15.
35 This is repeated a number of times in the *Analects*, "What I don't want others to do to me, so I should not do to others" (4.15). See also 5.12 and, in Slingerland, "Do not impose upon others, what you yourself do not desire" (12.2). For an

example of the debate about the negative and positive golden rule, see Robert Allinson, "The Golden Rule as the Core Value in Confucianism and Christianity: Ethical Similarities and Differences," *Asian Philosophy* 2.2, 173–85.

36   Hall and Ames define understanding or compassion as not imposing oneself on others. See David L. Hall and Roger Ames, *Anticipating China: Thinking Through the Narratives of Chinese and Western Culture* (Albany, NY: SUNY, 1995), 199.

37   *Analects* 5.20.

38   Lewis, *Sanctioned Violence*, 43.

39   David L. Hall and Roger Ames. *Thinking from the Han*, render *ren* as "authoritative person" and "self": see 27, 257–9. And they argue that "The problem [with translating *ren* as] benevolence is that it psychologizes *ren*, reducing a holistic and resolutely social conception of person to someone's particular moral disposition. 'Humanity,' a broader, and hence more adequate term, still fails to do justice to the profoundly religious dimension of *ren* and vitiates the uniqueness inherent in becoming *ren*" (263).Others note that, on one occasion, in the *Analects*, *ren* is referred to as love for others (*Analects* 12.22), but more often as "an all encompassing ethical ideal" (Shun Kwong-loi, "Ren and Li in the *Analects*," in *Confucius and the Analects: New Essays*, ed. Bryan Van Norden (New York: Oxford University Press, 2002), 53.

To add to the complexities of an English translation for "*ren*," the term is used only in certain layers of the *Analects*, reflecting later agendas. See E. Bruce Brooks and A. Taeko Brooks, "Word Philology and Text Philology in Analects 9.1", in *Confucius and the Analects: New Essays*, ed. Bryan Van Norden, especially 194f. The term evolved after Confucius, so one must be careful with it, but, as Benjamin Schwartz points out, for Confucius it is "an attainment of human excellence which – where it exists – is a whole embracing all the separate virtues" (*The World of Thought in Ancient China*, Cambridge, MA: Harvard University Press, 1985), 75.

40   *Analects* 4.2, 4.12.

41   *Analects* 12.1.

42   *Analects* 9.18.

43   The Chinese word *xin* means both mind and heart and is often translated as both or, as here, "mind/heart" (*Analects* 4.4).

44   For a description of early uses of ritual and the ways in which the term changes, see N. E. Fehl, *Li: Rites and Propriety in Literature and Life* (Hong Kong: Chinese University of Hong Kong, 1971).

45   See Lewis, *Sanctioned Violence*, 95f.

46   *Analects* 12.1.

47   *Analects* 8.2.

48   Others say this is a story about Wu Zixu (526–484) who was executed for giving good advice to the ruler of the state of Wu. His body was thrown in a river.

49   A gentleman, a *junzi*. This term has also been translated as "exemplary person" (Hall and Ames, *Thinking from the Han*), "superior man" (James Legge), and "superior person" (Liu JeeLoo). "Gentleman" conveys all of the class, political, and moral implications of the term, especially if one thinks of the way "gen-

tleman" was used, say, in Victorian England. A gentleman was upper-class, educated, and able to hold office in domestic or colonial government.

50 There are a number of phrases describing paradigmatic persons in the *Analects*: the good man (13.11, 13.29), and the complete man (14.12), but most of the discussion is aimed at the gentleman, and these terms "good" and "complete" seem to be other ways of saying "gentleman." Similarly a scholar/official seems to be another way of describing a paradigmatic individual who "must be strong and enduring for his burdens are heavy and the Way is long. Humanity is his burden – is it not a heavy thing? His Way ends only at his death – is it not long?" *Analects* 8.7.

51 *Analects* 4.11.
52 *Analects* 12.16.
53 *Analects* 13.23.
54 *Analects* 13.25.
55 *Analects* 13.26.
56 *Analects* 14.23. As Hall and Ames say, the "socially expansive and inclusive gentleman is opposed to the disintegrative and retarding qualities of the small person." Hall and Ames, *Thinking from the Han*, 160.
57 *Analects* 14.12.
58 *Analects* 14.30.
59 *Analects* 1.14.
60 *Analects* 12.5.
61 *Analects* 14.42.
62 *Analects* 4.5.
63 *Analects* 12.4. "The Way of the gentleman has three parts, yet I have achieved none of them. The humane do not worry; the wise are not confused; and the courageous are not afraid." *Analects* 14.28.
64 The idea that government administrators should be appointed on their merits, not according to their birth. would have been interesting particularly to the class of scholar/officials who were looking for these very jobs.
65 *Analects* 7.26, 7.34.

Notes to Chapter 3

1 *Analects* 8.13.
2 *Analects* 13.3. *Zheng ming* is often translated as "rectification of names." *Ming* can mean either "words" or "names." See *Analects* 12.17 for a play on words: "to govern, *zheng*, means to correct, *zheng*."
3 As is the ubiquitous, "We are sorry for *any* inconvenience." This is meant to mean, one supposes, that the fact that the flight has been cancelled may, just as an outside chance, cause someone a moment's pang, and for that they apologize. People who are forced to endure meetings full of this bafflegab have invented "buzzword bingo," where the numbers in a bingo card are replaced with jargon words. Players cross off the word in the square if it is used in the "presentation."
4 *Analects* 12.11.

5   *Analects* 13.3.
6   *Analects* 12.9.
7   *Analects* 12.7.
8   *Analects* 14.1.
9   *Analects* 8.9.
10 *Analects* 2.3.
11 Ibid.
12 Curiously, it was difficult to think of an example of behavior that would be considered shameful these days.
13 *Analects* 12.19.
14 *Analects* 12.18.
15 *Analects* 15.1.
16 *Analects* 13.30, 13.29.
17 The extent to which this meant that ritual was a semi-magical force in government and society, and whether the government was understood as held together by religious ritual and a transcendent moral vision, is debated. See Benjamin Schwartz, *The World of Thought in Ancient China* and the controversial views of Robert Eno, *The Confucian Creation of Heaven: Philosophy and the Defence of Ritual Mastery* (Albany: State University of New York Press, 1990).
18 *Analects* 17.5. Book 17 of the *Analects* contains a number of stories and conversations about this problem. The conversation in 17.15 points out that it is not just a corrupt ruler one has to deal with but also the small people who think only of holding on to the government job they have.
19 *Analects* 15.39.
20 *Analects* 8.9.
21 *Analects* 17.25. Not surprisingly, this passage in particular has been the subject of much discussion, with some modern commentators reading the passage as addressed to the problem of dealing with male and female servants. For an introduction to this discussion, see Slingerland's comments on the passage *Confucius: Analects* 211–12. For a further discussion of the role of women in Confucianism, see chapter 13. See also Paul R. Goldin, "The View of Women in Early Confucianism," and Lisa Raphaels, "Gendered Virtue Reconsidered: Notes from the Warring States and Han" in Li Chengyang, ed. *The Sage and the Second Sex: Confucianism, Ethics, and Gender* (Chicago: Open Court, 2000), 133–62; 223–48.
22 *Analects* 6.28. For the story of Nanzi and the long power struggle in the state of Wei that she was involved in, see the *Zuo Zhuan*, Duke Ling 14th year; compare Watson, trans., *The Tso Chuan [Zuo Zhuan]*, 195f. In the *Analects* 8.20, Confucius is seen dismissing the possibility of a good minister who is female when he refers to the ten good ministers of one of his heroes, King Wu. There were only nine good ministers, Confucius says. The female minister did not count.
23 Zigong, a student, told Confucius that he was tired of studying and was thinking of taking a rest in the company of his wife. Confucius replied, "A wife is difficult, how could you think about rest with her?" *Xunzi* 27.9. Compare Knoblock, trans., *Xunzi* 3, 230.

24 Book of Poetry *"Tang, Zhan Zhang"*; compare Legge, *The Chinese Classics. Volume 4: The She King [Shi Jing]* (1871; reprinted Hong Kong: University of Hong Kong Press, 1960), 561–2. The text also contains a number of charming poems, in a woman's voice, speaking of their love.

25 Book of Poetry *"Qi Fu, Si Gan"*; compare Legge, *The She King [Shi Jing]*, 306–7.

26 Book of Rites "Nei Ze"; compare Legge, *The Li Ki [Li Ji]* 1, 454–5.

27 Book of Rites "Nei Ze"; compare Legge, *The Li Ki [Li Ji]* 1, 470 and 454.

28 See Book of Rites "Hun Yi" (The Meaning of Marriage); compare Legge *The Li Ki [Li Ji]* 2, 434. Some commentators see this as a requirement for complementary responsibilities.

29 Book of Rites "Hun Yi"; compare Legge *The Li Ki [Li Ji]* vol. 2, 434. The context, however, is less equitable. The emperor, the Son of Heaven, is to regulate masculine energies by establishing what is proper to men; the empress regulates female energies by means of the obedience proper to women. The emperor guides all external affairs; the empress internal, household, affairs.

30 Nor do we find women's rituals around birth, for example, described in Confucian ritual texts.

31 *Zhan Guo Ce/Ch'an Kuo Ts'e, the Annals of the Warring States*, "Annals of Qin," SPPY ed., 4.8b.

32 *Analects* 7.21.

33 *Analects* 6.22.

34 *Analects* 3.12.

35 *Analects* 11.12.

36 *Analects* 2.4.

37 *Analects* 16.8. Along with the choice of Heaven, we should be in awe of the great men of our times and the teachings of the sages of the past.

38 *Analects* 17.19.

39 *Analects* 5.13.

40 *Analects* 11.9.

41 *Analects* 7.23.

42 *Analects* 9.5.

43 *Analects* 3.24.

44 *Analects* 14.35.

45 *Analects* 3.13.

46 Book of History *"Gao Zong, Rong Ri"*; compare Legge, *She King*, 264.

47 See David Schaberg, "Command and the Content of Tradition" in *The Magnitude of Ming: Command, Allotment, and Fate in Chinese Culture*, ed. Christopher Lupke (Honolulu: University of Hawai'i Press, 2005), 23–48.

48 *Analects* 14.36. See also 6.19 where the illness and death of Confucius' student is attributed to fate.

49 *Analects* 7.6.

50 *Analects* 4.8.

51 *Analects* 15.29.

52 Schwartz, *The World of Thought*, 120.

53 See Herbert Fingarette, *Confucius: the Secular as Sacred* (New York: Harper and Row, 1972).

Notes to Chapter 4

1 "School" or "-ism" is, in Chinese, *jia*, school, or *jiao*, teaching; see below.
2 "Scholars" or "scholar-bureaucrats" were learned men, the great majority from the upper classes, who looked for, and often achieved, jobs in government.
3 Mencius (see chapter 6) would not go to Jixia because he refused to accept payment from a ruler without being part of the government.
4 This led to other howlers: the abominable term "Muhammadanism" for Islam and "Lamaism" for Tibetan Buddhism. The issue of the development and use of the term "Confucianism" is ably set out in Lionel Jensen, *Manufacturing Confucianism: Chinese Traditions and Universal Civilization* (Durham, NC: Duke University Press, 1997).
5 Even the use of the term "*Ru*" has been rejected by some. Li-hsiang Lisa Rosenlee argues, oddly, that there was neither a literal nor a conceptual counterpart of "Confucianism" in the Chinese language. See *Confucianism and Women: A Philosophical Interpretation* (Albany, NY: SUNY, 2006), 17. Michael Nylan says that "the stable entity later scholars have called Confucianism never really existed. 'Confucianism' is an abstraction and a generalization – apparently useful but always obfuscating – a product of ongoing intellectual engagement as well as a subject of it," *The Five "Confucian" Classics*, 3.
6 Mozi calls Confucius a *Ru shi*, *Ru*-ist knight/worthy, and *Dao shi*, a knight/worthy of the Way.
7 The word "*Ru*" is not found in four of the Five Classics. The *Book of Rites* does use the term, but this may be a later addition. It is used only once in the *Analects*, where Confucius says that one wants to be a gentlemanly *Ru* not a petty *Ru* (6:13).
8 According to the *Zhou Li*, a Warring States text, *Ru* was first used as a name for a Zhou official whose duty was to teach the six accomplishments. It may also have been related to scholars and to teachers.
9 For a discussion of these stories, see Nylan, *The Five "Confucian" Classics*, 23.
10 This argument is based on an ancient dictionary *Shuo Wen Jie Zi*'s definition, "*Ru* means weak." Hu Shih (Hu Shi, 1891–1962) also argued that *Ru* was a term used prior to Confucius to refer to the shamans of the Shang dynasty.
11 See John Knoblock, *Xunzi* 1, 52.
12 Often, when modern scholars condemn the use of the term "Confucianism," they go on to use the terms *Ru* and *Ru*-ist in the same way they used to use the terms "Confucians" and "Confucianism."
13 See *Mozi*, "Condemnation of Confucians." The *Yanzi Chun Qiu* "Wai Pian," 8 is also full of the stock Mohist criticisms of the Confucians. It says that the Confucian connection to music was a deep one: "they wallow in music." Their music was heard everywhere bringing disorder to society; this kind of ornamentation was used to harm the world. These charges are much the same as the *Mozi*'s "Condemnation of Confucians" and "Condemnation of Music" chapters.
14 Later, both Zhuangzi and Han Feizi described Confucians in much the same way: these were people who emphasized ritual, particularly funeral rituals that

were elaborate and expensive; they insisted on a three-year mourning period for close family; they talked about filial piety and loyalty; they looked to antiquity and the ways of the early kings for their authority; they were identifiable by their antique clothing.

15 *Zhuangzi*, "Tian Xia"; see Burton Watson, *The Complete Works of Chuang Tzu [Zhuangzi]* (Columbia University Press, 1964), 363. Commentators agree that this refers to *Ru* dress.

16 Confucius himself became a model of behavior as well: his life became "the functional equivalent of a [guiding] concept or principle" (Hall and Ames, *Anticipating China*, 198).

17 In the *Xunzi*, for example, we find a discussion said to have taken place between Duke Ai of Lu and Confucius. Confucius describes scholars in this way: "Scholars are born in the present generation, but aspire to the Way of the ancient times; they live amid modern customs, but wear the clothes of ancient times." Duke Ai wants to know, however, if all who dress in this way are capable officials: "Of course, but of those who wear the Zhang Fu cap, ornamented shoes, and a large sash with the *hu* tablet, are they all worthy men?" Confucius answered, "Not necessarily. But, those who wear proper clothes with dark lower garments and a ceremonial cap while they ride in a carriage do not aspire to eat garlic. Those dressed in mourning clothes, wearing grass sandals, carrying a mourning staff, and drinking rice gruel, they do not have their aspirations set on meat and drink." *Xunzi*, "Ai Gong"; compare Knoblock, *Xunzi*, 3, 259.

18 *Shi Ji*, "Ru Lin Lie Zhuan." D. C. Lau points out that only 25 students are mentioned in the *Lun Yu*; see his *Analects*, Appendix 2.

19 See, for example, *Xunzi*, "Contra Physiognomy" (Knoblock, *Xunzi* 1, 208) and "Contra Twelve Philosophers" 1, 224. In the later Han dynasty, we find another description of Confucian groupings. In the *Han Shu*, the Han history, the "Di Li Zhi" chapter, which looks back at various states of the Warring States period, says of the state of Qi that it alone "loved the classics and the accomplishments" and of the state of Lu that "they honoured ritual and rightness." Scholarly discussions of who belonged to the various schools and what they argued about are numerous.

20 Conversely, Nylan argues that originally the term Ru meant "classicist" and indicated not a precise moral orientation or body of doctrines but a professional training with the general goal of state service; not all Ru were devoted to the Confucian Way identified with the ancients; *The Five "Confucian" Classics*, 3.

21 *Mozi*, "Fei Ru"; compare Burton Watson trans., *Mo Tzu [Mozi]: Basic Writings* (New York: Columbia University Press, 1963), 127.

22 There are other traditions about Mozi: that he studied Confucianism as a young man before rejecting it; that he was an expert in defensive fortifications; that he traveled widely to assist in defensive wars; and that he and his followers wore simple clothes and did not have much in the way of possessions. In the *Mozi* we are missing some chapters and now have only 53, some of which, scholars point out, are clearly from a much later date.

23 "Profit" can also be translated as "benefit" and "usefulness" as "accomplishment"; one can find these, and other, variations in a number of descriptions of Mozi.

24 "Universal love" was not always understood by Mozi's followers. There is
    a story that Master Dongguo, a follower of Mozi, once found a wolf being
    chased by hunters on Mount Zhongshan. Thinking that he should practice
    universal love, Master Dongguo put the wolf in a large bag and told the hunters
    that he had not seen any animal at all. When the hunters left, Master Dongguo
    released the wolf. The wolf said that he had nearly died from suffocation in the
    bag and, in compensation, Master Dongguo should let himself be eaten. Just
    then an old man came upon the scene and both the wolf and Master Dongguo
    explained their view of the situation. The old man suggested that the wolf get
    back in the bag so he could prove how much he had suffered. Once he was
    in, the old man told Master Dongguo to kill the wolf. Finally seeing the true
    situation, Master Dongguo did so. In Chinese, "Master Dongguo" (Dongguo
    Xiansheng) is a synonym for a pedant, while "wolf of Zhongshan" (Zhongshan
    lang) is used to refer to an ingrate.
25 See JeeLoo Liu, *Introduction to Chinese Philosophy*, 120f.
26 There is considerably more to Mozi's thought. For a good introduction to his
    logic and thinking, see the section on Mozi in JeeLoo Liu's *Introduction to
    Chinese Philosophy*, ch. 5.
27 *Mozi*, "*Fei Ru*"; compare Watson, *Mo Tzu [Mozi]*, 132.
28 *Mozi*, "*Jie Zang*"; compare Watson, *Mo Tzu [Mozi]*, "Moderation in Funerals."
29 *Mozi*, "*Fei Ming*"; compare Watson, *Mo Tzu [Mozi]*, "Against Fatalism."
30 See *Mozi*, "*Fei Yue*"; compare Watson, *Mo Tzu [Mozi]*, "Against Music."
31 Mohist, pronounced "moe-ist." The "h" is added to break the syllables; some-
    times you will see this as "Mo-ist" and "Moist."

Notes to Chapter 5

1 Burton Watson, trans., *The Complete Works of Chuang Tzu [Zhuangzi]*, 297.
   This episode is imaginary and the Confucius pictured here is fictional. Watson's
   translation is so good that I will quote his *Zhuangzi* translations directly
   throughout.
2 There is a Chinese family name, "Lao," but it is a different character from the
   "Lao" in Laozi. The later Han dynasty historian, Sima Qian, says that Laozi's
   name was Li Er or Lao Dan. He was said to have been a court archivist in
   the state of Zhou. There are traditional stories that Confucius visited him and
   that before he left China, Laozi was forced by the Keeper of the Pass to write
   the text we now have. He may also have been Lao Laizi, a contemporary of
   Confucius and an archivist. All of this information is vague, something Sima
   Qian admits.
3 The text's title is sometimes also rendered as the *Daodejing/Tao Te Ching*. The
   title comes from the first word of the first section, "Dao," and the first word
   of the second section "De." The version found at Mawangdui transposes the
   two sections. Estimates of the text's date of composition range from the 200s
   BCE to as early as the 600s BCE. Most scholars agree that much of the text
   was written in the 300s BCE, sometime after Mencius (see chapter 6), possibly
   incorporating older material, and put into the form we have now sometime

during the first century CE. The text has been found in a Han dynasty tomb dating from about 168 BCE and is very like the text we have now.

4 The text we have now has 33 chapters. The first seven, called the "Inner Chapters," are thought to have been written by Zhuangzi. Chapters 8–22 are called the "Outer Chapters" and were written by Zhuangzi or, at least, following Zhuangzi's thought. The rest, chapters 23–33, the "Miscellaneous Chapters," contain some pieces by Zhuangzi but are mostly by other hands.

5 The issue of what is, or is not, mysticism is greatly debated. While mysticism is a recognized tradition in the biblical religions, it is not easily transported to Daoist texts. For the beginnings of the discussion, see Steven Katz, *Mysticism and Philosophical Analysis* (New York: Oxford University Press, 1978).

6 *Laozi*, chs. 8, 78, 40, 125, 6. The *Laozi* is one of the most translated books in the world and there are hundreds of translations to choose from. However, the reader should be wary of many of them and check the credentials of the translator. The standard translation of the *Laozi* is D. C. Lau's *Lao Tzu: Tao Te Ching [Laozi: Dao De Jing]* (Penguin Books, 1963 and reprinted regularly). I am following Lau's chapter numbering. For a translation of the *Laozi* text from the Mawangdui finds, see Robert G. Henricks, *Lao Tzu's [Laozi's] Tao Te Ching [Dao De Jing]* (New York: Columbia University Press, 2000).

7 Non-action, *wu-wei*. We often find the *Laozi* saying, "The Dao does not act, but leaves nothing undone."

8 *Zhuangzi*, "Mastering Life", Watson, *The Complete Works of Chuang Tzu [Zhuangzi]*, 206–7.

9 *Laozi*, ch. 5.

10 *Laozi*, ch. 3.

11 *Laozi*, ch. 50.

12 The *Zhuangzi* also calls the sage the Holy Man, the Perfect Man, the True Man, or the Great Man.

13 *Laozi*, ch. 33.

14 *Laozi*, ch. 53.

15 *Laozi*, ch. 60.

16 Burton Watson, trans., *The Complete Works of Chuang Tzu [Zhuangzi]*, 112, 106. This view is also in the *Laozi*, ch. 80.

17 Burton Watson, trans., *The Complete Works of Chuang Tzu [Zhuangzi]*, 112.

18 *Zhuangzi*, "External Things," Watson, trans., *The Complete Works of Chuang Tzu [Zhuangzi]*, 296–7. Confucians have many sterling characteristics, but a sense of humor is not often one of them. These kinds of joking attacks must have been unbearable.

19 *The Art of War*, the *Sunzi Bingfa*. For a discussion of the formation of the text, see Michael Loewe, ed., *Early Chinese Texts: A Bibliographic Guide* (Berkeley, CA: Society for the Study of Early China, 1993).

20 *Sunzi Bingfa*; see the chapter "Employing Spies." Ralph D. Sawyer, *Sun-tzu [Sunzi] The Art of War* (New York: Barnes and Noble, 1994), 299f.

21 *Sunzi Bingfa* "*Shi Ji*"; compare Ralph D. Sawyer, *Sun-tzu [Sunzi] The Art of War*, 168.

22 Logicians are also called the School of Disputation, the School of Names/Words, or the Later Mohists.

23 See the Mohist Canons, which have long discussions about the rules of logic and how arguments should be structured as well as discussions about similarity and difference and how they are decided. A. C. Graham, *Later Mohist Logic, Ethics, and Science* (Hong Kong: Chinese University Press, 2003).

24 Hui Shi, Zhuangzi's friend as portrayed in the *Zhuangzi*. We have no firm dates for him. It is possible that he lived from about 380 to 305 BCE.

25 *Zhuangzi*; see Watson, *The Complete Works of Chuang Tzu [Zhuangzi]*, 374–5.

26 There are no firm dates for Gongsun Long. Some place him from about 325–250 BCE; others date him about 380 BCE. Most of Gongsun Long's writings have been lost. There are only six essays in a text, *Gongsun Long*, which contains the white horse argument.

27 See Wing-tsit Chan, *A Source Book in Chinese Philosophy* (Princeton: Princeton University Press, 1963), 235f.

28 Terms like "white" are what Gongsun Long calls *zhi*, "to point to" an idea, an abstract concept.

29 Similarly, he argues that a white stone is not hard. This is because when we see the stone, we can see the "white," but we cannot see "hard." When we feel the stone, we can feel "hard," but we cannot feel "white." So we have epistemological proof that "hard" and "white" are separate universals. We know them in different ways, they cannot be the same, and they do not "interpenetrate" each other. This is a position that later Mohists will argue against.

30 See J. J. L. Duyvendak, *The Book of Lord Shang: A Classic of the Chinese School of Law* (Chicago: University of Chicago Press, 1963), and Liu Yongping, *The Origins of Chinese Law: Penal and Administrative Law in its Early Development* (Hong Kong: Oxford University Press, 1998).

31 See H. G. Creel, *Shen Pu-hai [Shen Buhai]: A Chinese Political Philosopher of the Fourth Century B.C.* (Chicago: University of Chicago Press, 1974).

32 See the "*Han Feizi*, ch. 50, "Eminence in Learning."

33 *Han Feizi*, "*Wu Du*"; compare Burton Watson, trans., *Han Fei Tzu [Han Feizi]: Basic Writings* (New York: Columbia University Press, 1964), 111.

34 Han Feizi was sent as an envoy from the state of Han to the state of Qin, where he met his fellow student Li Si, by then prime minister of the state of Qin. Li Si thought in the same way as Han Feizi and so had Han Feizi imprisoned. Fittingly enough, Han Feizi died in prison, likely on the orders of Li Si, in 233 BCE.

35 See the *Mencius* 7A.26. For Mencius and citations from the *Mencius* see below.

Notes to Chapter 6

1 The *Mencius* 6.B.15. My translations follow Lau's numbering system and readers can consult alternate translations for comparison. An excellent modern translation of the *Mencius* with explanatory notes and a discussion of how Neo-Confucian readings of the text have affected our understanding is Bryan W. Van Norden's *Mengzi [Mencius] with Selections from Traditional Commentaries* (Indianapolis: Hackett Publishing, 2008). An older, though standard, translation of the *Mencius* is by D. C. Lau (New York: Harmondsworth, Penguin,

1970). David Hinton's *Mencius* (Washington: Counterpoint, 1999) is also a good introductory translation. Mencius, 371–289 BCE, was a contemporary of Alexander the Great (d.323 BCE).

2 Mengzi's given name is "Ke," also styled Ziyu.

3 These stories, and others, can be found in later Han dynasty works, the *Han Shi Wai Zhuan* and *Biographies of Women*; see chapter 9.

4 *Mencius* 2A.2 and 2B.13.

5 *Mencius* 3B.9.

6 The only thing Confucius says about human nature is one statement where he says that people are born alike but differ through practice. *Analects* 17.2.

7 *Mencius* 6A.6.

8 "Anyone who assumes that babies are just little egoists who enter the world needing to be socialized so they can learn to care about others and become good citizens is overlooking other propensities every bit as species-typical," Sarah Blaffer Hrdy, *Mothers and Others: The Evolutionary Origins of Mutual Understanding* (Cambridge, MA: Belknap Press, 2009), 6.

9 Gaozi, for example, says that human nature is the appetite for food and sex. See the *Mencius* 6A.4.

10 *Mencius* 6A.7.

11 *Mencius* 2A.6.

12 *Mencius* 6A.8.

13 We know nothing about Gaozi, other than his appearances in the *Mencius*. In 6A.4, Gaozi seems to argue that morality is taught to us, but is not natural. See *Mencius* 6A.1.

14 *Mencius* 6A.10.

15 See Kim-chong Chong, "Confucianism (II): Meng Zi and Xun Zi" in *History of Chinese Philosophy*, ed. Bo Mou, Routledge History of World Philosophies (New York: Routledge, 2009), vol. 3, 193, 197.

16 *Mencius* 6A.10, 6A.14–15. For Mencius, goodness is also reflected in the face and appearance: see 7A.21 and 7A.38. Mencius also says, "A great man is one who does not lose his child-like mind/heart" (4B.12). And that, while people have the sense to go after straying chickens or dogs, they do not go after the mind/heart when it strays (6A.11).

17 *Mencius* 4B.28.

18 *Mencius* 7A.1. See also 6A.15.

19 *Mencius* 4B.29 and 4B.19.

20 *Mencius* 4B.12.

21 *Mencius* 2A.2.

22 *Mencius* 6A.16

23 *Mencius* 1B.6.

24 *Mencius* 7B.14. The spirits of the land and grain represented the territory of the state.

25 *Mencius* 1B.8.

26 *Mencius* 5A.6.

27 JeeLoo Liu argues that Mencius did indeed mean revolution against corrupt rulers, as a corrupt ruler is no longer, according to setting words right, a ruler.

Mencius wanted the ministers of the government to overthrow such a ruler; he was not looking for a popular revolution from the people.

28 *Mencius* 1A.1.
29 *Mencius* 1A.7.
30 *Mencius* 6A.7.
31 This is the "well field" system ("well" refers to the Chinese character for a well, which looks like #). The central square is public, the crop goes to the ruler; the others are privately owned. The land all belongs to the state, and is given to the people; so the tax goes to the state, not to feudal lords (*Mencius* 3A.3).
32 *Mencius* 1A.7.
33 Ibid.
34 Ibid.
35 *Mencius* 6A.10.
36 *Mencius* 1A.5 and 7B.4.
37 *Mencius* 4A.14.
38 *Mencius* 4B.28.
39 *Mencius* 4A.4.
40 *Mencius* 7A.39.
41 *Mencius* 4A.18.
42 *Mencius* 3.A.5.
43 *Mencius* 4A.17.
44 *Mencius* 3B.2.
45 *Mencius* 7A.13.
46 *Mencius* 2A.2.
47 As I have argued elsewhere: see "Mencius and his Vast, Overflowing *Qi* (*Haoranzhiqi*)," *Monumenta Serica* 46, 93–104 (1998).
48 *Mencius* 7A.1.
49 *Mencius* 4A.12.
50 *Mencius* 7A.4.

Notes to Chapter 7

1 *Xunzi*, "Confucian Teachings"; compare Knoblock, *Xunzi* 2, 79. See the Glossary for pronunciation.
2 Xunzi's given name was Kuang, but he is most often referred to as Xun Qing.
3 For an excellent biography of Xunzi, a description of Xunzi's times, and an overview of the text, see John Knoblock, *Xunzi: A Study and Translation of the Complete Works* (Stanford, CA: Stanford University Press, 1988), vol. 1, "General Introduction," 3f. Knoblock's translation, in three volumes, is the most thorough and modern available. For a shorter introduction to the *Xunzi* see Burton Watson's translation, *Hzun Tzu [Xunzi]: Basic Writings* (New York: Columbia University Press, 1967).
4 The text we now have was assembled in the Han dynasty from shorter works. For a discussion of the composition of the text, see Knoblock, *Xunzi*, 1, 105f and 240f.

5 *Xunzi*, "On Getting Rid of Blindness." The Duke of Zhou was a Confucian hero, a paragon of moral and political behavior. The Three Kings are the founders of the three dynasties, the Xia, Shang, and Zhou. Compare Knoblock, *Xunzi* 3, 103.

6 *Xunzi*, "Human Nature is Evil"; compare Knoblock, 3, 150f.

7 See Knoblock, *Xunzi* 3, 139 for a discussion of the term.

8 *Xunzi*, "Human Nature is Evil"; compare Knoblock, *Xunzi* 3, 155.

9 *Xunzi*, "Human Nature is Evil"; compare Knoblock, *Xunzi* 3, 152.

10 *Xunzi*, "Human Nature is Evil"; compare Knoblock, *Xunzi* 3, 151: "They are called the emotions given to us by nature." "Discussing Nature"; compare Knoblock, *Xunzi* 3, 17. For a more detailed discussion of the constitution of human nature and the emotions according to Xunzi, see Kim-chong Chong, "Confucianism (II): Meng Zi [Mencius] and Xun Zi [Xunzi]," 203f.

11 *Wei* has been translated as "artificial," "man-made," "conscious activity," "human artifice," "deliberate effort." See Liu, *Introduction to Chinese Philosophy*, 94.

12 *Xunzi*, "Human Nature is Evil"; compare Knoblock, *Xunzi* 3, 153.

13 *Xunzi*, "Human Nature is Evil"; compare Knoblock, *Xunzi* 3, 158.

14 *Xunzi*, "Human Nature is Evil"; compare Knoblock, *Xunzi* 3,153. See also section 19.1. In discussing the "dilemma of the early sages" Liu argues that the early sage-kings used the moral rules that they had devised to become moral themselves; Liu, *Introduction to Chinese Philosophy*, 102–3.

15 *Xunzi*, "Human Nature is Evil"; compare Knoblock, *Xunzi* 3, 151.

16 *Xunzi*, "A Discussion of Ritual"; compare Knoblock, *Xunzi* 3, 65.

17 *Xunzi*, "Enriching the State"; compare Knoblock, *Xunzi* 2, 126–7.

18 *Xunzi*, "Enriching the State"; compare Knoblock, *Xunzi* 2, 121.

19 *Xunzi*, "On Kings and Dictators," ch. 11.

20 Knoblock argues that, when Xunzi visited the state of Qin in about 260 BCE, he was an orthodox Confucian, teaching many of the same things we have seen in Confucius and Mencius. What he saw in Qin was such a shock that he had to re-examine his thinking, and we can see a change in his attitudes, particularly about government and the effect of moral teachings in government. See Knoblock, *Xunzi* 1, 22f.

21 "Dictator" is also translated as "hegemon" or Knoblock's "Lord Protector." This title had been given to various overlords in the Zhou and Warring States era whose authority came from military force. For a discussion of the origin and use of the term, see Knoblock, *Xunzi* 2, 140f.

22 *Xunzi*, "On Kings and Dictators"; see Knoblock, *Xunzi* 2, 151.

23 *Xunzi*, "On Putting Words Right"; see Knoblock, *Xunzi* 3, 130-31.

24 *Xunzi*, "On Putting Words Right"; see Knoblock, *Xunzi* 3, 129f.

25 See *Xunzi*, "On Putting Words Right," ch. 19.

26 *Xunzi*, "Discussing Nature"; compare Knoblock, *Xunzi* 3, 14.

27 *Xunzi*, "Discussing Nature"; compare Knoblock, *Xunzi* 3, 17.

28 *Xunzi*, "Discussing Nature"; compare Knoblock, *Xunzi* 3, 18-19. For the terms "yin" and "yang," see chapter 9.

29 *Xunzi*, "Discussing Nature"; compare Knoblock, *Xunzi* 3, 19. For the *Book of Changes* see chapter 8.

30 *Xunzi*, "On Getting Rid of Blindness"; compare Knoblock, *Xunzi* 3,109.
31 *Xunzi*, "Against Twelve Philosophers"; see Knoblock, *Xunzi* 1, 223f.
32 *Xunzi*, "On Getting Rid of Blindness"; see Knoblock, *Xunzi* 3,102f.

Notes to Chapter 8

1 *Xunzi*, "You Zuo"; compare Knoblock, *Xunzi* 3, 249. Prince Bi Gan, uncle of the last Shang emperor, tried to give good advice to his nephew. The emperor, having heard that a sage's heart had seven openings, cut out Bi Gan's heart to inspect it. Guan Longfeng was an advisor to the last emperor of the Xia dynasty. Wu Zixu was a loyal and wise minister in the state of Wu who was ordered to commit suicide by his lord. His dying words drove the King of Wu to have Wu's body mutilated and thrown in the Yangzi River. Like them, Confucians might offer expert and proper advice, but that advice was not always followed, nor were Confucians necessarily popular with the rulers of the Warring States period. Confucians often portray themselves as neglected advisors and, in the Confucian classics, again and again, rulers find themselves facing disaster for not following Confucian advice.
2 *Han Feizi*, "Xian Xie."
3 *Han Shu*, "Di Li Zhi."
4 See, for example, *Xunzi*, "Against Physiognomy," Knoblock, *Xunzi* 1, 208 and "Against the Twelve Philosophers," Knoblock, *Xunzi* 1, 224.
5 He is frequently seen in the *Analects* where he asks questions, but Confucius criticized him for his rashness. The *Han Feizi* says that Zi Zhang's group emphasized caps and dress and attracted a great many followers. Zi Zhang is also found caricatured in the *Zhuangzi*, "Dao Zhi."
6 He is seen in the *Analects* as a teacher in his own right, but Confucius criticizes him for not being "a gentleman Confucian" (*Analects* 6.13). He is credited with the transmission of many of the classics in the *Shi Ji* "Ru Lin Lie Zhuan" and is prominent in the *Book of Rites*. The followers of Zi Xia were called "petty men" because they performed only the outer forms of ritual (bowing, advancing, and retiring); see the *Analects* 19.12.
7 Zi Si is traditionally credited with some of the writing in the *Book of Rites* and with writing the *Doctrine of the Mean*. It is now known that the *Doctrine of the Mean* was probably compiled at the beginning of the Qin dynasty. Xunzi says that in his time, some Confucians used Confucian ideas and tied them to the *wu xing*, five phases or processes theory. They then claimed that these were the ideas of Zi Si and Mencius; see Knoblock, *Xunzi* 1, 214–15; see chapter 9 for *wu xing*. Xunzi might not have wanted to attack Confucius' grandson, but he did frequently criticize Mencius and his ideas. The *Han Feizi* credits Mencius with almost 1,000 students. There is speculation that Zi Si, Yue Zheng, and Mencius formed one group that might, in turn, have been related to Zi You's group.
8 See the *Xunzi*, "Ru Xiao." He is mentioned in the *Analects* 6.6, 6.1, 13.2, and the *Shiji* 67.9. Scholars think Xunzi may have meant Ran Yong (whose style was Zhong Gong) but little is known of him.

9   *Han Feizi*, "Xian Xue"; compare Watson, *Han Fei Tzu [Han Feizi]: Basic Writings*, 118f. The *Han Feizi*'s reference to a "Sun" group has led to a debate about who this is, with many scholars arguing that it is, in fact, Xunzi. For further information, see Slingerland's *Analects*, Appendix 2, "Disciples of Confucius."

10   Mark Csikszentmihalyi, *Material Virtue: Ethics and the Body in Early China* (Leiden: Brill Sinica Leidensia, 2004), vol. LXVI, 31f.

11   Michael Nylan, "Boundaries of the Body and Body Politic in Early Confucian Thought" in *Confucian Political Ethics*, ed. Daniel A. Bell (Princeton: Princeton University Press, 2008), 85.

12   *Zhuangzi*, "Tian Dao"; compare Watson, *The Complete Works of Chuang Tzu [Zhuangzi]*, 149 and 165. Confucius is described as talking about the twelve *jing*, classics, which commentators take to mean that there were actually six classics, *jing*, with six accompanying commentaries. In the list of classics we have seen above, the *Zhuangzi* lists four: *Poetry, History, Rites*, and *Music*. A set of the Confucian classics in Chinese can be found at the "Chinese Text Project" by Donald Sturgeon, http://chinese.dsturgeon.net. The English translations given there are often from James Legge's translations from the late 1800s.

13   See John B. Henderson, *Scripture, Canon, and Commentary: A Comparison of Confucian and Western Exegesis* (Princeton: Princeton University Press, 1991) for a description of the various versions of the *Documents*.

14   *The Book of Poetry*, the *Shi Jing* is also called the *Book of Odes*, the *Book of Songs* or just the *Songs*. See Arthur Waley, trans., *The Book of Songs*, edited and added to by J. R. Allen (New York: Grove Press, 1996). The text has also been used by linguists; see Bernhard Karlgren, *The Book of Odes* (Stockholm: Museum of Far Eastern Antiquities, 1954).

15   *The Book of History*, the *Shu Jing* or *Shang Shu*, is also called the *Classic of Documents*, the *Classic of History*, the *Book of Documents* or just the *Documents*.
     In 1993, the archaeologists at the Jingmen City Museum excavated a tomb in the town of Guodian, Hubei, near the capital of the Warring States state of Chu, finding 804 bamboo strips of texts, mostly philosophical texts. The tomb is dated to 300 BCE so these are the earliest versions of the texts that are extant. In 1994, a cache of 1,200 bamboo strips was bought by the Shanghai Museum in the antiques market of Hong Kong (likely from tomb robbers). Both of these discoveries are described in the first section of Edward L. Shaughnessy, *Rewriting Early Chinese Texts* (Albany, NY: SUNY Press, 2006). The discovery of these texts has corroborated the authenticity of several texts we have now, including the *Laozi*. For *The Book of History*, see Liao Mingchun, *A Preliminary Study on the Newly-Unearthed Inscriptions of the Chu Kingdom: An Investigation of the Materials from and about the Shangshu in the Guodian Chu Slips* (Taipei: Taiwan Guji, 2001).

16   *Mencius* 7B.3. Nylan says that the text was not put into a continuous history until sometime at the end of the Warring States era or in the Han dynasty. See the *Five "Confucian" Classics*, 122f. Nylan gives an excellent description of these texts and their development. See also her bibliography and long endnotes on the Yale University Press website.

17 *Mencius* 3B. 9.

18 *Spring and Autumn Annals*, Duke Zhuang, 22nd year; compare Legge, *The Ch'un Ts'ew with the Tso Chuen [The Spring and Autumn Annals and the Zuo Zhuan]*, The Chinese Classics vol. 5 (1872; reprint) (Hong Kong: University of Hong Kong Press, 1960), 101–2 . We do not have annals from any state other than Lu. Like *The Book of History* and the *Book of Rites*, the only complete translation of the *Spring and Autumn Annals and the Zuo Zhuan* are these very old texts from the end of the 1800s.

19 The *Book of Changes* is also called the *Classic of Change, Zhou Yi* or *Yi*. For a discussion of the *Zhou Yi*, the *Book of Changes* as found in the Shanghai Museum purchase of bamboo strips, see Edward L. Shaughnessy, "A First Reading of the Shanghai Museum Bamboo-Strip Manuscript of the *Zhou Yi*" in *Early China* 30 (2005–6), 1–25.

20 Because it is the source of cosmology and moral ideas for both Confucian and Daoist thinkers, Liu argues that it "… is the single most important work in the history of Chinese philosophy," Liu, *Introduction to Chinese Philosophy*, 26. Fascination with this book of divination continues among scholars even today. There have been recent translations and discussions of the text that look at the layers in the text and the historical development of the text; see Edward L. Shaughnessy, trans., *I Ching: The Classic of Changes* (New York: Ballantine, 1997) and Richard John Lynn, trans., *The Classic of Changes: A New Translation of the I Ching* (New York: Columbia University Press, 1994).

21 The *Book of Rites, Li Ji*, is also called the *Book of Ritual* or the *Record of Rites*. There are a number of ritual texts in addition to the *Book of Rites*. For a description of them, see Nylan, *The Five "Confucian" Classics*, ch. 4, 168f.

22 *Great Learning*, the *Da Xue*.

23 *Doctrine of the Mean*, the *Zhong Yong*.

24 The *Xunzi's Discussion of Music* was probably written between 300 and 200 BCE; most of the *Book of Rites' Record of Music* was written about the same time, but edited by Han Confucians; the *Shi Ji's Book of Music* repeats the *Record*; and the passages from the *Lu Shi Chun Qiu* were written around 293 BCE. This means that the bases of most of our major sources were written around much the same time.

25 Its authorship is now considered to be unknown. For a description of the chapters of the *Classic of Filial Piety* and their contents see Rosemont and Ames, *The Chinese Classic of Family Reverence*, 6–7, and see the rest of the text for a good discussion of the issues involved and a modern translation.

26 Prime minister Li Si's advice to the First Emperor. Burton Watson, trans., *The Records of the Grand Historian* (New York: Columbia University Press, 1993), 185.

27 See Denis Twitchett and Michael Loewe, *The Cambridge History of China: the Ch'in [Qin] and Han Empires, 221B.C.–A.D. 220* (Cambridge: Cambridge University Press, 1986), 34f. They quote Shang Yang's biography, "Whoever did not denounce a culprit would be cut in two; whoever did denounce a culprit would receive the same reward as he who decapitated an enemy; whoever concealed a culprit would receive the same punishment as he who surrendered to an enemy" (36).

28 Qin intrigue includes the tale of Lu Buwei, a very wealthy merchant, who made friends with an heir to the Qin throne, giving this heir his own favorite concubine. The concubine, according to the later Han dynasty historian, Sima Qian, was already pregnant by Lu. When she bore a son, this son went on to become the ruler of Qin. Lu Buwei continued as Qin's chancellor with his illegitimate son on the throne. Lu, unwisely, continued his relations with the concubine and was forced to commit suicide in 235 BCE. Lu Buwei is also known as a patron of scholars who wrote the *Lu Shi Chun Chiu*, an encyclopedic work. The possibly illegitimate son went on to become the First Emperor of China.

29 Qin Shi Huangdi. One of those things that people say about China is that the English word "China" is based on the word "Qin." There is no evidence for this. There are many of these so-called "facts" floating around, like the mistaken notion that Chinese has no verb "to be."

30 The Great Wall of China that we know today was mostly built in the Ming dynasty. The First Emperor's wall was more modest in construction and in length.

31 In modern-day Qufu, one can see the wall where it is said that the Kong family and the people of Lu hid the Confucian texts.

32 See Nylan, *The Five "Confucian" Classics*, 29f.

33 In 208 BCE Li Si had his ears, nose, fingers, and feet amputated, was whipped, and decapitated. His head was then displayed.

Notes to Chapter 9

1 The Former or Early Han dynasty, 206 BCE–23 CE, the Later Han dynasty, 25–220 CE.

2 *Shi Ji*, "Ru Lin Lie Zhuan."

3 Other inventions included iron ploughs that not only were better at cutting into the soil, but also raised and turned the soil at the same time. The invention of the seed drill made sowing seeds more even; grain was winnowed with a crank-driven machine, the first in the world. Many of these developments were not seen in Europe for over a thousand years.

4 More inventions of the time: the cog-wheel, the water mill, a caliper with decimal scale, belt drives, the suspension bridge, descriptions of blood circulation, and negative numbers. See Joseph Needham, *Science and Civilization in China* (Cambridge: Cambridge University Press, 1959) 3, 627–8, and Robert Temple, *The Genius of China: 3,000 Years of Science, Discovery, and Invention* (New York: Simon and Schuster, 1989), 218–24. Like the Roman empire, the Han dynasty extended its borders and developed sophisticated technology and government structure. Both empires fell due to "barbarian" invasions, the rich's possession of enormous estates, intrigue and weakness at court, and the rise of religion (Christianity and Religious Daoism). But the Chinese empire was land-based, was more culturally homogeneous, and had a common writing system. It would rise again, while the Roman empire was never duplicated (Roberts, *A History of China*), 39.

5   Keith N. Knapp, *Selfless Offspring: Filial Children and Social Order in Medieval China* (Honolulu: University of Hawai'i Press, 2005), 21. See 22f for a discussion of the debate on the Confucianization of the Han dynasty.

6   There is disagreement here. Hall and Ames argue that by the first century BCE Confucianism had become a victor over all the contending voices: "Its success was due in an important degree to its ability to accommodate within a ritually grounded society many of the profound elements of Daoism, Legalism, and Mohism, a pattern that would be repeated in Confucianism's gradual appropriation of Buddhist elements by its medieval adherents" (Hall and Ames, *Anticipating China*, 210).

7   For a description of this process, see Edward L. Shaughnessy, *Rewriting Early Chinese Texts.*

8   Chinese title "*Chun Qiu Fan Lu.*" Recent scholarship has shown that this text was written by a number of authors and over centuries. For good scholarly discussions of the yin-yang texts, see Robin S. Yates, *Five Lost Classics: Tao [Dao], Huanglao, and Yin-Yang in Han China* (New York: Ballantine, 1997) and Sarah A. Queen, *From Chronicle to Canon: the Hermeneutics of the Spring and Autumn, According to Tung Chung-shu [Dong Zhongshu]* (Cambridge: Cambridge University Press, 1996).

9   Yin-yang theorists were active by the time of Xunzi. Zou Yan (*c.*340 BCE) is thought to have been at the Jixia academy with Xunzi; his works, once extensive, are now lost. Even though he is considered to be the person most associated with yin-yang thought, texts describe him as more deeply involved with the five phases theory or some variation of it. Sima Qian says he assigned the "five virtues to things so as to explain the transformations of these five virtues." The *Records of the Historian* also says that Zou Yan used yin-yang thought in order to end immorality at court; he "looked deeply into the increases and decreases of yin and yang." See *Records of the Historian* 74.5–6. See Knoblock, *Xunzi* 1, 64f for a brief introduction to Zou Yan's thinking.

10   The actions of yin and yang depend on their own natures, not on a germ of yin inside yang nor yang inside yin. The idea that yin and yang interpenetrate to some degree is not found until the Song dynasty where we see it in Zhou Dunyi's Diagram of the Supreme Ultimate (*Tai Ji*); see chapter 11.

11   *Chunqiu Fan Lu*, ch. 53, section 12.

12   Issues around the yin-yang theory are still very much debated. For the view that the yin-yang theory does work as a complementary system, see Hall and Ames, *Anticipating China*, 261f. Sherry J. Mou argues that the yin-yang systems of the Han defined relationships hierarchically, and that this included gender relations and, as she points out, these were then reinforced with ideas of loyalty, filial piety, rightness, and so on, and regulated by rituals. See *Gentlemen's Prescriptions for Women's Lives: A Thousand Years of Biographies of Chinese Women* (New York: M. E. Sharpe, 2004), 7.

13   The word is often used oddly. There is an advertisement that claims that using the featured product will result in "a state of *qi*." As everything is made of *qi*, everyone already has a state of *qi*. Many Westerners have heard the term used in the martial arts where often it means something more like "energy."

14 In addition to yin-yang and five phases theories, the New Text school was influenced by another strand of thought, Huang-Lao, named after the sage-king, the Yellow Emperor (Huangdi), and Laozi, believed to be the author of the *Daodejing*. In the Western Han, Huang-Lao developed as a combination of Legalist ideas about the structure of government along with Daoist ideas of non-action. When a government organization was set up well and laws were understood, a ruler did not need to involve himself in government. While Huang-Lao thought died out in the early Han, it is thought to have influenced the yin-yang thought of the New Text school. In 1973 at Mawangdui (near modern Changsha in Hunan province) manuscripts associated with Huang-Lao thought were discovered.

15 *Chunqiu Fanlu*, ch. 19, section 6.

16 *Chunqiu Fanlu*, ch. 56, section 13.

17 The five phases, *wu xing*, is also translated as the five elements or five stages.

18 Because it is the center, there is no yin or yang position for earth/center/yellow.

19 Uncrowned, or unrecognized, king.

20 Hall and Ames, *Anticipating China*, 201.

21 For a description of changes in the figure of Confucius, see Mark Csikszentmihalyi, "Confucius and the *Analects* in the Han" in *Confucius and the Analects: New Essays*, ed. Bryan Van Norden (New York: Oxford University Press, 2002), 134–62; for a list of Han stories about Confucius, see ibid., 136.

22 Wang Chong was said to have been so poor that he read the classics by frequenting the bookstores of Luoyang and reading the texts while pretending to buy. His text is the *Lun Heng, Balanced Discourses*, which he wrote in obscurity. It only came to light when one of his in-laws tried to pass off Wang Chong's thinking as his own. Wang Chong is open about his dependence on Daoist thought, but says that Daoists did not understand how to prove their arguments, while he did.

23 *Chunqiu Fanlu*, "Yin Yang Yi," ch. 49.

24 *Lun Heng*, "Ziran"; compare A. Forke, trans., *Lun Heng* (1907 reprint) (New York: Paragon, 1962), 1, 99.

25 *Lun Heng*, "Ziran"; compare Forke, *Lun Heng* 1, 92.

26 *Lun Heng*, "Han Wen"; compare Forke, *Lun Heng* 1, 278; 283.

27 *Lun Heng*, "Bian Dong"; compare Forke, *Lun Heng* 1, 109–10. "Human beings are creatures; even though they are noble lords or rulers, their nature is no different from the nature of all other creatures," *Lun Heng*, "Dao Xu"; compare Forke, *Lun Heng* 1,335–6.

28 Liu Xiang's *Biographies of Women* has 104 biographies, divided among seven chapters. The chapter titles are: "The Highest Standard of Motherhood," "The Wise and Intelligent," "The Humane and Knowledgeable," The Incorruptible and Obedient," "Those with Principles and Rightness," "Those Who Pass on Examples and Have Good Opinions," and "The Evil and Depraved." See Mou, *Gentleman's Prescriptions*, 11f. and Appendix A.1, 201f. for her translations. This organization set the standard for many biographies of women to come.

29 See Knapp, *Selfless Offspring*, 24.

30 *Shuoyuan Zhuzi Suoyin* 3.8 by Liu Xiang, cited in Knapp, 29.

31 Knapp, *Selfless Offspring*, 25.

Notes to Chapter 10

1   Down to modern times, Chinese people refer to themselves as "Han ren," people of the Han, or "Tang ren," people of the Tang. These are the only two dynasties to be so distinguished.

2   You may have seen the movie *The Matrix*. The hero, Neo, is offered a red pill that allows him to see that the world he believed was real is a hoax. It is a computer simulation that creates an artificial reality called the Matrix. If you take the red pill, you can begin to understand one of the most complex of Buddhist philosophical schools, Yogacharin Buddhism. It began in India about 300 CE. It argues that central to all things, central to reality itself, is the Tathagata-garbha, the storehouse consciousness. This storehouse contains seeds that are all the ideas and mental impressions of consciousness. Consciousness shares these seeds so that trees look like trees. But the world we see and know through our senses is not real, it is more like a movie. We think it is real, but only because the mental seeds look real. This view is similar to what we see in *The Matrix*. We are caught up in events, situations, and things that are not really real. What is real is Consciousness, the storehouse, also understood to be the real, eternal Buddha, called the Tathagata. Enlightenment then is realizing that the world we think is real, the one that makes us suffer, is not real at all.

3   Fazang went on to argue that all phenomena are mutually interpenetrating. For more on Hua Yan and its arguments with the Tiantai school of Buddhism, see essays in Peter N. Gregory and Daniel A. Getz Jr., eds., *Buddhism in the Sung [Song]*, (Honolulu: University of Hawai'i Press, 1999).

4   Knapp, *Selfless Offspring*, 4f. Extraordinary service including making life-saving medicines for one's parents from pieces of one's own flesh. This, in turn, led to a number of jokes. An old one is about a doctor who says that the only thing that will save a father is a medicine made with the flesh of a filial son's thigh. The son then went out to the mansion's gate and found a beggar sound asleep there. He cut a slice of the beggar's thigh and the beggar screamed in pain. The son told the beggar to calm down, saying, "Your flesh is going to save the life of a dying father. What's the matter with you, don't you understand the importance of filial piety?"

5   Knapp, *Selfless Offspring*, 136. He points out that women appear in filial piety stories usually only in the absence of brothers and often have to die to show their filial piety, that is, go further in service to prove it. In the early medieval period, stories about filial daughters or daughters-in-law were rare; by the Song-Yuan period, about one quarter of the tales are about women (185–6).

6   Through time, the details of the examination system varied; this is only a general description. See Ichisada Miyazaki, *China's Examination Hell: the Civil Service Examinations of Imperial China*, Conrad Schirokauer, trans. (Yale University Press, 1981), 31.

7   See Miyazaki, *China's Examination Hell*, 36f.

8   Ibid., 57.

9   In the Han dynasty, it is estimated that China's population was about 60 million, reaching that height again in the Tang dynasty and, by the Song

dynasty, doubled to about 120 million people. Capital cities, like Kaifeng, were four to five times the size of ancient Rome. See Fairbank and Goldman, *China: a New History*, 89. For population and government officials numbers, see ibid., 106.

10   For an entertaining insight into the roles of a magistrate in the imperial period, see R. H. van Gulik's series of Judge Dee murder mysteries, such as *The Chinese Lake Murders* and *The Chinese Nail Murders*. For a description of the duties of magistrates and the problems they faced, see John H. Berthrong and Evelyn Nagai Berthrong, *Confucianism: An Introduction* (Oxford: Oneworld, 2000), 107f.

11   As one old story has it, a very successful pirate was only diverted from his life of crime by being offered the post of a government official. The pirate said, "Officials take their posts and then become thieves, but I was a thief before becoming an official."

12   Greatest Sage and Ancient Teacher, *Zhi Sheng Xian Shi*, or the most complete sage and the first master.

13   At the 2008 ceremony in Taipei on the 2,558th birthday of Confucius, unusually, the eight-row ceremonial dance, the *bayi*, reserved for performance in front of emperors, was performed. Taipei city councilors complained that Confucian temple officials were "fawning" over the new president, Ma Ying-jeou (Ma Yingjiu).

14   For a description of the Confucian temple in Taipei, see the government website at http://www.ct.taipei.gov.tw/EN/01-history/hst1.html. For the Confucian temple in Qufu, see www.china.org.cn/english/kuaixun/74944.htm. The Confucian temple in Indonesia is the Boen Bio temple, originally built in 1883, rebuilt in 1907, and dedicated to "the Prophet Confucius." Refurbished Confucian temples in China include those in Nanjing, Tianjin, and Ganzhou; the old Confucian temple in Xian is now the tourist site the "Forest of Steles." Korea has the largest number of Confucian temples outside of China and some still continue Confucian rites.

15   For a fascinating discussion of the changing iconography of Confucius and the debates around it, see Julia K. Murry, " 'Idols' in the Temple: Icons and the Cult of Confucius" in the *Journal of Asian Studies* 68.2 (May 2009), 371–411.

16   For a description, see http://academics.hamilton.edu/asian_studies/home/chrono.html, the link to "chronology of enshrinement." The Hanlin (forest of scholars) academy was established in the Tang in 725.

17   For the view that Confucius is a god, see, for example, Henri Maspero, *Taoism and Chinese Religions*, F. Kierman, trans. (Amherst: University of Massachusetts Press, 1981), 1–2. See Hall and Ames, *Anticipating China*, 202 for the view of Confucius as a guide.

18   Before the Choson dynasty, there were private and government academies; the government created a publishing house for the Confucian classics; a Hanlin academy (Korean: Hallim-won) was established; and, in 958, a civil service examination system began.

19   For a detailed description of Choson dynasty Confucianism see James Huntley Grayson, *Korea: A Religious History* (New York: Routledge Curzon, 2002), especially 112–20, 126–38.

20   See Grayson, 178f.
21   See Lee Seung-hwan, *A Topography of Confucian Discourse*, ch. 4. Lee says, "The authentic Confucian spirit has never been achieved in modern Korean history. Confucianism has been used as an ideological apparatus for the protection of the capitalist system, labor suppression, and the stability of the regime" (170).
22   See Prince Shotoku's "Constitution" of 604 for the use of Confucian terms and ideas like proper behavior, rightness, loyalty, and so on.
23   But some Confucian scholars used government support to criticize the government: their work on the enormous 226-volume history of Japan, which began in 1657 and was completed in 1906, was motivated by the idea of "using the past to criticize the present," a common theme in early Confucianism. See Masaharu Anesaki, *History of Japanese Religion* (Rutland, VT: Charles E. Tuttle, 1963), 272f.
24   "[T]he Vietnamese manifested some longstanding familiarity with Confucian teachings, but the impact was far less extensive than in either Korea or China. Confucianism, as a systematic and coherent body of beliefs had faded in importance by midcentury, and very few institutions specifically aimed at the propagation of its teachings remained. But, if one forgoes a search for a coherent organized set of beliefs and searchers instead for concepts (like loyalty or filial piety) with clear Confucian origins, then Confucianism remained quite common"; Shawn Frederick McHale, *Print and Power: Confucianism, Communism and Buddhism in the Making of Modern Vietnam* (Honolulu: University of Hawai'i Press, 2004), 94. See also his article, "Mapping a Vietnamese Confucian Past and Its Transition to Modernity" in Benjamin A. Elman et al., eds., *Rethinking Confucianism: Past and Present in China, Korea, and Vietnam* (Los Angeles: UCLA Press, 2002), 397–430.

Notes to Chapter 11

1   See Fairbank and Goldman, *China: a New History*, 92.
2   There have been theories that, through the influence of the Mongol conquests of Asia and parts of Europe, knowledge of both woodblock and moveable-type printing spread from China to Europe. Others disagree and describe the independent historical progression of printing techniques in Europe. See Tsien Tsuen-hsun, "Paper and Printing" in *Science and Civilisation in China. Volume 5: Chemistry and Chemical Technology*, part 1, ed. Joseph Needham (Cambridge: Cambridge University Press, 1985).
3   See Ari Borrell, "Ko-wu [Gewu] or Kung-an [Gongan] Practice, Realization, and Teaching in the Thought of Chang Chiu-Ch'eng [Zhang Jiucheng]" in *Buddhism in the Sung [Song]*, ed. Gregory and Getz, 62–109 for a description of the complex relationship between Buddhist thought and Neo-Confucianism.
4   Han Yu is better known as an excellent writer and his works can be found in collections of prose. See Sjoj Shun Liu, *Chinese Classical Prose: the Eight Masters of the T'ang [Tang]-Sung [Song] Period* (Hong Kong: Chinese University Press of Hong Kong, 1979), 45f.

5 "Metaphysical" is a word that is not helpful. Its literal meaning is "after the Physics" in Aristotle's books, but the makeup of the word does not tell us what it means. The Chinese phrase for "metaphysical" is more helpful: it is *xing er shang*, what is above the forms and shapes that we perceive. "Metaphysical" describes something that is not perceivable by the senses and that is abstract as opposed to concrete. "Transcendent" means beyond our world of time and space. Early Daoist texts often refer to the Dao as something so far beyond language that one can say it both exists and does not exist. The Buddhist idea of Tathagata, the eternal state of the Buddha, is also described as both existing and not existing.

6 The Buddha taught that all things are made up of two or more other things and that all things will change over time. This would mean that there is nothing eternal, like God or a soul. In Buddhist terms, this means things are *sunyata*, "empty." Yogacharin Buddhism, developed in India in the 300s CE, posed another view that is much like the one found in the movie *The Matrix*.

7 *Western Inscription, Xi Ming*, ch. 17 of his *Discipline for Beginners*. It is called the "Western" inscription because a scroll with the passage hung on the west side of his study. For an introduction to the writings of the Neo-Confucians, see Wing-tsit Chan, *A Sourcebook of Chinese Philosophy* (Princeton: Princeton University Press, 1969). For the *Western Inscription* see ibid., 497–8.

8 *Recorded Sayings*, ch. 94. See Chan, *Sourcebook*, 638.

9 In at least one passage, though, Zhu Xi sees the distinction between human nature and mind/heart as simply one of language: "such words as feeling, nature, mind, and ability all mean the same thing" (*Collected Works of Lu Xiangshan (Lu Jiuyuan)*), ch. 35. Bryan W. Van Norden points out that Zhu Xi changes Mencius' dictum "human nature is good" to read "human nature is basically good." This is a reflection of Zhu Xi's belief that one had to uncover the basic principle (human nature) within, while Mencius argued that one had to develop human nature outwardly. See *Mengzi*, xliiif.

10 The mind/heart is not principle, human nature is principle. The mind/heart relates to concrete life and activity and is a union of principle and *qi*.

11 *The Book of History, The Book of Poetry*, the *Spring and Autumn Annals* with the *Zuo Zhuan* commentary, the *Book of Changes (Yi Jing)* and the *Book of Rites*.

12 This Confucian orthodoxy was enforced especially severely by the emperors Yongzheng (1723–36) and Qianlong (1736–96), who are both well known for their censorship of books and thinkers.

13 Ding-hwa E. Hsieh, "Images of Women in Ch'an Buddhist Literature" in *Buddhism in the Song*, 178–9. Zhu Xi also opposed the idea of women becoming Buddhist nuns, as it took them away from their family duties. He banned the practice when he held the post of assistant magistrate. See Bettine Birge, "Chu Hsi [Zhu Xi] and Women's Education" in *Neo-Confucian Education: the Formative Stage*, ed. W. T. de Bary (Berkeley: University of California Press, 1989), 357–9. For stories of loyal widows, see Patricia Ebrey, "Widows Loyal Unto Death" in Patricia Ebrey, ed., *Chinese Civilization: A Sourcebook* (New York: Maxwell Macmillan, 1993).

14   Bettine Birge, *Women, Property, and Confucian Reaction in Sung [Song] and Yuan China (960–1368)* (Cambridge: Cambridge University Press, 2002).
15   It was still possible even in the mid-1990s to meet elderly women with bound feet in various parts of China. Footbinding was not generally practiced by non-Han Chinese groups, and when the Manchus conquered China in 1644 they tried to stop the practice, but were unsuccessful. This has led Li-Hsiang Lisa Rosenlee to make the astonishing argument that one of the functions of footbinding was to express Han Chinese nationalism during the Mongol and Manchu invasions. See *Confucianism and Women: a Philosophical Interpretation*, 143f.
16   See Patricia Ebrey, *The Inner Quarters: Marriage and Lives of Chinese Women in the Sung [Song] Period*, (Berkeley: University of California Press, 1993). For a nuanced description of the influence of Confucianism on women, especially in the Ming and Qing dynasties, see Fangqiu Du and Susan Mann, "Competing Claims on Womanly Virtue in Late Imperial China," in Dorothy Ko, Hyun Kim Haboush, and Joan R. Piggott, eds, *Women in Confucian Cultures in Premodern China, Korea, and Japan* (Berkeley and Los Angeles: University of California Press, 2003), 219–47.
17   See Kenneth Ch'en, *Buddhism in China: a Historical Survey* (Princeton: Princeton University Press, 1964), especially 471–3.
18   Wang Yangming, *Instructions for Practical Living*; see Chan, *Sourcebook*, 669.

Notes to Chapter 12

1   It was the Manchus who decreed that all Chinese men must wear the queue – sometimes derogatorily called a "pigtail."
2   Which is why the British government put such a high tax on tea sold in the Americas, leading to the "Boston tea party," and why taxation on tea was one of the reasons for the American Revolution in 1776.
3   Kang's proposal was in part to imitate, in part to prevent, Christian practice in China. The *Kongjiao xueyuan*, a Confucian academy along the lines of a Christian church, was set up in Hong Kong. This academy exists today and its head is recognized by the Hong Kong government as the head of the Confucian religion. Confucianism is recognized in Hong Kong as an official religion, though not in the rest of China; see John Makeham, *Lost Soul: "Confucianism" in Contemporary Chinese Academic Discourse* (Cambridge, MA: Harvard-Yenching Institute Monographs 64, 2008), 306.
4   There was also some attempt at military reform and in 1907 the Dowager Empress, Cixi, announced the setup of federal and provincial assemblies, but they had no real power.
5   The founder of the republic, Sun Yat-sen (1866–1925), wrote that the Confucian family model, based on filial piety and the second-class status of women, was one of the biggest problems facing China. See Nylan, *The Five "Confucian" Classics*, 316–17.
6   *Pohuai Kongjia dian*, "smash the Confucian family shop." Wu Zhihui's slogan was, "All thread-bound books [the printing style of old books, including the Confucian classics] should be thrown away down the toilet."

7 Some of the titles give us a taste of their time: the *Dawn, Young China, New Society*, the *New Woman*.

8 Lu Xun, "A Madman's Diary." He refers to the great practice of filial piety, using one's own flesh to make a medicine for ailing parents.

9 Chiang Kai-shek is the version of his name best known in the West; in Mandarin, his name is Jiang Jieshi.

10 The New Life Movement's short rules, however, contain little one would recognize as Confucian: "Don't smoke when walking; look straight ahead; button up your buttons; sit up straight; be on time."

11 Slavery in ancient and imperial China is a difficult and disputed issue. The Marxist interpretation of the Shang and Zhou dynasties as slave-holding societies has not brought clarity to the debates.

12 See Kenneth Lieberthal, ed., *Governing China: From Revolution to Reform* (New York: Norton, 1995), 71.

13 In 1949, the Communist government of China set up the People's Republic of China, the PRC. Having retreated to the island of Taiwan, Chiang Kai-shek and the Guomindang continued to maintain that they were the real government of China as the Republic of China, the ROC. Foreigners often find it hard to distinguish between the PRC and the ROC.

14 When French leaders criticized China's crackdown on Tibet in early 2008, Carrefour stores in China, incorrectly identified as being anti-Chinese, were besieged by demonstrators and the Internet was full of an outpouring of Chinese patriotism from young people inside China and abroad.

15 Tang Junyi, Mou Zongsan, Xu Fuguan, and Zhang Junmai issued in 1958 "*Wei Zhongguo wenhua jinggao shijierenshi xuanyan*" [Declaration concerning Chinese culture respectfully announced to the people of the world]. In it, Confucianism is declared to be religious. This continues in the thinking of Mou Zongsan and Tang Junyi who call Confucianism a humanist religion, *renwen zongjiao*. See Makeham, *Lost Soul*, 280.

16 In Chinese, *Xin Ruxue*, new Confucian learning.

17 Foremost among Western commentators was Max Weber, who argued that Confucianism and capitalism were antithetical and that one of the reasons that Confucianism could not cope with modern society was that a Confucian society could not deal with economic, capitalist growth. This is all nonsense, of course. There are many, many factors involved in the development of both Western and Asian countries. Confucianism's role was considerably less important than the processes of imperialism, for example.

18 Tu Wei-ming (Du Weiming) was particularly involved in the establishment of the Confucian–capitalism thesis, but he does not see it as a causal connection. See John Makeham, *Lost* 22; 30. Makeham notes that in the early 1980s Confucianism became associated with capitalist modernity "almost overnight" (ibid.).

19 Tu Wei-ming (Du Weiming) is the Harvard-Yenching Professor of Chinese History and Philosophy and of Confucian Studies at Harvard University. See his *Centrality and Commonality: An Essay on Confucian Religiousness* (Albany, NY: SUNY Press, 1989).

20   Umberto Bresciani, *Reinventing Confucianism: the New Confucian Movement* (Taipei: Taipei Ricci Institute for Chinese Studies, 2001), 491.

21   For a discussion of the details and implications see Makeham, *Lost*, chs. 6, 7, 10, 12, and 13.

22   Western values are function, application, *yong*, while Confucian humanism, based on the learning of mind/heart, is the substance/principle, *li* (Lee Seunghwan, *A Topography of Confucian Discourse*, 34–5).

23   Apologists say things like "it is important to distinguish between pure doctrines and their historical realizations," Bresciani, *Reinventing*, 484. He expands on this in an endnote: "Any apologist for any religion would request that such a distinction be made. Therefore it should not be the case to discard Confucianism based on historical realities (authoritarian dynastic regimes, cruel family rules, backward social customs, and the like). All these negative aspects attributed to Confucianism in its historical realization arguably might be only slightly related, or not related at all, to the basic Confucian world-view. Liu Shuxian observes, 'Although the "Confucian state" has been used by historians in the English-speaking community to characterize the Han and subsequent dynasties, the Confucian state is no more Confucian than Christendom is Christian, this is another myth in need of further scrutiny' "; Bresciani, *Reinventing*, 632, note 58. For another example of the argument that there is a difference between an ideal and a practiced Confucianism see Rosemont and Ames, *The Chinese Classic of Family Reverence*, 4.

24   "Mysticism" is a word that seems to mean whatever the speaker wants it to mean. Too often it is used as a way to say "unexplainable" or "I am not going to explain it." For New Confucians, it seems to indicate developing a sense of oneness with the universe. For a discussion of "mysticism" and the ways it has been applied to Asia, see Richard King, *Orientalism and Religion: Postcolonial Theory, India, and the "Mystic East"* (New York: Routledge, 1999). While King focuses on the Indian traditions, much of his discussion can apply to studies in China as well. Important scholars like Tang Junyi and Mou Zongsan have declared Confucianism a religion.

25   Bresciani, *Reinventing*, 464f. Liu Shuxian says, "[it is a misunderstanding when] they consider Confucianism as just a set of moral rules. They utterly ignore the whole network of doctrines of Confucianism concerning the meaning and destiny of human beings and concerning the communion between human beings and Heaven. We New Confucians continuously stress these religious dimensions of Confucianism" (Bresciani, *Reinventing*, 466). See Bresciani for a more complete description of the history of, and the similarities among, New Confucians.

26   Tu Weiming, on the other hand, argues that Confucianism is both a philosophy and a religion, not an exclusively analytical philosophy, nor a religion that talks about faith and souls; Bresciani, *Reinventing*, 466. This attitude has affected scholarship. When the Shanghai strips were published (see notes, chapter 8), one can see, for example at www.confucius2000.com and www.jianbo.org, that many of the pieces have been understood as texts from a school associated with Mencius and Confucius' grandson. Thus the texts are read as emphasizing a more religious or transcendent aspect of Confucianism. See Makeham, *Lost*, ch. 10.

27 See Bresciani, *Reinventing*, 33.
28 In discussions of this sort, I find that there is rarely any distinction made among the countries of North America and Europe. All are tarred with the same brush.
29 See the 1998 article by Wang Mekui, Chief of the National Affairs Bureau, quoted in Lee Seung-hwan, *Topography*, 62.
30 See Huang Chun-chieh and Wu Kuang-ming, "Taiwan and the Confucian Aspiration: Toward the Twenty-first Century," in *Cultural Change in Postwar Taiwan*, ed. Steven Harrell and Huang Chun-chieh (Boulder, CO: Westview Press, 1994).
31 Joseph B. Tamney and Linda Hsueh-Ling Chiang, *Modernization, Globalization, and Confucianism in Chinese Societies* (London: Praeger, 2002), 6. Tamney also points out that in Taiwan Confucianism is often identified with the people who came to the island with the Guomindang, and folk religion is identified with the Taiwanese. With the growth in Taiwanese nationalism, it may well be that we will see Confucianism as a detachable part of Chinese culture; see 85f.
32 Yu Ying-shih (Yu Yingshi) from Yale and Tu Wei-ming of Harvard. It may be that more study in Confucianism is needed. In Singapore in 2000, a sizeable increase in ministerial salaries was justified by one minister saying that paying officials well was an ancient Confucian idea and quoting Sunzi, "It is impossible to have good people come forward without the proper rewards" (Tamney, 76–7). But Sunzi is not a Confucian, and the idea of rewards and punishments to organize the behavior of civil servants is a Legalist idea.
33 "While it is impossible to calculate the amount of loss incurred by bureaucratic corruption in China, it is estimated that four times the amount of the national GDP is siphoned from the national treasure to private safes every year." Lee Seung-hwan, *Topography*, 63.
34 When I traveled in China in the early 1980s and people asked me what I taught, I would get a blank look when I said, "Chinese philosophy." I found that adding "Kongzi, Mengzi" (Confucius, Mencius) would evoke some recognition. It is only in the past decade that I have found a general recognition of Kongzi's name, but still only rare recognition of the names of other thinkers of the Warring States like Laozi or Mozi who are not generally taught in schools. Makeham argues that teaching about Confucianism has been only with test groups and Confucius is not widely taught in schools; see Makeham, *Lost* 313f.
35 Lee Kwan Yew is the journal's honorary director. In another approach, John Makeham makes a strong argument that it is wrong to think that the party-state promotion of Confucianism in China is what is promoting Confucianism as cultural nationalism. State nationalism explains it better. Confucian centered Chinese cultural nationalism is a movement of academics; Makeham, *Lost*, 7,16.
36 Tamney, *Modernization*, 74.
37 The relationship is reciprocal: many New Confucian academics have their careers and funding tied to a state-sponsored Confucianism; see Nylan, *The Five "Confucian" Classics*, 337. South Korea, and to a lesser extent Japan, have also followed this model. "A *Straits Times* [Singaporean newspaper] editorial (16 October 1989) repeated a point about Confucianism: 'The most damning

of charges is that it is so easily harnessed by politicians to lend respectability to their tyrannical ways. ... Philosophy usually loses its moral worth when drafted for dubious political purpose and Confucianism, which has much that is humanist, deserves better than that.' However, political leaders in mainland China and Singapore are prone to using Confucianism selectively to support their own desire for power, and in the process give Confucianism generally a bad name"; Tamney, *Modernization*, 80. John Makeham argues that the Chinese government's promotion of Chinese cultural or traditional values is not actually closely related to New Confucianism. New Confucianism, he says, is a separate phenomenon. The equation of traditional culture = Chinese-ness = Confucianism is to a large extent a response to perceived threats from the West and a way to define all these things as different from the West. For a summary, see Makeham, *Lost*, 342f. He goes on to say that "Academic discourse on *ruxue* [New Confucianism] in China and Taiwan bears little evidence of a sustained or robust philosophical creativity in *ruxue* philosophy" (344).

38   For a description of the criticism of Zheng Kezhong see Lee Seung-hwan, *Topography* 55; for a description of the criticism by Zhu Riayao, see ibid., 56.

39   The Beijing Olympics in 2008 made no mention of Mao Zedong, but leaned heavily on the figure of Confucius, particularly in the opening ceremonies.

Notes to Chapter 13

1   "Confucian discourse has been couched under the same rubric of 'Confucianism' which inadvertently produces a vast range of different meanings for this one term. ... Although expressed by the identical signifier Confucianism, the meaning of Confucian discourse cannot be the same; it is carried out by different agents in different contexts. What really matters is 'who' wants to select, distribute, and use 'what part of the tradition for which purpose' "; Lee, Seung-hwan *Topography*, ix–xi.

2   See Makeham, *Lost*, 2.

3   See Tu Wei-ming et al., eds., *The Confucian World Observed: a Contemporary Discussion of Confucian Humanism in East Asia* (Honolulu: University of Hawai'i Press, 1992), 17.

4   For Tu Wei-ming see chapter 12. Robert Neville is Dean of the Boston School of Theology, see his *Boston Confucianism* (Albany: SUNY, 2000). See also John Berthrong, "Boston Confucianism: the Third Wave of Global Confucianism," *Journal of Ecumenical Studies* Winter/Spring, 2003.

5   For a fascinating and lively discussion of Confucianism in present-day China, its relationship to society, and the possibilities for its development, see Daniel A. Bell, *China's New Confucianism: Politics and Everyday Life in a Changing Society* (Princeton: Princeton University Press, 2008).

6   Lee Kuan Yew, *The Economist*, April 27, 1994, 5. Quoted in Richard Madsen, *Democracy's Dharma: Religious Renaissance and Political Developments in Taiwan* (Berkeley: University of California Press, 2007), xx.

7   Along with this is a view that one can still frequently encounter, namely that the jury system is a terrible idea. It is much better, elitists argue, to be judged

by a judge who knows the law than by ordinary people who may be very ignorant.

8   *Analects* 12.19.

9   *Analects* 7.16.

10 We are encouraged to pamper ourselves. If you want to see this in action, advertisements are the best place to look. Many are based on "you know you want it," "you deserve it," or "if you don't reward yourself, who will?" with no thought for the moral consequences, or financial impact, on life. Others are more blatant: a recent Christmas ad says, "How can I give to my friends and family, while showing myself how much I care about me?" Another says that, after you have bought gifts for others, "You'll have money left over for – dare I say it? – yourself. It won't even matter if you've been naughty or nice."

11 Li-hsiang Lisa Rosenlee, *Confucianism and Women*, 45f., is a good example of the latter point of view.

12 Novels like the *Dream of the Red Chamber* imply that women with education tended to be more unfaithful and meet tragic ends, but in general the idea was that education for women helped society, taught morals, and provided better early education of children. By the Ming dynasty, women's education was a topic of debate. The Ming saying was, "In women, lack of talent is a virtue," and this was followed by a Qing dynasty saying, "Ignorance in women is a virtue."

13 A radical alternative can be found in *Ching Hua Yuan, Flowers in the Mirror*, by Li Ru-chen, 1763–1800. In this novel, everything is turned around. The hero is kept as a concubine and has his feet bound and his ears pierced and is covered in makeup. He is in a household ruled by women who also sit for the civil service exams. There are, however, many Confucian ideas such as filial piety, chastity, and widows committing suicide, and the villain is that Confucian arch-enemy, Empress Wu of the Tang dynasty.

14 The earliest version of this story dates from about the fifth century CE, but there are many variations on it. For a modern version of this story, ignore Disney and see Maxine Hong Kingston's novel, *Woman Warrior*.

15 Joseph Chan, "Confucian Attitudes toward Ethical Pluralism," in *Confucian Political Ethics*, ed. Daniel A. Bell (Princeton: Princeton University Press, 2008), 129. "I shall argue that this conception of gender [in the *Analects* and the *Mencius*] is primarily a functional distinction assigning women to inner/domestic duties, and men to outer/public duties. I shall then show how this conception of gender plays out in the context of the Confucian relationship role system. Finally I shall argue that this conception of gender can neither justify those forms of subordination of women, nor itself be justified on Confucian grounds. One can discard this early Confucian conception of gender, without relinquishing one's commitment to the core doctrines of early Confucianism" (Sin Yee Chan, "Gender and Relationship Roles in the *Analects* and the *Mencius*" in *Confucian Political Ethics*, 147).

16 Discussing imperial China, "Ru [Confucian] learning was not identical to, nor dependent on, state power. ... Ru official-literati did not possess substantial political power which was in the hands of the ruling house," Rosenlee, *Confucianism and Women* 5.

17   Such as Voltaire, Montesquieu, Rousseau, Leibniz, and Wolff. "Confucius –
     as the Jesuits constructed him –offered testimony through his writings of the
     natural theology of the Chinese and the prospect of its union with the Jesuits'
     own revealed theology. ... 'Confucius' was their Christian other" (Jensen,
     Manufacturing Confucianism, 94).

18   The issues in defining much of Chinese religiosity are extremely complex.
     Modern scholars have moved away from labeling Chinese religiosity as simply
     the traditions of Buddhism, Religious Daoism, and possibly Confucianism.
     Scholars now look at the "synthetic-syncretic" practice of religiosity that
     includes everything from ancestral veneration to shrines in homes and busi-
     nesses to funeral rituals to the belief in ghosts and spirits. They do this as a way
     to deal with the ubiquitous comment one hears in China, where people will
     tell you that they are not religious. This applies in the West as well. In census
     data from 2001 Statistics Canada reports that 58.6% of Canadians of Chinese
     origin reported "no religious affiliation." Meanwhile religious activity is going
     on in homes and in the community that is not institutional or text-based. For
     a great example of syncretism in Chinese practice, see the autobiography of
     Kong Demao, *The House of Confucius*, Rosemary Roberts, trans. (London:
     Hodder and Stoughton, 1988). In her memoirs as one of the daughters of the
     Kong family in the period from the early 1900s to the 1970s, she describes
     "very Confucian" family rituals that are syncretic. For an introduction to these
     issues, see Adam Yuet Chau, *Miraculous Response: Doing Popular Religion in
     Contemporary China* (Stanford, CA: Stanford University Press, 2006).

Glossary of Names and Terms

You will find the English, the Pinyin version, then the Wade–Giles transliteration, if it differs. As Pinyin can be confusing to non-Sinologists, an approximate pronunciation is in quotation marks, followed by the Chinese character.

English	Pinyin	Wade–Giles	Pronunciation	Chinese character(s)
accomplishments, arts	*yi*	*i*	"yee"	藝
Analects	*Lun Yu*			論語
artificiality	*wei*		"way"	僞
	Ban Zhao	Pan Chao		班昭
Book of Changes	Yi Jing	Yi Ching	"yee" "jing" rhymes with "ring"	易經
or	Zhou Yi	Chou Yi	"Zhou, Joe"	周易
Book of History	Shu Jing	Shu Ching		書經
Book of Poetry	Shi Jing	Shih Ching		詩經
Book of Rites	Li Ji	Li Chi	"Lee gee"	禮紀
	Cheng Hao	Ch'eng Hao	"ch'ung" "hao, how"	程顥
	Cheng Yi	Ch'eng Yi	"ch'ung" "yi, yee"	程頤
	Chiang Kai-Shek		"Chiang, chee-ahng" "Kai," rhymes with "high" "shek" rhymes with "check"	蔣介石

English	Pinyin	Wade–Giles	Pronunciation	Chinese character(s)
choice of Heaven	Tian ming	T'ien ming	"tea-anne" "ming" rhymes with "ring"	天命
Chu, state of			"chew"	楚
classic	jing		"ching" rhymes with "ring"	經
Classic of Music	Yue Jing	Yueh Ching	"you-eh"	樂經
Confucius	Kungzi	K'ung Tzu	"Kong" rhymes with "lung" "zi, dzzuh"	孔子
also	Kongfuzi	K'ong Fu Tzu	"fu, foo"	孔夫子
also	Kong Qiu	K'ung Chiu	"chee-oh"	孔邱
also	Kong Zhongni	K'ung Chong-ni	"j-uhng"	孔仲尼
Confucians (see "Ru" below)	*Ru*	*Ju*	"roo"	儒
courage	*yong*	*yung*	"y-uhng"	勇
Dao, Tao, the Way	Dao	Tao	rhymes with "how"	道
Dao De Jing, Tao Te Ching	Dao De Jing	Tao Te Ching	"De" rhymes with "they"	道德經
a knight/worthy of the Way	Dao shi	Tao shih	"sure"	道士
the orthodox transmission of the Dao of Confucius	Dao Tong	Tao t'ung	"tong, tongue"	道統
school of the Dao	Daoxue	Tao Hsueh	"xue, shoe-eh"	道學
Deng Xiaoping	Deng Xiaoping	Teng Hsiao-p'ing		鄧小平
dictator, local lords, hegemon	*ba*	*pa*		霸
Doctrine of the Mean	Zhong Yong	Chung Yung	"zhong, zh-uhng"	中庸
dutifulness, loyalty	*zhong*	*chung*	"zhong, zh-uhng"	忠
	Dong Zhongshu	Tung Chung-shu	"dong, d-uhng" "zhong, zh-uhng" "shu, shoe"	董仲舒

English	Pinyin	Wade–Giles	Pronunciation	Chinese character(s)
fate, choice, mandate	*ming*		rhymes with "ring"	命
	Fazang	Fa-tsang	"faw", "dz-ahng"	法藏
filial piety	*xiao*	*hsiao*	"she-ow"	孝
	Gaozi	Kao Tzu	"Gao" rhymes with "how"	告子
Gaozu (emperor)	Gaozu	Kaotzu	"Gao" rhymes with "how" "zoo"	高祖
gentleman	*junzi*	*chun-tzu*	"j-one" "dzzuh"	君子
ghosts and spirits	*guishen*	*kuei-shen*	"g-way" "sh-hen"	鬼神
gods	*shen*			神
	Gongsun Long	Kung-sun Lung	"Gong" and "Long" rhyme with "lung" "sun, s-one"	公孫龍
Great Learning	Daxue	Ta Hsueh	"da" "shoe-eh"	大學
	Guomindang	Kuomintang	"Guo, g-woe" "min, mean" "dang, d-ahng"	國民黨
Han dynasty			"h-ahn"	漢
Han Fei, Han Feizi			"fay" "dzzuh"	韓非
Han, the state of				韓
Hanlin Academy	Hanlin Yuan		"lin of Linda"	翰林院
	Han Yu		"Yu, you"	韓愈
Heaven	Tian	T'ien	"tea-en"	天
Heaven's Choice, or the Mandate of Heaven	Tian Ming	T'ien Ming		天命
honesty	xin	hsin	"shin"	信
	Hua Yan	Hua-yen	"h-wah" "yen"	華嚴
	Huang-Lao		"huh-wahng" "Lao" rhymes with "how"	黃老

English	Pinyin	Wade–Giles	Pronunciation	Chinese character(s)
	Hui Shi	Hui Shih	"Hui, h-way" "Shi, sure"	惠施
humanity, humaneness, co-humanity, benevolence, Goodness and so on	*ren*	*jen*	rhymes with "hen"	仁
intuitive knowledge	*liang zhi*	*liang-chih*	"lee-ahng" "zhi, zh-ure"	良知
Jixia/Chi-hsia Academy	Jixia	Chi-hsia	"Ji, cheee" "xia, she-a"	稷下
a gentleman	*junzi*	*chun-tzu*	"jun, j-one"	君子
	Kang Youwei	K'ang Yu-wei	"Kang" "k-ahng" "You, yo" "wei, way"	康有爲
knight, scholar	*shi*	*shih*	"sure"	士
knowledge	*zhi*	*chih*	"j-ure"	知
the "female" basic hexagram from the *Book of Changes*	*kun*	*k'un*	"k-one"	坤
	Laozi	Lao Tzu	"Lao" rhymes with "how" "zi, dzzuh"	老子
Lee Kuan Yew			"lee" "k-wan" "you"	李光耀
Li Ao			"lee" "ow"	李翱
	Li Si	Li Ssu	"lee" "s-uh"	李斯
the school of principle	Li Xue	Li Hsueh	"lee" "shoe-eh"	理學
original mind	*liang xin*	*liang hsin*	"lee-ahng" "shin"	良心
Lin Yutang			"Lin" the "lin" of "Linda;" "you" "t-ahng"	
loyalty, dutifulness	*zhong*	*chung*	"zh-ohng"	忠
Lu, state of			"loo"	魯

English	Pinyin	Wade–Giles	Pronunciation	Chinese character(s)
	Lu Jiuyuan	Lu Chiu-yuan	"lew" "gee-oh" "you-ahn"	陸九淵
	Lu Xun	Lu Hsun	"Lu, lew" "Xun, sh-one"	魯迅
Luoyang			"lwo-yahng"	洛陽
	Mao Zedong	Mao Tse-tung	"m-ow" "z-uh" "d-uhng"	毛澤東
Mencius	Mengzi	Meng Tzu	"Meng" rhymes with "lung" "dzzuh"	孟子
mind/heart	*xin*	*hsin*	"shin"	心
	Mozi	Mo Tzu	"Mo" rhymes with "toe" "dzzuh"	墨子
movement	*dong*	*tung*	rhymes with "lung"	動
Perfect Sage and Ancient Teacher	*zhi sheng xian shi*	*chih sheng hsien shih*		至聖先師
phenomenon	*shi*	*shih*	"sure"	事
principle	*li*		"lee"	理
energy and matter	*qi*	*ch'i*	"chee"	氣
Qi, the state of			"chee"	齊
the "male" basic hexagram from the *Book of Changes*	*qian*	*ch'ien*	"chee-en"	乾
Qin, the state of, later the dynasty	Qin	Ch'in	"chin"	秦
Qing/Ch'ing dynasty	Qing	Ch'ing	rhymes with "ring"	清
	Qu Yuan	Ch'u Yuan	"chew" "you-anne"	屈原
	Qufu	Ch'u Fu	"chew-foo"	曲阜
ritual, rites, propriety	*li*		"lee"	禮
rightness, right, righteousness	*yi*	*i*	"yee"	義
	Ru	Ju	"roo"	儒

English	Pinyin	Wade–Giles	Pronunciation	Chinese character(s)
Ru-ist knight, worthy	Ru shi		"roo" "sure"	儒士
the school of Ru	Ru jia	Ju chia	"roo" "gee-ah"	儒家
Ru teachings	Ru jiao	Ru chiao	"roo" "gee-ow"	儒教
school (of thought)	*jia* *jiao*	*chia* *chiao*	"gee-ah" "gee-ow"	家 / 教
setting words right	*zheng ming*	*cheng ming*	"zh-uhng" "ming" rhymes with "ring"	正名
	Shandong	Shantung	"sh-an" "d-uhng"	山東
Shang dynasty			"Sh-ahng"	商
Shang Yang			"sh-ahng" "y-ahng"	商鞅
	Shen Buhai	Shen Pu-hai	"Shen" rhymes with "pen" "Buhai, boo-high"	申不害
Records of the Historian	Shi Ji	Shih Ch'i	"sure gee"	史記
	Sima Qian	Ssu-ma Chien	"suh-mah" "chee-en"	司馬遷
	Sima Tan	Ssu-ma T'an	"suh-mah" "tan"	司馬談
sincerity, integrity	*cheng*	*ch'eng*		誠
spirits	*guishen*	*kuei-shen*	"g-way" "shen"	鬼神
Song/Sung, state of, or dynasty	Song	Sung	rhymes with "lung"	宋
Spring and Autumn	Chunqiu	Ch'un Ch'iu	"ch-one" "chee-oh"	春秋
still, stillness, quiescence	*jing*	*ching*	rhymes with "ring"	靜
Sui dynasty			"sway"	隋
	Sunzi	Sun Tzu	"s-one" "dzzuh"	孫子
Sunzi Bingfa, the *Art of War*			"bing" rhymes with "ring" "fah"	孫子兵法

English	Pinyin	Wade–Giles	Pronunciation	Chinese character(s)
sympathy, compassion	shu		"shoe"	恕
	Taishan	T'ai Shan	"tie" "sh-anne"	泰山
	Taibei	Taipei	"tie" "bey"	臺北
Taiwan			"tie" "wan"	台灣
Supreme Ultimate	Tai Ji	T'ai Chi	"tie" "gee"	太極
Tang/T'ang dynasty	Tang	T'ang	"t-ahng"	唐
	Wang Chong	Wang Ch'ung	"wa-ahng" "ch-uhng"	王充
	Wang Yangming	Wang Yang-ming	"wa-ahng" "y-ahng" "ming" rhymes with "ring"	王陽明
Wei, state of,			"way"	魏
Wey, state of			"way"	衛
wisdom, wise	*zhi*	*chi*	"j-ur"	智
Supreme Ultimate-less	Wu Ji	Wu Chi	"Wu" "woo" "gee"	無極
Xia/Hsia dynasty	Xia	Hsia	"shaw"	夏
filial piety	*xiao*	*hsiao*	"she-ow"	孝
mind and heart	*xin*	*hsin*	"shin"	心
New Confucians	Xin Ruxue	Hsin Ju Hsueh	"shin" "roo" "shoe-eh"	新儒學
the school of mind/heart	Xinxue	Hsin Hsueh	"shin shoe-eh"	心學
Xuanzong, Tang emperor			"t-ahng" "sh-wan" "z-uhng"	唐玄宗
	Xunzi	Hsun Tzu	"Xun" rhymes with "done" "dzzuh"	荀子
	Yan Hui or Yan Yuan	Yen Hui	"Yan" rhymes with "hen" "h-way"	顏回 or 顏淵
	Yang Guifei	Yang Kuei-fei	"y-ahng" "g-way" "fay"	楊貴妃
	yin-yang			陰陽
Yan/Yen, state of	Yan	Yen		燕
Zhao, state of			"zh-ow"	趙
	Zhang Zai	Chang Tsai	"j-ahng" "sigh"	張載

English	Pinyin	Wade–Giles	Pronunciation	Chinese character(s)
Zhou/Chou dynasty	Zhou	Chou	"Joe"	周
	Zhou Dunyi	Chou Tun-yi	"done" "yee"	周敦頤
	Zhu Xi	Chu Hsi	"Jew" "shee"	朱熹
	Zhuangzi	Chuang Tzu	"zh-wahng"	莊子
Zi Si/Tzu Ssu, Confucius' grandson	Zi Si	Tzu Ssu	"dzzuh" "suh"	子思
Zou or Zouyi		Tsou yi	"z-oh" or "z-oh yee"	陬邑
	Zuo Zhuan	Tso Chuan	"Z-woe" "j-wahn"	左轉

Suggestions for Further Reading

Chapter 1

Mark Edward Lewis, *Sanctioned Violence in Early China*. Albany: State University of New York Press, 1990.
Shigeki Kaizuka, *Confucius: His Life and Thought*, trans. Geoffrey Bownas. New York: Macmillan, 1956.
Burton Watson (trans.), *The Tso Chuan [Zuo Zhuan]: Selections from China's Oldest Narrative History*. New York: Columbia University Press, 1989.

Chapter 2

Roger Ames and Henry Rosemont, *The Analects of Confucius: A Philosophical Translation*. New York: Ballantine Books, 1998.
E. Bruce and Taeko Brooks, *The Original Analects: Sayings of Confucius and His Successors*. New York: Columbia University Press, 1998.
Edward Slingerland, *Confucius: Analects with Selections from Traditional Commentaries*. Indianapolis/Cambridge: Hackett Publishing, 2003.

Chapter 3

Daniel A. Bell (ed.), *Confucian Political Ethics*. Princeton: Princeton University Press, 2008.
David L. Hall and Roger Ames, *Thinking Through Confucius*. Albany: State University of New York Press, 1987.
Yao Xinzhong, *An Introduction to Confucianism*. New York: Cambridge University Press, 2000.

Chapter 4

Philip J. Ivanhoe and Bryan W. Van Norden, *Readings in Classical Chinese Philosophy*. New York: Seven Bridges, 2001.

Yuri Pines, *Foundations of Confucian Thought: Intellectual Life in the Chunqiu Period*. Honolulu: University of Hawai'i Press, 2002.

Burton Watson (trans.), *Mo Tzu [Mozi]: Basic Writings*. New York: Columbia University Press, 1963.

Chapter 5

D. C. Lau (trans.), *Lao Tzu: Tao Te Ching [Laozi: Dao De Jing]*. London: Penguin Books, 1963.

Liu JeeLoo, *An Introduction to Chinese Philosophy*. Oxford: Blackwell, 2006.

Benjamin I. Schwarz, *The World of Thought in Ancient China*. Cambridge, MA: Harvard University Press, 1985.

Burton Watson (trans.) *The Complete Works of Chuang Tzu [Zhuangzi]*. New York: Columbia University Press, 1964.

Chapter 6

David Hinton, *Mencius*. Washington, DC: Counterpoint, 1999.

Kwong-loi Shun, *Mencius and Early Chinese Thought*. Stanford, CA: Stanford University Press, 1997.

Bryan W. Van Norden, *Mengzi [Mencius] with Selections from Traditional Commentaries*. Indianapolis: Hackett Publishing, 2008.

Chapter 7

John Knoblock, *Xunzi: A Study and Translation of the Complete Works*, 3 vols. Stanford, CA: Stanford University Press, 1988.

Burton Watson (trans.), *Hzun Tzu [Xunzi]: Basic Writings*. New York: Columbia University Press, 1967.

Chapter 8

Michael Loewe (ed.), *Early Chinese Texts: A Bibliographic Guide*. Berkeley, CA: Society for the Study of Early China, 1993.

Henry Rosemont, Jr. and Roger Ames, *The Chinese Classic of Family Reverence: A Philosophical Translation of the Xiaojing*. Honolulu: University of Hawai'i Press, 2009.

Edward L. Shaughnessy (trans.), *I Ching: The Classic of Changes*. New York: Ballantine, 1997.

Edward L. Shaughnessy, *Rewriting Early Chinese Texts*. Albany: State University of New York Press, 2006.

Chapter 9

David L. Hall and Roger Ames, *Thinking from the Han: Self, Truth, and Transcendence in Chinese and Western Culture*. Albany: State University of New York Press, 1998.
Michael Nylan, *The Five "Confucian" Classics*. New Haven: Yale University Press, 2001.
Sarah A. Queen, *From Chronicle to Canon: the Hermeneutics of the Spring and Autumn, According to Tung Chung-shu [Dong Zhongshu]*. Cambridge: Cambridge University Press, 1996.
Robin S. Yates, *Five Lost Classics: Tao [Dao], Huanglao, and Yin-Yang in Han China*. New York: Ballantine, 1997.

Chapter 10

Keith N. Knapp, *Selfless Offspring: Filial Children and Social Order in Medieval China*. Honolulu: University of Hawai'i Press, 2005.
Ichisada Miyazaki, *China's Examination Hell: the Civil Service Examinations of Imperial China*, trans. Conrad Schirokauer. New Haven: Yale University Press, 1981.
Sherry J. Mou, *Gentlemen's Prescriptions for Women's Lives: a Thousand Years of Biographies of Chinese Women*. New York: M. E. Sharpe, 2004.

Chapter 11

John H. Berthrong and Evelyn Nagai, *Confucianism: A Short Introduction*. Oxford: Oneworld, 2000.
Wing-tsit Chan (trans.), *Instructions for Practical Living, and Other Neo-Confucian Writings by Wang Yang-ming*. New York: Columbia University Press, 1963.
Carson Chang, *The Development of Neo-Confucian Thought*, 2 vols. New York: Bookman, 1962.
Patricia Ebrey, *The Inner Quarters: Marriage and Lives of Chinese Women in the Sung [Song] Period*. Berkeley: University of California Press, 1993.

Chapter 12

Daniel A. Bell, *China's New Confucianism: Politics and Everyday Life in a Changing Society*. Princeton: Princeton University Press, 2008.
Umberto Bresciani, *Reinventing Confucianism: the New Confucian Movement*. Taipei: Taipei Ricci Institute for Chinese Studies, 2001.

Joseph B. Tamney and Linda Hsueh-Ling Chiang, *Modernization, Globalization, and Confucianism in Chinese Societies*. London: Praeger, 2002.
Tu Wei-ming, *Centrality and Commonality: an Essay on Confucian Religiousness*. Albany: State University of New York Press, 1989.

Chapter 13

Seung-hwan Lee, *A Topography of Confucian Discourse: Politico-philosophical Reflections on Confucian Discourse Since Modernity*, trans. Jaeyoon Song and Seung-hwan Lee. Paramus, NJ: Homa and Sekey Books, 2006.
John Makeham, *Lost Soul: "Confucianism" in Contemporary Chinese Academic Discourse*. Harvard-Yenching Institute Monographs 64. Cambridge, MA, 2008.
Robert Neville, *Boston Confucianism*. Albany: State University of New York Press, 2000.

Bibliography

Ames, Roger and Henry Rosemont. *The Analects of Confucius: A Philosophical Translation*. New York: Ballantine Books, 1998.

Bell, Daniel A. *China's New Confucianism: Politics and Everyday Life in a Changing Society*. Princeton: Princeton University Press, 2008.

Bell, Daniel A., ed. *Confucian Political Ethics*. Princeton: Princeton University Press, 2008.

Berthrong, John. "Boston Confucianism: the Third Wave of Global Confucianism." *Journal of Ecumenical Studies* (Winter/Spring 2003).

Berthrong, John H. and Evelyn Nagai. *Confucianism: A Short Introduction*. Oxford: Oneworld, 2000.

Birge, Bettine. "Chu Hsi [Zhu Xi] and Women's Education." In *Neo-Confucian Education: the Formative Stage*, ed. W. T. deBary, pp. 337–59. Berkeley: University of California Press, 1989.

Birge, Bettine. *Women, Property, and Confucian Reaction in Sung [Song] and Yuan China (960–1368)*. Cambridge: Cambridge University Press, 2002.

Bresciani, Umberto. *Reinventing Confucianism: the New Confucian Movement*. Taipei: Taipei Ricci Institute for Chinese Studies, 2001.

Brooks, E. Bruce and Taeko A. Brooks. *The Original Analects: Sayings of Confucius and His Successors*. New York: Columbia University Press, 1998.

Chan Wing-tsit, trans. *Instructions for Practical Living and Other Neo-Confucian Writings, by Wang Yang-ming*. New York: Columbia University Press, 1963.

Chan Wing-tsit, trans. *A Source Book in Chinese Philosophy*. Princeton: Princeton University Press, 1963.

Chang, Carson. *The Development of Neo-Confucian Thought*, 2 vols. New York: Bookman, 1962.

Chang Chun-shu. *The Rise of the Chinese Empire. Volume 1: Nation, State, and Imperialism in Early China, ca. 1600 B.C.–A.D. 8*. Ann Arbor: University of Michigan Press, 2007.

Chang Kwang-chih. *Early Chinese Civilization: Anthropological Perspectives*. Cambridge, MA: Harvard University Press, 1976.

Creel, H. G. *Shen Pu-hai [Shen Buhai]: A Chinese Political Philosopher of the Fourth Century B.C.* Chicago: University of Chicago Press, 1974.

Csikszentmihalyi, Mark. "Confucius and the *Analects* in the Han." In *Confucius and the Analects: New Essays*, ed. Bryan Van Norden, pp. 134–62. New York: Oxford University Press, 2002.
Csikszentmihalyi, Mark. *Material Virtue: Ethics and the Body in Early China*. Leiden: Brill Sinica Leidensia, 2004.
Dawson, Raymond. *Confucius*. New York: Hill and Way, 1981.
Du Fangqui and Susan Mann, "Competing Claims on Womanly Virtue in Late Imperial China." In *Women in Confucian Cultures in Premodern China, Korea, and Vietnam*, ed. Dorothy Ko, 219–47. Los Angeles: University of California Press, 2003.
Duyvendak, J. L. *The Book of Lord Shang: A Classic of the Chinese School of Law*. Chicago: University of Chicago Press, 1963.
Ebrey, Patricia, ed. *Chinese Civilization: A Sourcebook*. New York: Maxwell MacMillan, 1993.
Ebrey, Patricia, ed. *The Inner Quarters: Marriage and Lives of Chinese Women in the Sung [Song] Period*. Berkeley: University of California Press, 1993.
Eno, Robert. *The Confucian Creation of Heaven: Philosophy and the Defense of Ritual Mastery*. Albany: State University of New York Press, 1990.
Fairbank, John K. and Merle Goldman. *China: a New History*. Cambridge, MA: Belknap Press, 1998.
Fingarette, Herbert. *Confucius: the Secular as Sacred*. New York: Harper and Row, 1972.
Graham, Angus C. *Later Mohist Logic, Ethics, and Science*. Hong Kong: Chinese University Press, 2003.
Hall, David L. and Roger Ames. *Thinking Through Confucius*. Albany: State University of New York Press, 1987.
Hall, David L. and Roger Ames. *Anticipating China: Thinking Through the Narratives of Chinese and Western Culture*. Albany: State University of New York Press, 1995.
Hall, David L. and Roger Ames. *Thinking from the Han: Self, Truth, and Transcendence in Chinese and Western Culture*. Albany: State University of New York Press, 1998.
Henricks, Robert G. *Lao Tzu's [Laozi's] Tao Te Ching [Dao De Jing]*. New York: Columbia University Press, 2000.
Hinton, David. *The Analects*. Washington: Counterpoint, 1998.
Hinton, David. *Mencius*. Washington: Counterpoint, 1999.
Hrdy, Sarah Blaffer. *Mothers and Others: The Evolutionary Origins of Mutual Understanding*. Cambridge, MA: Belknap Press, 2009.
Hu Pingsheng. *An Annotated Translation of the Xiaojing [Classic of Filial Piety]*. Beijing: Zhonghua Shuju, 1999.
Ichisada Miyazaki. *China's Examination Hell: the Civil Service Examinations of Imperial China*. Conrad Schirokauer, trans. New Haven: Yale University Press, 1981.
Ivanhoe, Philip J. and Bryan W. Van Norden. *Readings in Classical Chinese Philosophy*. New York: Seven Bridges, 2001.
Jensen, Lionel. *Manufacturing Confucianism: Chinese Traditions and Universal Civilization*. Durham, NC: Duke University Press, 1997.

Kaizuka, Shigeki. *Confucius: His Life and Thought*. Geoffrey Bownas, trans. New York: Macmillan, 1956.

Knapp, Keith N. *Selfless Offspring: Filial Children and Social Order in Medieval China*. Honolulu: University of Hawai'i Press, 2005.

Knoblock, John. *Xunzi: A Study and Translation of the Complete Works*, 3 vols. Stanford, CA: Stanford University Press, 1988.

Lau, D. C. *Confucius: The Analects*. New York: Penguin, 1979.

Lau, D. C. *Lao Tzu: Tao Te Ching [Laozi: Dao De Jing]*. London: Penguin, 1963.

Lee, Seung-hwan. *A Topography of Confucian Discourse: Politico-philosophical Reflections on Confucian Discourse since Modernity*. Jaeyoon Song and Seung-hwan Lee, trans. Paramus, NJ: Homa and Sekey Books, 2006.

Lewis, Mark Edward. *Sanctioned Violence in Early China*. Albany: State University of New York Press, 1990.

Lewis, Mark Edward. *The Construction of Space in Early China*. Albany: State University of New York Press, 2006.

Leys, Simon. *The Analects of Confucius*. New York: W.W. Norton and Co., 1997.

Li Chengyang, ed. *The Sage and the Second Sex: Confucianism, Ethics, and Gender*. Chicago: Open Court, 2000.

Li Feng. *Landscape and Power in Early China: the Crisis and Fall of the Western Zhou 1045–771BC*. Cambridge: Cambridge University Press, 2006.

Liao Mingchun. *A Preliminary Study on the Newly-Unearthed Inscriptions of the Chu Kingdom: An Investigation of the Materials from and about the Shangshu in the Guodian Chu Slips*. Taipei: Taiwan Guji, 2001.

Liu JeeLoo. *An Introduction to Chinese Philosophy*. Oxford: Blackwell, 2006.

Liu Yongping. *The Origins of Chinese Law: Penal and Administrative Law in its Early Development*. Hong Kong: Oxford University Press, 1998.

Loewe, Michael, ed. *Early Chinese Texts: A Bibliographic Guide*. Berkeley, CA: Society for the Study of Early China, 1993.

Lynn, Richard John, trans. *The Classic of Changes: A New Translation of the I Ching*. New York: Columbia University Press, 1994.

Makeham, John. *Transmitters and Creators: Chinese Commentators on the Analects*. Cambridge, MA: Harvard University Press, 2003.

Makeham, John. *Lost Soul: "Confucianism" in Contemporary Chinese Academic Discourse*. Cambridge, MA: Harvard-Yenching Institute Monographs 64, 2008.

McHale, Steven. "Mapping a Vietnamese Confucian Past and Its Transition to Modernity." In Benjamin A. Elman et al., eds., *Rethinking Confucianism: Past and Present in China, Korea, and Vietnam*, pp. 397–430. Los Angeles: University of California Press, 2002.

Miller, James, ed. *Chinese Religions in Contemporary Society*. Santa Barbara, CA: ABC-CLIO, 2006.

Mou, Sherry J. *Gentlemen's Prescriptions for Women's Lives: a Thousand Years of Biographies of Chinese Women*. New York: M. E. Sharpe, 2004.

Murray, Julia K. " 'Idols' in the Temple: Icons and the Cult of Confucius." *Journal of Asian Studies* 68.2 (May 2009), 371–411.

Needham, Joseph. *Science and Civilization in China*. Cambridge: Cambridge University Press, 1959.

Neville, Robert. *Boston Confucianism.* Albany: State University of New York Press, 2000.

Ng On-cho and Q. Edward Wang. *Mirroring the Past: The Writing and Use of History in Imperial China.* Honolulu: University of Hawai'i Press, 2005.

Nylan, Michael. *The Five "Confucian" Classics.* New Haven: Yale University Press, 2001.

Peerenboom, R. P. *Law and Morality in Ancient China: the Silk Manuscripts of Huang-Lao.* Albany: State University of New York Press, 1993.

Pines, Yuri. *Foundations of Confucian Thought: Intellectual Life in the Chunqiu Period.* Honolulu: University of Hawai'i Press, 2002.

Puett, Michael J. *To Become a God: Cosmology, Sacrifice, and Self-Divinization in Early China.* Harvard University Asia Center, 2002.

Queen, Sarah A. *From Chronicle to Canon: the Hermeneutics of the Spring and Autumn, According to Tung Chung-shu [Dong Zhongshu].* Cambridge: Cambridge University Press, 1996.

Rosenlee, Li-hsiang Lisa. *Confucianism and Women: A Philosophical Interpretation.* Albany: State University of New York Press, 2006.

Rosemont, Henry, Jr. and Roger Ames. *The Chinese Classic of Family Reverence: a Philosophical Translation of the Xiaojing.* Honolulu: University of Hawai'i Press, 2009.

Sawyer, Ralph D. *Sun-tzu [Sunzi] The Art of War.* New York: Barnes and Noble, 1994.

Schwarz, Benjamin I. *The World of Thought in Ancient China.* Cambridge, MA: Harvard University Press, 1985.

Sellmann, James D. *Timing and Rulership in Master Lu's Spring and Autumn Annals Lushi chunqiu.* Albany: State University of New York Press, 2002.

Shaughnessy, Edward L., trans. *I Ching: The Classic of Changes.* New York: Ballantine, 1997.

Shaughnessy, Edward L. *Rewriting Early Chinese Texts.* Albany: State University of New York Press, 2006.

Shun, Kwong-loi. *Mencius and Early Chinese Thought.* Stanford, CA: Stanford University Press, 1997.

Shun, Kwong-loi. "Ren and Li in the *Analects*." In *Confucius and the Analects: New Essays,* ed. Bryan Van Norden, pp. 53–72. New York: Oxford University Press, 2002.

Slingerland, Edward. *Confucius: Analects with Selections from Traditional Commentaries.* Indianapolis/Cambridge: Hackett Publishing, 2003.

Tamney, Joseph B. and Linda Hsueh-Ling Chiang. *Modernization, Globalization, and Confucianism in Chinese Societies.* London: Praeger, 2002.

Temple, Robert. *The Genius of China: 3,000 Years of Science, Discovery, and Invention.* New York: Simon and Schuster, 1989.

Tsien Tsuen-Hsuin. *Written on Silk and Bamboo: the Beginning of Chinese Books and Inscriptions.* Chicago: University of Chicago Press, 2004.

Tu Wei-ming. *Centrality and Commonality: An Essay on Confucian Religiousness.* Albany: State University of New York Press, 1989.

Tu Wei-ming et al., eds. *Humanity and Self-Cultivation: Essays in Confucian Thought.* Berkeley: University of California Press, 1979.

Tu Wei-ming et al., eds. *The Confucian World Observed: a Contemporary Discussion of Confucian Humanism in East Asia*. Honolulu: University of Hawai'i Press, 1992.

Van Norden, Bryan W. *Mengzi [Mencius] with Selections from Traditional Commentaries*. Indianapolis: Hackett Publishing, 2008.

Waley, Arthur, trans. *The Book of Songs*, ed. and added to by J. R. Allen. New York: Grove Press, 1996.

Wang Ch'ung [Wang Chong]. *Lun Heng*, 2 vols. A. Forke, trans., 1907; repr. New York: Paragon, 1962.

Watson, Burton, trans. *Mo Tzu [Mozi]: Basic Writings*. New York: Columbia University Press, 1963.

Watson, Burton, trans. *The Complete Works of Chuang Tzu [Zhuangzi]*. New York: Columbia University Press, 1964.

Watson, Burton, trans. *Han Fei Tzu [Han Feizi]: Basic Writings*. New York: Columbia University Press, 1964.

Watson, Burton, trans. *Hzun Tzu [Xunzi]: Basic Writings*. New York: Columbia University Press, 1967.

Watson, Burton, trans. *The Tso Chuan [Zuo Zhuan]: Selections from China's Oldest Narrative History*. New York: Columbia University Press, 1989.

Watson, Burton, trans. *The Records of the Grand Historian*. New York: Columbia University Press, 1993.

Yao Xinzhong. *An Introduction to Confucianism*. New York: Cambridge University Press, 2000.

Yates, Robin S. *Five Lost Classics: Tao [Dao], Huanglao, and Yin-Yang in Han China*. New York: Ballantine, 1997.

Index

Sunzi Bingfa, The Art of War 80
Supreme Ultimate
  Zhou Dunyi 162–3, 164, 165
  Zhu Xi 165, 166, 168, 173, 174,
    175, 205

Tamney, Joseph 189
Tang dynasty 146, 147, 154, 158,
    160, 161, 174, 176
timeliness 40, 53
Tu Wei-ming 183, 190, 193

uncrowned king 12, 16, 140
understanding/sympathy 32–3
unequal treaties 176
universal love 71, 72, 74
usefulness 70, 89, 111, 117

Vietnam 152, 157–8

Wang Chong 141–3, 145
Wang Yangming 159, 172–4
Warring States 5–9
Wei, state of 6, 13, 17, 51, 55, 56, 57,
    120, 128
Wei Zheng 174
Western Inscription 164, 173, 184
women 156, 178, 179, 180
  Confucius 55
  footbinding 170–1
  in Confucian texts 55–7, 143
  Mencius 101–2, 117
  modern Confucianism 190, 192,
    194, 198–202
  Neo-Confucianism 169–70, 175

Xia dynasty 2
Xiang Yu 132
Xu Fuguan 189
Xuanzong, emperor 200
Xunzi 66, 68, 84, 105–18
  artificiality 108–9
  government 111–13

Heaven 114–16
human nature is evil 106–9
language 113
life 105–6
morality is artificial 109–10
ritual 110–11

Yan Hui 55, 59, 120, 153
Yan, state of 128
Yan Zhizai 12, 16
Yang Guifei 200
Yang Zhu 85
yin-yang
  in the Han dynasty 135–7
  in the Supreme Ultimate 162, 163
Yu Yingshi 193

Zhang Zai 163–4, 174
Zhao, state of 105, 106, 128
Zhong Liang 120
Zhou Dunyi 162–3
Zhou dynasty 2–4, 7, 9, 12, 15, 17,
    32, 42, 44, 53, 59, 66, 120, 125,
    162
  breakdown 4–6
Zhu Xi
  and Buddhism 168, 171
  life 165
  orthodox transmission 169
  principle 165–6, 168
  Supreme Ultimate 166
  the Four Books 269
  women 169–70
Zhuangzi 75–80, 84, 121, 122, 127,
    161
Zi Si 88, 89, 120, 125, 126
Zi Xia 120
Zi You 120
Zi Zhang 120
Zigong 120
Zilu 46, 48, 58
Zou 16, 88
Zuo Zhuan 123, 124, 127, 134, 199